PROMOTION AND
CAREERS IN TEACHING

Promotion and Careers in Teaching

S. Hilsum and K. B. Start

NFER Publishing Company Ltd.

Published by the NFER Publishing Company Ltd.

Registered Office: The Mere, Upton Park, Slough, Bucks, SL1 2DQ
Book Division: 2 Jennings Buildings, Thames Avenue,
Windsor, Berks, SL4 1QS

First Published 1974
© National Foundation for Educational Research, 1974

SBN 85633 043 4

Printed in Great Britain by
Staples Printers Ltd., at the Stanhope Press, Rochester, Kent

Distributed in the USA by Humanities Press Inc.,
Hillary House—Fernhill House, Atlantic Highlands,
New Jersey, 07716 USA

Contents

Acknowledgements

The project reported here was sponsored by the Social Science Research Council, and a supplementary grant was received from the Department of Education and Science.

As in all large-scale investigations, thanks are due to several colleagues who worked with the project at different times: these include Vernon Ward, Judy Dean, Tony Udall, and James Bunton; and throughout the project Wendy Fader acted as project statistician. In addition secretarial assistance provided during the project by Marilyn Smith, Eunice Hulford, Alma Hilsum and Jean Day was much appreciated.

The NFER wish also to thank the representative bodies of the Local Education Authorities and of the Teachers' Associations for their co-operation throughout the project, but most of all, acknowledgement should be made of the debt owed to the teachers, heads and LEA officials, without whose participation this report could not have been written.

H.S.

SECTION I

Introduction

CHAPTER ONE

Issues and Origins

It will surprise no one that promotion is a subject on which a great many grievances are aired within the teaching profession. Many of these no doubt stem from disappointment; and the complaints of the most vocal individuals cannot be regarded as hard research evidence. Nevertheless, it is worth devoting some attention, at the outset of this survey, to the tenor of published correspondence on the subject, as it indicates the depth of feeling about promotion among ordinary teachers, and what the commonest points of contention are.

The quotations that follow are culled from letters published in journals that circulate widely among teachers.[1] They are cited here not because they are necessarily representative—no such claim is made—but as indicators of some of the salient points at issue. We can make no judgement, at this point, on the validity of the individual cases, nor have we troubled to make reference to the rejoinders that were sometimes made, or to the more sanguine views of the promotion system which can also at times be found in the pages of educational journals.

Some correspondents condemn the promotion system in the most general terms:

'No teacher can feel satisfied that the present system for promotion is just' (G, 14.5.71)

'It is apparent that (the system of teacher promotion) is open to sycophantism and subtle manoeuvring' (TES, 20.11.70)

'Teachers' career prospects are determined by a high-level grapevine of letters and telephone calls between headmasters, heads of department and local education authorities' (G, 14.5.71).

Other letters refer to specific abuses such as the 'rigging' of appointments:

'A headmistress has been heard to boast how a local councillor had

[1] Sources of quotations are abbreviated as follows: G = The *Guardian* NS = *New Schoolmaster*, TES = *Times Educational Supplement*, T = *The Teacher*, TW = *Teacher's World*, TI = *The Times*.

told her that if she applied for a headship when he was on the board, she would get it—and, for whatever reason, she did' (TES, 25.6.71) 'There we all were (husbands with wives applying for a double post in a remand home). Some of us had come across England for the interview. Then the interviewers arrived—and as they went past us into the room where they sat, they all went and shook hands with one particular local couple, who—surprise—got the job' (TES, 25.6.71).

Between the two levels of generalization are comments that allege the unfairness of certain norms within the system:

'All will agree that the major posts should go to the best people, but what constitutes best? My authority appears to define it in graduate terms only' (TES, 23.6.72);

'There are 28 mixed comprehensive schools in . . . and they have 28 headmasters. So women have equal access to top jobs, do they?' (TI, 26.2.71);

'Teachers of physical education, like teachers of other practical subjects, tend to be looked upon professionally as second-class citizens in the competition for promotion with their academic colleagues' (TES, 22.1.71);

'Teachers in "closed" authorities . . . where promotions are made only from within the authority, are nonetheless able to apply for jobs in "open" areas, thus getting what appear to be an unfair two bites at the headship cherries' (TW, 4.12.70);

'Promotion in teaching means gradually changing to administration . . . There should be possible rewards in finance, respect and status for class teachers, comparable to those offered to administrators' (TES, 20.11.70).

Other published comments highlight specific aspects of the appointing procedure such as long periods of waiting or brusque treatment by interviewers.

The composition of an interviewing panel has often been a subject of complaint:

'I was disgusted with the constitution and the quality of the interview board . . . The board consisted of the divisional education officer (in an advisory capacity only); an administrative assistant from County Hall, who was obviously bored by the whole proceedings; an old gentleman . . . who saw some i.t.a. on the wall and said "What's that?" . . . Not one of those men knew anything about infant schools . . . They bandied about a few in-phrases, asked a lot of totally irrelevant questions' (TES, 25.6.71).

The non-professional men and women who sit on interviewing panels in their capacity as school managers or governors or members of an education committee are frequently regarded by teachers as unfit to judge the educational qualifications of candidates, though it has been countered that

'managers are merely lined up to pay lip-service to appointment procedures which are laid down by local education authorities. . . . Let's stop pretending the managers have a say in appointments' (TES, 12.11.71).

A major source of grievance appears to be the process by which information about applicants is gleaned—through testimonials, references, and confidential reports. Open testimonials are sometimes seen as suspect. It is often alleged that a head will compile a laudatory reference or testimonial in order to be rid of a teacher, while the opposite may also occur:

'Often, (the system) is recognized as working fairly. But examples are on record of maliciously inaccurate references by headmasters—who perhaps do not wish the applicant to leave their school—wrecking a man's prospects for job after job' (G, 14.5.71).

And a practice that is purported to cause teachers much anxiety is the 'telephone confidential', when one head communicates directly with a prospective employer in private.

Concern about the methods of reporting on teachers has at times led to the suggestion of an appeals procedure:

'There should be protection for the individual teacher by an impartial, ombuds committee, against the blatant misuse of authority' (TES, 20.11.70);

'There must be protection against irregular assessments made outside accepted channels' (G, 14.5.71).

The alleged defects of the promotion system are seen by some writers as resulting in promotion having been given to the wrong people:

'We have on our staff a young woman who has an extra allowance for being in change of the library, and who admits that she never reads a book . . . My feelings are that people are promoted for the wrong qualities' (TES, 25.6.71);

'I recently was interviewed for a post in a girls' high school . . . to teach history and geography up to O-level. I was rather dumbfounded when

a candidate who freely admitted he had not looked at any geography
since his own A-level was given the job' (TES, 30.7.71);
'It is to (the teacher's) advantage to seek an end to the hit-or-miss
procedures which are commonly used today, resulting in too many
square pegs being forced into too many round holes' (NS, Dec. 1971).

What, then, is an observer, trying to be objective, to make of it all?
From contributions to the educational press it is evident that the topic
is of great interest to teachers even if opinions conflict. Proper study
of the promotion system has been proposed at various teacher union
conferences over the last decade, but (until the present survey) no
full-scale inquiry had materialized.

Obviously the topic is delicate. The different sectional interests
within the profession would have a natural wariness over their own
specific sensitivities. The professional conduct of teachers, the
efficiency of employers and the integrity of interviewing panels are
all at issue. To establish the facts in specific cases teachers must
provide verifiable details of their own experiences. However, they
might well believe that doing so would be liable to jeopardize their
careers.

In 1970, the National Foundation for Educational Research proposed
that it should undertake this inquiry into careers and promotion in
teaching. It was felt that the NFER was particularly suitable to conduct this inquiry as most interested parties would recognize the NFER
as an inquiring body which had no particular axe to grind and no
sectional interest to serve. With representatives of both employers
and employees on its Board of Management, the NFER would pursue
as objective and non-partisan an approach as possible. The Social
Science Research Council agreed to sponsor the project, and the
DES later contributed a supplementary grant. There was considerable
initial discussion with representative bodies of both LEAs and
teachers, to acquaint them with the aims of the project and seek their
co-operation. With their support the two-year investigation began in
January 1971, and it is the report of that investigation that is presented
in this book.

Supplementary data

The statistical evidence on which the findings of this report are
based is included, chapter for chapter, in tabular form. A great deal
of the statistical and analytical matter could not, however, be included,
and this has been lodged with the National Library, from whom
copies can be obtained on payment of a fee. This material is in the
form of seven appendices, each with its own National Library reference

number. Each can be obtained separately, but material within a single appendix cannot be split up. Requests for copies should be sent to the British Library, Boston Spa, Yorkshire, UK, quoting the appropriate Supplementary Publication number given below. Requests should be accompanied by payment, either as prepaid coupons or their equivalent in cash. Supplies of BLL photocopy coupons are held by many universities and technical libraries throughout the world, and by British Council offices. A single coupon purchases up to 10 pages of photocopy or a microfiche for any complete item. Photocopies of items in excess of 10 pages may be purchased *pro rata*, i.e. one coupon for every 10 pages or part thereof. Prepaid coupons may be purchased in books, and the latest cost quoted at time of going to press is: UK and Eire—£10 for 50, or 25p each; Europe—£7 for 20, or 35p each; elsewhere—£10 for 20, or 50p each.

The content of the supplementary appendices is as follows:

Appendix A: *Design, Sampling and Response.* Tables with accompanying description. 6 pages. British Library Supplementary Publication No. SUP 80010.

Appendix B: *Questionnaires.* Copies of questionnaires used in the research. 44 pages. British Library Supplementary Publication No. SUP 80011.

Appendix C: *Details of the Teacher Sample.* Characteristics of the sample of teachers used in the research—their career patterns, biographical features, age, education, qualifications, experience, specialist subjects, subjects now taught and mobility. In the form of tables with accompanying brief description. 17 pages. British Library Supplementary Publication No. SUP 80012.

Appendix D: *An Analysis of Application Forms for Teaching Posts.* By S. Hilsum and J. Bunton. A comparison of 120 application forms used by different Local Education Authorities for recruiting teachers, with a proposed standard application form. 9 pages. British Library Supplementary Publication No. SUP 80013.

Appendix E: *An Analysis of Advertisements.* A comparison of the style and content of advertisements of vacant teaching posts in two successive issues of the *Times Educational Supplement* in April 1971. Table with a brief introduction. 6 pages. British Library Supplementary Publication No. SUP 80014.

Appendix F: *Responses to Advertisements.* Tables, with a brief textual introduction, on the numbers of responses received to advertisements of vacant teaching posts, mostly headships. 8 pages. British Library Supplementary Publication No. SUP 80015.

Appendix G: *Promotion and Careers, Part I: Characteristics of Post-holders.* Tables only on: average ages of post-holders; distribution of levels of post by school type, sex, qualifications, age, career type and experience; type of promotion, number of schools in which served, length of experience, courses attended, evening lecturing, home moves, and number of LEAs in which served. 35 pages. British Library Supplementary Publication No. SUP 80016.

Appendix G: *Promotion and Careers, Part II: Views and Aspirations, Advertisements and Appointments.* Factors favouring promotion and factors that ought to favour promotion, teachers' views on; placement of advertisements, Heads' involvement in shortlisting and interviewing, teachers' satisfactions and dissatisfactions with teaching and with appointment procedure, and teachers' job aspirations and expectations. Tables only. 49 pages. British Library Supplementary Publication No. SUP 80017.

CHAPTER TWO

Objectives and Procedures

Aims of the project

The project was concerned with full-time teachers in maintained schools in England and Wales. Its chief aims were to explore:

(a) the promotion structure and appointment procedures in the teaching profession;

(b) the career patterns of teachers and the factors that appeared to determine promotion;

(c) the opinions of both teachers and their employing local authorities regarding promotion opportunities and efficiency of appointment procedures.

In addition to a study of the overall situation, the project looked at the career patterns and promotion prospects for different groups of teachers (e.g. primary/secondary, men/women, graduate/non-graduate) and their opinions about the promotion system. The researchers inquired also into any differences that might exist among LEAs in their appointment procedures. As 'wastage' was a topic currently being discussed, teachers were also asked about their professional plans. And, finally, the inquiry sought the teacher's views about teaching as a career.

Note on the changed promotion structure

When the project was launched in January 1971, changes in the promotion structure of the teaching profession were in the offing. The NFER decided to go ahead with the research because (a) the greater part of the project's brief—career patterns, appointment procedures and factors influencing promotion—would probably not be radically altered under any new system; and (b) where the system did undergo change, the views of teachers about the pre-change situation would provide a sound reference point for discussion of the later position. As far as can be judged in the short time since the system was re-structured (during 1971), the decision to continue this study in the proposed manner proved justified, as most of the findings in this report are substantially unaffected by the new structure. The nomenclature of the new posts is different, but this is covered by cross-referencing in order to relate the structure as investigated to that now existing. Where the findings might have been affected by the 1971 changes comment has been made.

Sampling and methods of inquiry

The researchers were well aware of the sensitive nature of this kind of inquiry, and they consulted carefully with the LEAs and teacher representatives about the procedures to be used.

Three media were used for the collection of the data: questionnaires to teachers, headteachers and LEAs, interviews with teachers and LEAs, and (content analyses of) application forms, advertisements and their responses. These data were then analysed within the framework of the Burnham Committee's recommendations over the past 25 years, which are reviewed in Chapter Three.

The draft questionnaires and interview schedules were discussed fully with representatives of the teachers and LEAs before finalization. The respective associations received specimen blanks of all documents relating to their members, and the LEAs received copies of material circulated to the schools.

It was planned to survey all the LEAs in England and Wales, and about 12,000 teachers. To make contact with LEAs was no problem; obtaining the teacher sample proved much more difficult. The 12,000 teachers had to be selected randomly, and stratified to represent teachers of different types. The DES has a register of all teachers in maintained schools, and in theory they could have identified the teacher sample required. But we needed the teachers' names and addresses so that they could be contacted directly and personally to preserve confidentiality, and this conflicted with the Department's policy to withhold such information from any outside agency or enquirer.

As the names and addresses of schools were available, the second-best alternative was employed, a random sample of schools, up to a teacher total of about 12,000. First the head of each school was asked for a list of teachers' names so that we might then write in confidence to each teacher at the school inviting him or her to participate. Apart from increasing costs, this method increased the potential for non-participation by teachers. If a head did not answer, all teachers in that school would be denied the opportunity even to consider participation.

A random sample of 963 maintained schools was obtained from the DES. This represented an overall sampling fraction of one in 30 schools.

From DES records it was estimated that this school sample contained 11,591 full-time teachers.

1. *Heads' questionnaires*

The head of each of the 963 schools was sent a letter explaining the project and inviting his co-operation. Enclosed was a brief preliminary questionnaire asking for basic information on the school circumstances and head's involvement in appointment procedures. Attached was a request for a list of the school's full-time teachers including the head himself. The head was assured that returning the questionnaire and list did not commit any of his staff, as their participation would be sought subsequently and independently.

After the original despatch in spring 1971, and some later reminders, 881 heads' questionnaires were returned, representing 91.5 per cent of the original school sample. The schools which did not return staff lists were estimated to contain 1549 teachers (13.4 per cent of the original sample of 11,591) and left 10,042 full-time teachers as our teacher sample to be contacted.

2. *Teachers' questionnaires*

During May and June the teachers' questionnaires, which covered biographical and professional background, career experience, future plans, and opinions on teaching and promotion, were despatched to the 10,042 teachers (including heads) in the 881 schools from which we had earlier recieved teacher lists. Each questionnaire was sent independently and privately to the individual teacher at his school address, together with a covering letter explaining the project and inviting his or her co-operation, and a pre-paid, addressed envelope for return of the completed questionnaire.

After the initial despatch and subsequent reminders, 6,722 teacher questionnaires were returned, representing 67.0 per cent of those sent (these 6,722 teachers represent 58.0 per cent of the estimated original 11,591 teachers).[1]

The non-response varied from 28 per cent to 39 per cent for the main school types, with 32 per cent and 33.9 per cent for men and women respectively. As far as school type and sex of teacher were concerned, the final sample appeared to have little systematic bias which would invalidate the general findings of the project. This conclusion was later reinforced when it was found that the distribution of the main

---

[1] Details of the school and teacher samples are given in Appendix A in the supplement—see p. 13.

posts of responsibility in the responding sample were similar to the national figures given in the DES's *Statistics of Education.*

3. *LEA questionnaires*

In April 1971 every local education authority in England and Wales was sent a questionnaire which asked about LEA policy on staffing, appointment procedures, and opinions about the system operated. All authorities had been contacted earlier in the year with a letter concerning the project generally, and specifically seeking their permission to invite participation from any schools that might be sampled in their area; none had refused permission. However, the sources of detailed LEA information were the 155 LEA questionnaires which were returned from the 164 despatched.

4. *Teacher interviews*

Certain issues relating to promotion and appointments needed more than a postal questionnaire and could be discussed adequately only through structured personal interviews. From the responding schools, a small pool was randomly selected, representing primary and secondary schools and all geographical regions. In each of these schools teachers who had returned the teacher questionnaire were randomly chosen (one, two or three teachers, depending on the school's size) for an interview with one of the researchers. Schools unwilling or unable to take part were replaced by others in our sample pool. If one teacher refused, another respondent at his school was randomly picked. In addition, the researchers interviewed the head of the school, where this was possible. The interviews took place between November 1971 and March 1972, and all teachers were assured of complete confidentiality. The researchers believe that the 135 interviews which were recorded and transcribed supplied a reasonably adequate representation of the kind of qualitative information that was sought, and provided some extremely valuable data to supplement the teacher questionnaire.[1]

When visiting a few of these 'interview schools' the researchers tried to make incidental contact with teachers who had not responded to the teacher questionnaire; 17 such teachers were seen and agreed to be interviewed. The reasons given for non-return of the questionnaire were based on forgetfulness, indifference or lack of time, rather than hostility to the project. This small group's answers to the interview questions displayed no radical differences from those of teachers who had returned questionnaires.

5. *LEA interviews*

A small sample of 20 LEA officers in different parts of the country were interviewed to illuminate some topics briefly covered in the LEA questionnaires.

6. *Application forms*

The LEAs were asked to provide copies of application forms issued to teachers who inquired about specific appointments. This is to our knowledge the first collection of the application forms issued by almost all authorities in England and Wales. The differences and similarities among the forms used by LEAs were noted and a possible standardized form suggested. An assessment of the validity of teachers' criticisms of current forms was also possible. This will be found in Appendix D in the supplement (see p. 13).

7. *Advertisements*

The extent of the analysis of advertisements of jobs was limited by the time and staff resources available. Two consecutive issues of the *Times Educational Supplement* were selected at random during the early period of the project, April 2nd and 9th, 1971, and the details of every advertisement of a post of responsibility in maintained schools were collated. A summary of the chief findings is given in Appendix E in the supplement (see p. 13).

8. *Response to advertisements*

In the spring of 1972 we wrote to every LEA asking for brief details of any headships recently advertised or about to be advertised, together with the number of actual applications received for each post. In addition we contacted the heads of a random sample of 100 primary and 100 secondary schools taken from our pool of 881 schools, asking for details. Replies were received from about 75 per cent of the LEAs and 75 per cent of the schools (both primary and secondary). All the data, which do not appear to have been collected before, were received in the late summer or early autumn of 1972, and were then collated and analysed. Comments drawn from this analysis have been inserted in the text of this report where it seemed appropriate, and the details of the analysis are included in Appendix F in the supplement (see p. 13).

It may be thought that because the 'response to advertisement' data related to 1972 it should not be used to illuminate our other findings collected in 1971. However, the main object of the 1972 exercise was to help interpret any differences in the 1971 findings between different groups of teachers; and while the *general* rate of application, i.e. the 'demand' for promotion, might have changed between 1971 and 1972 (possibly owing to a new 'supply' position as a result of the new promotion structure) such a change would probably have affected all teachers alike, and there is no reason to suggest that one group of teachers rather than another suddenly increased or reduced their rate of applications for promotion between 1971 and 1972.

9. *Burnham reports*

In order to understand the background to the system of promotion, the reports of the Burnham Committee since 1945 were studied. A brief history of the main items possibly affecting our sampled career patterns is provided in Chapter 3.

The analysis of the information

We wanted first to discover the general nature of the promotion system, i.e. how it affected most teachers, and then probe more deeply to see how different groups of teachers or schools were affected.

i. Although a vast range of data was collected, limited finance, time and staffing dictated that we studied only matters considered top priority. However, general information about several items of interest which could not be studied in detail is presented in Appendix C in the supplement (see p. 13).

ii. It proved necessary to treat primary and secondary teachers separately, but where it was thought important (and feasible) to provide a 'total' picture the data were combined.

iii. The teacher sample was divided into three 'career groups': (a) the 'N' group—those with 'Normal' uninterrupted careers; as these formed the large majority of our sample, the greater part of the analysis was related to this group; (b) the 'R' group (Re-entrants)—those whose careers had been interrupted for some reason, e.g. war service, family commitment, etc. (an arbitrary interval of 5 or more years was chosen as a criterion); (c) the 'L' group (Late entrants)—those who began their teaching career after work experience in industry or elsewhere (an arbitrary criterion for this group was set at 15 years after leaving school). Appendix C includes details of the numbers in the various sub-samples.

v. As the questionnaires to teachers referred to the statuses current in spring 1971, these formed the framework for our analysis and for this report. For readers who have become accustomed to the new status levels under the new promotion structure introduced since our survey we have compromised by keeping the old terms of graded post and head of department, but making cross-reference to the corresponding new Scales where appropriate. Deputy head and head are retained as the highest statuses, and teachers who were, under the old scheme, called second or senior masters/mistresses are treated as deputy heads. In Chapter three the relationship between the statuses in the old and new system is explained more fully.

vi. For a variety of reasons not all questions were answered fully by all respondents. Hence the number of teachers in a particular group appears to vary from one questionnaire topic to another. This explains why some tables quote different numbers for the same teacher group. Appendix C, however, shows how the main characteristics (variables) of teachers were distributed across the whole sample.

SECTION II

Influences on Promotion

CHAPTER THREE

Burnham

Just what is the context within which the promotion system for teachers in England and Wales is supposed to function? Of the several statutory committees which periodically recommend to the Secretary of State for Education and Science scales of salaries for employees within the educational system, the salaries of teachers in primary and secondary schools are the purview of the *Burnham Primary and Secondary Committee*. Named after its first chairman, the committee consists of a Teachers' Panel, made up of representatives of the main teacher organizations, and a Management Panel comprising representatives of teachers' employers and the DES. Although teachers are paid directly by their employers at local level, their salary scales are negotiated at national level. Recommendations of the Burnham Committee are usually accepted by the DES, and the Secretary of State incorporates them in the necessary Order in Council. (If the committee fails to agree on a recommendation, the Secretary of State in the Department of Employment sets up an arbitral body whose recommendation is binding on the DES Secretary of State, unless rejected by both Houses of Parliament.)

The Burnham Committee not only recommends specific salary levels but also the 'structure', i.e. the establishment of various statuses to which those salaries are to apply. While salary scales are re-negotiated every year or two, formal reappraisal of the basic structure is much less frequent. Obviously any radical change in structure such as that in 1971 may easily open up or close down avenues of promotion. Sometimes what seem minor changes, e.g. introduction of the points system or graded posts, had quite major effects on salary prospects of teachers in different types of school.

The Burnham Committee began functioning in 1919 as 'The Standing Joint Committee on the Salaries of Elementary School Teachers'. Prior to the second World War there were separate scales for primary and secondary teachers. Hence up to 1945 there may have been a financial incentive for graduates to go into secondary rather than primary schools. Separate Burnham committees dealt with the salaries of teachers in public elementary schools, secondary schools and technical and similar schools. These three committees were consolidated into one Burnham committee towards the end of the war and it was this committee which negotiated the 1945 Burnham Report which governed the post-war situation. We were unable to discover any single published source that traced the history of Burnham settlements,[1] so the following brief history has been sifted from the Burnham reports since 1945, and presents the chief items that formed the context for the career patterns and prospects of our sample of teachers.

Following the fundamental policy statement of the 1944 Education Act, the Burnham Committee's recommendations in 1945 established the basic structure of the teaching profession for the next two decades. All full-time teachers in maintained primary and secondary schools were paid according to two basic scales, one for men and one for women, and they spanned, by equal annual increments, a range of 15 years for men and 13 for women. In determining a teacher's salary point on the basic scale, incremental credit was granted on a 'one-for-one' basis for war service and previous teaching experience, while usually one increment was allowed for every three years of 'gainful employment' outside teaching.

Superimposed on the basic scale, and therefore operative at all points on the scale, allowances could be awarded for additional study or training, a degree, working in special schools or classes, working in the London area, holding a 'post of special responsibility'—often referred to as a PSR—and being a headteacher. The PSR allowance had to be between £50 and £100, and between 14 per cent and 16 per cent of the teaching staff employed by an LEA could hold the allowance. The headship allowance rose by £30 for each 100 pupils on roll (up to a maximum of £150), and by £50 for each group of 30 pupils over fifteen years old (these amounts being higher for heads of special schools).

Thus, in 1945, the promotion statuses open to the teacher were a PSR or a headship, and to a great extent the number and age of pupils on the school roll determined both. Placing a differential on pupils of fifteen and older effectively separated grammar schools, with their

---

[1] Mr. E. L. Britton, General Secretary of the National Union of Teachers, has subsequently informed us of an unpublished stencilled 'history' going back to 1913, and also an unpublished thesis by Stanley Barnes in the University of London library.

fifth and sixth forms, from the secondary modern schools, which at that stage did not have children over fifteen, and from the primary schools. In a grammar school the head's salary and the number of PSRs increased because the 15-plus children not only added to the basic numbers on the roll; they brought with them the financial loading for age and the possibility of teaching advanced or special academic work, which was one of the main criteria used by an LEA when awarding individual PSRs. This use of the number and age of pupils as a factor in teachers' promotion openings has been continued during the entire period of negotiated settlements up to the present time.

These were the chief elements which, in 1945, shaped a teacher's current and future prospects. In succeeding years changes occurred which reflected not only the particular sectional interests of the participants in the Burnham negotiations but also wider considerations, like the continuing reorganization of the school system, the raising of the school-leaving age, fluctuations in the school population, national requirements for specialists in different fields, sporadic demands for more and different education, growing concern for disadvantaged children and so on.

The major change of the 1948 settlement was that it restructured the basis on which school size was estimated: the term 'unit total' took over from 'school roll'. Each school unit (i.e. pupil) was allocated points: each of those under fifteen was assigned one point, those between fifteen and sixteen four points, those between sixteen and seventeen seven points, and those over seventeen ten points. (The allocation of points to pupils in special schools was arranged on a different basis.) The total number of points assigned to a school was its 'unit total', and schools were placed in Groups according to their unit totals. Schools with unit totals of less than 100 were to be Group I schools, those with unit totals of 101–200 were to be Group II schools, and so on progressively to the largest possible, a Group XXII school with a unit total of over 3,000. Each head's allowance was now related to his school's Group (I to XXII), which increased the differentiation between heads. Previously, when school size meant school roll, only five groups had been recognized, Group V being those with more than 500 pupils.

This change provided a financial incentive to grammar schools to develop their sixth forms at a time when the premature leaving from grammar schools was the subject of a special DES report. The enlargement of the sixth form provided a higher salary for the heads and more opportunities for PSRs for assistant teachers, thereby increasing the career prospects of both teachers and headteachers appointed to grammar schools. On the other hand, the points system did little to differentiate between the primary and secondary modern schools, since one point was allocated to all children to the age of fifteen. The 1948 settlement also differentiated among graduates—those with first class honours to be paid an allowance over and above the normal graduate allowance.

In 1951 the unity of graduate allowance was restored and schools with unit totals of less than 40 were called Group 0, those with 40–100 now comprising Group I. The allocation of PSRs was no longer to depend on the staff complement but on the unit total. An LEA allocated a school a sum of money which increased with its unit total. This sum could be assigned to one PSR or shared among several PSRs, provided no PSR was allocated less than £40. The large majority of LEAs had schemes for allocating PSRs, and schools conformed with these, though the heads exercised considerable power in deciding which teacher should receive a PSR.

The Special Salary Award in 1952 offered no change in structure, whilst the 1954 agreement restored a difference between 'ordinary' and 'good honours' graduates, the latter receiving an allowance in addition to his graduate allowance.[1]

The 1956 agreement saw three changes of radical importance. Equal pay for men and women was initiated, the process to be completed by 1961. In a change crucial to the structure, the old PSR was expanded from being a single status level, though embracing sizeable variations in the actual allowance received, into 39 different status levels, each with a specific salary allowance. And three main types of post were distinguished: graded post, head of department, and deputy head.

There were three levels of graded post, each carrying its own specific allowance and not, in fact, a scale as their names, scales I, II and III, suggested. Every school was allocated, in Burnham, a 'score' depending on its Group, varying from one (for Group IV) to 30 (for Group XXII). A school's score was then distributed among graded posts, with graded posts I, II, and III counting as one, two and three points respectively. The form of distribution could vary. For example, a school of Group VI with a score of three could distribute the points as

---

[1] The terms of the 1955 amendments, and a commentary on them will, be found in *Burnham Report Appendix X, Allowances for Advanced Teaching* by (as he then was) Dr. W. P. Alexander, published by Councils and Education Press Ltd., March 1955.

three graded posts I, or one graded post I and one graded post II, or a single graded post III.

Head of department allowances were to be allocated in secondary schools only, being *mandatory* in schools with GCE O-level work and *permissible* where this level was not taught. There were different grades of head of department and each had its own specific salary allowance. The general recommendation was that regard should be paid to the School Group and to the particular responsibilities of the post in question. Whether a post was awarded at all, and the grade if awarded, should depend on the responsibilities undertaken by the teacher: generally these should entail supervision of a department, but LEAs had discretion in this matter. Burnham suggested that the highest grade awarded ought to be A in schools up to Group VII, B in Groups VIII to XII, C in XIII to XVII, and D ought to be allowed only in schools of over Group XVII. Unlike graded posts, therefore, the number of possible head of department posts was determined very much by the decision of the LEA, usually after consultation with the head, and was not governed by any stipulated maximum 'score' allocated by Burnham.

Many teachers had criticized the old PSR system because it lacked a clear and precise definition of the specific duties or responsibilities to be discharged by the status-holder, and because of the discretion the system allowed to heads and LEAs when establishing such posts. The new system of graded posts and heads of department, however, was not at all dissimilar in this respect. Although a head of department often performed the function the status implies, he might easily be awarded the status without having a 'department' to supervise, and a teacher holding a graded post need have no observable special responsibilities. However, the discretion permitted to heads and LEAs in this matter would be claimed by many as its great advantage, for in this way highly valued teachers could be induced to remain at a school (or join a school) regardless of their having no apparent additional responsibility.

All schools from Group III to XXII (and even below III under special circumstances) were to have a deputy head, and all schools from Group XI to XXII could, at the LEA's discretion, appoint a second master/mistress. Deputy headship allowances were tied to the School Group, as headship allowances had been since 1948. The allowance granted to a second master/mistress, if such a post existed, was to be 'appropriately related' to that received by the deputy head, so that in effect this also was tied to the School Group. Deputy heads of special schools were paid higher allowances than deputies in ordinary schools.

The whole structure of status levels remained linked to the unit total system. Graded post allocation depended on the *school's score*, which depended on the *School Group;* maximum grades permitted to heads of departments were related to the School Group; deputy headship and second master/mistress allowances rose as the School Group rose; and *School Groups* were determined by *unit totals*. Allied to the re-structuring of statuses was a major change in the way unit totals were to be calculated.

From 1956 each pupil under thirteen years old was to count one point as before, but those between thirteen and fifteen were not counted two points. Those between fifteen and sixteen counted four points, between sixteen and seventeen six points, and over seventeen ten points. This increased the unit totals for all secondary schools, but effectively doubled those of secondary modern schools. This raised their School Group numbers, thereby enlarging the allowances for head, deputy head and second master/mistress, and expanding the range of head of department posts and augmenting the number and range of graded posts. It created a financial incentive to take a post in a secondary modern rather than a primary school or possibly even than a junior post in a grammar school, thereby attracting some graduates to the secondary modern schools. With this improved staffing, fifth forms were built up which in turn increased the point value of the schools and enabled them to attract further well-qualified staff, leading to the establishment of sixth forms, this in turn further increasing the point total and the opportunities for promotion and consolidating staff quality. Thus the raising of the point value of 13- to 15-year-old children was an important pump-priming operation for the secondary modern school.

The fact that the 1956 arrangements generated a great change in the number of status levels open to the teacher should not be taken to imply that thereby an enormous number of new actual promotion posts suddenly appeared. The major part of the change was basically of nomenclature; the teacher previously holding a PSR was now to be called a deputy head, or head of department, or holder of a graded post. There were a number of teachers whose posts as ungraded assistants in secondary schools were suddenly transformed into status posts carrying allowances, but there were a much larger number of post-holders after 1956 than before. This could not have resulted from the change in structure alone but was associated with other, possibly related, causes such as a larger global sum being made available for teachers' salaries, or relatively more money being allocated to above-scale posts than formerly. The crucial point was that from 1956 a teacher could see his prospects in terms of a series of fairly well-defined stages, each of which, if reached, conferred upon the teacher not just financial rewards but also recognition of his status level in the professional hierarchy. Many teachers, when deliberating on a particular step in their career plans, often made status considerations override salary implications (e.g. going from a head of department post to a moderate deputy headship, with no appreciable increase—even a reduction—in allowance).

Like most far-reaching changes, the effects produced were not by any means regarded as entirely beneficial. Some teachers foresaw in the new structure a harmful intensification of the growing trend towards discriminating among different groups of teachers. A particular concern was that the creation of more promotion levels would generate a search for posts at those levels, with a consequent increase in teacher movement from one school to another. The 1956 changes influenced greatly the career patterns and related factors described in succeeding chapters. Its effects no doubt also contributed in great measure to the teachers' opinions reviewed in various sections of this report.

In 1959 the School Groups expanded beyond XXII up to XXVII. In 1961 head of department Grade E was permitted in School Groups XXI and above. From 1961 to 1971 there were notionally three basic scales, for non-graduates, ordinary graduates and good honours graduates, but in effect this was no different from the earlier situation of one basic scale, with additions for degree and good honours degree allowed at minimum and maximum. The 1961 agreement also introduced unequal increments at specific points in the Salary Scales, with the idea of accelerating the salaries of long-service teachers—the 'booster increments'.

The 1963 settlement contained an important recommendation for primary schools in that head of department posts at Grade A level could be awarded in schools of Group V and over.

1965 saw both innovation and streamlining. The 'Head's Allowance' was discontinued, and in future heads were to be paid according to a scale which differed for each School Group. Each scale ranged across three or four years, depending on the School Group. The only additional allowance permitted heads was the 'London area' allowance.

The cumbersome structure involved in having 28 School Groups was telescoped to produce 14 groups, now identified as Group 0, Group

1, 2, 3 etc. up to 13. The unit total for a school did not alter; it was simply assigned to the new grouping, and the allowance for the deputy head was made appropriate to that new group.

The permitted maximum grades for secondary heads of department became: Grade A in School Groups below 6, B in Group 6, C in Groups 7 and 8, D in Group 9, and the highest Grade, E, in Groups 10 and over. In primary schools, the Grade A was permitted in schools of Group 4 and above. The school 'score' governing the allocation of graded posts was adjusted to a score appropriate to the school's new group.

The allowance awarded for approved additional study or training was to apply only as far as the maximum of the basic scale. A new allowance, generally known as a 'merit' allowance, and permissible at both the minimum and maximum of the basic scale, was awarded for attendance at certain supplementary or advanced courses.

In 1967 primary schools of Group 4 and over were allowed to allocate a head of department Grade B post. Also, any teacher whose status might be affected by school reorganization was to have his salary and future increases at that level safeguarded, provided no alternative equivalent post was refused, right up to retirement.

1969 saw a small change in the scoring system for unit totals which had a considerable impact on many schools: a pupil under thirteen was to count as one-and-a-half points instead of one. This frequently raised the School Group, which in turn could affect the head's salary scale and would probably increase the number and range of a school's status allowances. The fact that the points change was at the young end of the pupil range meant that a large number of primary schools benefited. Another innovation was the creation of a School Group 14, for schools with unit totals of over 7,600.

When, in 1965, the School Groups were telescoped from 28 to 14 groups, each new group spanned a much wider range of unit totals, and all schools within that wider range received the same graded posts 'score' because the score was tied to the new School Group. The 1969 settlement restored the link between 'score' and unit total, and allowed larger schools within the same School Group to be allocated larger scores.

A new allowance was created for teachers and headteachers working in 'schools of exceptional difficulty', usually in Educational Priority Areas (hence the allowance being called an EPA).

It was at this point that the NFER undertook the survey described in this book, and therefore the questionnaires from teachers relate, as far as their career patterns and 'present status' are concerned, to the situation created by the history of Burnham up to this period. To help readers view our findings in present day terms, we continue with a brief résumé of subsequent change in promotion structure up to the time of writing.

In the 1971 settlement, scales for heads were to continue as before, but deputy heads were to have separate scales, each scale related to the School Group in the same way that heads' scales were arranged. There were 14 School Groups, now beginning with Group 1 (the former Group 0 being assimilated into Group 1).

All other teachers were to be paid according to one of five scales. A new teacher would be placed on Scale One, which spanned, in unequal annual increments, 15 years. Incremental credit would be given for war service, previous teaching experience, 'other' gainful employment (less credit for this), approved additional study/training, ordinary degree, good honours degree and special advanced courses. Only the good honours credit was allowed to extend beyond the Scale One maximum. Scales Two to Five were to be, in general, promotion scales, and placement would be either A at the minimum of the relevant scale, or B at the salary entitled to on the scale formerly applicable plus a 'promotion increase' which varied according to the scales to and from which the teacher was being promoted (whichever route, A or B, gave the higher salary was applied). If a teacher moved up more than one scale, he received all the promotion increases allowed for movement between each scale, subject to the maximum of the scale to which he was promoted. The good honours degree credit was not allowed beyond the maximum if the teacher was on Scale Four or Five.

The basis for allocating to schools any post above Scale One was similar to that for the old graded posts. Each Scale was assigned points: Scale Two: one point, Scale Three: two, Scale Four: three and Scale Five: four points. Each school was allocated by its LEA a 'score' within a given range of points, the range being tied to the school's unit total. The LEA was to decide—and, as before, such decisions usually considered the heads' recommendations—how the score for a particular school was to be distributed among the scales. For example, a school of unit total 450 was entitled to a score within the range three to eight and if the LEA assigned it five points, there could be created five Scale 2 posts, or three Scale 2 posts and one Scale 3, or one Scale 2 post and two Scale 3 posts. It was recommended that schools under Group 4 should not have any promotion-scale posts, Groups 4 and 5 should not have posts higher than Scale 2, Groups 6 to 8 none higher than Scale 4, and only Groups 9 to 14 should be permitted Scale 5 posts.

The recommended transition from old to new structure should be as follows: graded post 1 = Scale 2; graded post II and head of department A = Scale 3; graded post III and heads of departments Grades B and C = Scale 4; head of department Grades D and E = Scale 5.

Schools of Group 10 and over could have two deputy heads, a second master/mistress should receive the same salary as the deputy head, and allowances could be added for working in (a) special schools or classes, (b) EPA schools, (c) the 'London area'.

In 1972 a new post of senior teacher was created, to be paid according to a separate scale. The post could be awarded only in schools of Group 10 or over, and up to three senior teacher posts per school were permitted. They were to be allocated within the points score of the school, a senior teacher counting 4 points. Henceforth Group 3 schools were to be allowed one Scale 2 post.

Three comments are worth noting about the 1971/72 reports. The LEA's power in the allocation of promotion posts has increased because it can decide where, within a given range, a school's 'score' is to be placed. Nowhere in the reports is the award of a promotion post on Scale 2 to senior teacher made dependent on a responsibility to be undertaken by the incumbent teacher. These changes have increased the possibility of rapid promotion; and in divorcing responsibility from salary has thereby enabled the deployment of funds to attract teachers on scarcity subjects and to retain teachers who might otherwise move to a promotion in another school.

To summarize, there are three main factors determining the context within which career patterns and opportunities in the teaching profession are shaped:

1. the supply of status levels forming a sequence of steps up the promotion ladder;
2. the supply of actual appointments at each status level;
3. the demand by teachers for those appointments.

The supply of status levels is largely the purview of the Burnham Committee and is the framework around which promotion structure is built. The main foundation for this framework rests on the unit total system for determining the School Group.

The *supply* of actual appointments at each status level is primarily a matter—first at national then at local authority level—of financial and educational policy, insofar as such policy applies to the number of schools built, their size, their pupil age range and their internal organization. The *demand* for promotion appointments is determined by the career aspirations of individual teachers. The supply of status levels has been studied by reference to the Burnham context. The relationship between supply of actual promotion posts and the demand for them is the subject of succeeding chapters.

CHAPTER FOUR

Career Patterns

To what career pattern can a teacher look forward? What is the probability of promotion to each of the different levels within teaching? How long does it take teachers who are promoted to get that promotion?

As was indicated in Chapter Three, the structure of the teaching profession has changed considerably over the years. Undoubtedly a watershed for teachers like those in this study was the 1956 Burnham recommendations. Many status levels were re-designated, others created, and the number at each level increased. There was an increase in promotion opportunities. An experienced teacher with 10 or 15 years' experience may only have been promoted after 1956 when the post was there to be offered. Teachers who entered the profession subsequently have had more status posts to aim for and could gain promotion more quickly.

Neither have teachers been static. When teachers are grouped by their school type it is the school in which they were serving when the study was undertaken that is used. Yet many teachers have moved across school types from infant to junior, or grammar to secondary modern. Also there will have been movement between subjects. The obvious changes which spring to mind are usually from specific to less-specific areas: subject teachers who move to general studies or 'remedial', and the general trend for teachers of physical education in middle age to move into a specific subject or general area.

The situation is obviously not ideal for constructing patterns and profiles. It has been too changeable for that. In attempting to provide profiles, the authors are conscious of the many ways they could have been compiled, and of the weaknesses of any one of them. Three approaches were chosen: (a) an examination of the length of teaching experience of current holders of posts. This effectively removed from the calculations all teachers who had held that status previously but who had since moved up the promotion ladder. (b) We looked at what proportion of each group of teachers were promoted, as the probability of promotion was as important as the speed of those who were successful. (c) Finally, we took the small group of teachers who had reached the position of headteacher, and looked retrospectively at the pattern of their career in schools.

A great variety of career patterns was, of course, encountered, and it would have been misleading to construct an overall profile of 'the career of a typical teacher'. This would in fact have amounted to the profile of a fictitious *average* teacher made up of the median points of a wide variety of career patterns. Profiles for sub-groups (men, women, graduates, non-graduates, and so on) give a more accurate indication of the real position, and have been constructed in such a way as to show both the median point and the spread of cases within that sub-group (Figures 1 to 4.14).

A. Career profiles

The profiles presented in this section are an index of the length of teaching experience associated with appointment to various career stages. The stages, though arbitrary, seem to represent a logical sequence of increasing status, and take some account of salaries. Because the sequence of feasible stages is not common to both primary and secondary teachers, profiles are presented separately for each sector. Within both primary and secondary groups, profiles are then shown for various types of teacher.

The confounding factor of 'change in school type' has to be borne in mind, as the method of compilation of profiles could not include this consideration. We do not, however, believe that our general or detailed interpretation of the profiles is unduly affected. Teachers' changes between school types are noted in Appendix C, Tables C24 and C25.

For each status the profile shows the average (median) length of teaching experience of the present holders when they were appointed to the post. In addition, the variation in the length of this experience can be judged from the 25th and 75th percentile values (represented in the Figures as a dotted line) between which the middle 50 per cent of appointees fall. The profiles are based on our 'N' (normal) sample of teachers, those whose careers were neither delayed nor interrupted (see Chapter Two).

Interpreting the profiles

The profiles (Figures 4.1 to 4.14) indicate the length of experience of teachers who have made their way up some or all of the promotion ladder, i.e. the relatively successful teachers. Fewer and fewer teachers reached the increasing status levels. When interpreting the profiles different aspects are of significance according to whether one is interested in the characteristics of a particular group or in comparing the profiles of the different groups.

a) Each profile

While the *median point* for any particular status gives a rough idea of the average time it took present holders to reach that status, it is important to note how that length of time varied among the teachers—and the dotted line between the 25th and 75th percentiles shows this. Between these two limits lie half the promoted teachers. These did not have their promotion exceptionally accelerated or delayed. These we call the typical teachers.

In presenting the progress graphically the status levels are treated as a equal units. This is obviously an oversimplification. The 'status' distance between level 1 (Scale 2) and level 2 (Scale 3) is hardly that between deputy and head. But to estimate the 'true' comparability of distance between status levels would have introduced insoluble problems, and we feel it is sufficient to alert the reader to this possible misreading of the figures.

As can be seen in the figures, some teachers at a high status reached it after the same or even less experience as teachers at a lower status. There are obvious explanations: (i) For some teachers length of service may have little effect in achieving higher status. (ii) Some teachers 'skipped' a particular level and aimed for, and attained, a higher level. (iii) Teachers who were passed over earlier when status posts were in short supply have been awarded these 'lower' posts later when they became more available. (iv) Some teachers were given status posts in recognition of long service rather than as an indication of suitability for greater responsibility.

b) Comparing profiles of different teacher groups

For a *particular status*, it is important to compare not only the average (median) length of experience when the holders in each teacher group were awarded the status, but also the variation in such experience for each group (i.e. comparing where the respective 25th and 75th percentiles lie).

Where our sample contained so few of that particular teacher group who held the highest statuses that a reliable median could not be calculated, the profile will not run to these higher levels. As our sample was a random one, a truncated profile would suggest that for a particular teacher group these higher status levels were either unavailable or not in demand. Unavailability of the 'highest status' is an important aspect to examine when comparing groups. It has great relevance for a teacher deciding on the kind of teaching sphere he or she proposes to enter or continue in. However, one teacher group may be denied the highest statuses but progress rapidly to the moderate statuses, perhaps more quickly than another group whose ambitions appear to have no upper limits imposed.

A particular profile may have a *missing status*, but a comparison between profiles in this respect is not always justified: the omission of the status may be due entirely to the fact that we selected for our 'standard' profile those intermediate statuses that seemed to form a logical sequence of career steps, but such 'logic' may not apply to all teacher groups equally.

Career profiles of primary teachers

i. *Primary teachers generally* (Fig. 4.1) One quarter of *promoted* teachers received their first elevation after three years or less experience, another between three and seven, and the next between seven and 15. Typically therefore half of level 1 appointments were to teachers with between three and 15 years experience. The 25 per cent promoted latest had served more than 15 years, by which time more than half of the deputy heads had been appointed and nearly a third of the headships had been won.

As not all teachers appointed to graded posts (new scale 2) were subsequently promoted to head of department (new scale 3) or the latter to deputy heads, there were many teachers for whom a particular level was terminal. As a result one expected and found that the slopes increase progressively from lowest to highest status levels. The range in the length of teaching experience of those typically promoted to a particular status was largest (14 years) for level 2 (head of department A, new scale 3) followed by status levels 1 (12 years), 3 (11 years), but narrowed a little when headships were gained (nine and seven years). The variation in itself was interesting, but was it different for different types of primary teacher.

ii. *Sex* (Fig. 4.2) The profiles show that men gained promotion more quickly than women. The intervals were 5, 10, 3, 3 and 2 years at the five levels from graded level (scale 2) to head of a large school. The biggest difference is enlarged by school type issues, as the simplest schools not warranting head of department Grade A (present scale 3), and certainly not a deputy head, are infant schools. Such schools are staffed almost entirely by women, for whom these status levels effectively become ceilings and are obtained only after long service.

Both men and women who were appointed to the various promotion posts had taught for widely differing lengths of time. It is interesting to note that in the lowest two levels while the median is to the left (young end) of the 'typical' range for men, it is central and to the right (older end) for women. Hence a much higher proportion of older women

FIGURE 4.1: *Post-holders in primary schools*

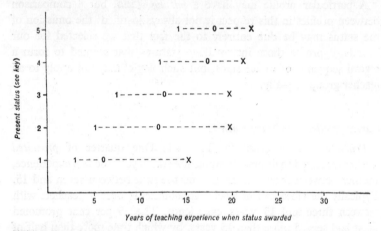

Years of teaching experience when status awarded

KEY

Status 1 Graded Post (New Scale 2)
   „   2 Head of Department, A (New Scale 3)
   „   3 Deputy Head
   „   4 Head (Small/Medium-size school)
   „   5 Head (Large school)

0 Median
X 75th Percentile
1 25th Percentile

were appointed to these levels. Perhaps it reflects the award of a status increment for long service and experience rather than as an inducement or an index of suitability for additional responsibility and future advancement.

The typical range for first appointments to these levels is much wider for women than for men: longer by 5, 4, 4, 0 and 6–7 years as one ascends the status levels.

Explanations for these differences go beyond the simple dominance of men. Certainly there *may* be a sex bias on the part of employers. There may be a different supply at levels dominated by women teachers. But one must also consider the demand factor. This is discussed more fully later, but a quick reference to some major issues is in place here. Many women might not apply for promotion because they do not expect to be preferred to a man. Married women may delay taking on additional professional responsibility whilst raising a family, and this, ironically is the reverse for a man, who may feel the need for additional finance with the onset of domestic responsibility. Mobility of married

FIGURE 4.2: *Post-holders among primary men and women*

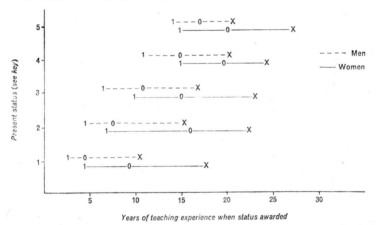

KEY

Status 1 Graded Post (New Scale 2)

   ,,   2 Head of Department, A (New Scale 3)

   ,,   3 Deputy Head

   ,,   4 Head (Small/Medium-size school)

   ,,   5 Head (Large school)

0 Median

X 75th Percentile

1 25th Percentile

women is limited, so that whereas a male teacher will move his family to take up a higher status post, the woman rarely does so. Thus the number of opportunities open to the woman are limited to those within a commutable distance of home.

iii. *Type of primary school* (Figure 4.3) First it must be remembered that the infant pattern must reflect the careers of women as well as teachers in infant schools, because the latter are staffed almost entirely by women. The infant profile tends to lag behind the other primary pattern by one to five years, except that the deputy head stage is reached one to two years earlier. The small size of infant schools usually meant that there were no Head of Department posts, promotion being to deputy head.

iv. *Qualification* (Figure 4.4) Our sample, following the national teacher population, contained relatively few primary graduates, and a full profile for graduates could not therefore be drawn. It is noteworthy that those graduates who held a graded post 1 or were heads of large schools

FIGURE 4.3: *Post-holders, primary teachers by school type*

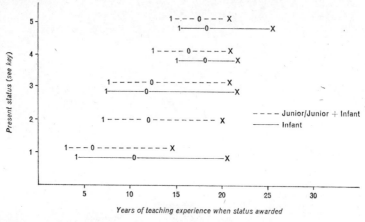

KEY

Status 1 Graded Post (New Scale 2)

   ,,   2 Head of Department, A (New Scale 3)

   ,,   3 Deputy Head

   ,,   4 Head (Small/Medium-size school)

   ,,   5 Head (Large school)

0 Median

X 75th Percentile

1 25th Percentile

were in general awarded these statuses after the same length of teaching experience as non-graduates.

Comparing primary and secondary teachers

Before examining secondary profiles (Figures 4.5 to 4.14) it is important to note that they will differ from primary profiles in two ways—both crucial to teachers' careers. Secondary teachers have more status levels to aim for than primary teachers. The highest status on both primary and secondary profile frameworks includes headship of a large school, and it is true that in both school types the peak of aspiration for those who want to scale the entire status ladder is 'headship of a large school'. But that term conceals real differences in range of opportunity: in fact primary schools range up only to about Group 6, while secondary extend to Group 14. For the purpose of the profiles we arbitrarily selected as primary highest status the headship of a school in Group 4 and over (i.e. in practice Groups 4, 5 and 6), and as secondary highest status the headship of a school in Groups 8 and above (i.e. in practice Groups 8 up to 14).

FIGURE 4.4: *Post-holders, primary, non-graduates and graduates*

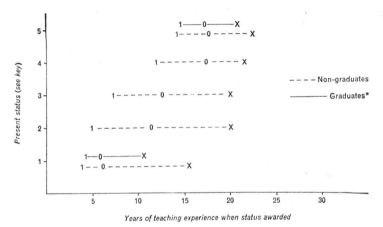

Years of teaching experience when status awarded

KEY

Status 1 Graded Post (New Scale 2)
   ,,   2 Head of Department, A (New Scale 3)
   ,,   3 Deputy Head
   ,,   4 Head (Small/Medium-size school)
   ,,   5 Head (Large school)
0 Median
X 75th Percentile
1 25th Percentile

Career profiles of secondary teachers

Secondary teachers generally (Figure 4.5) Because of the age range of the children, the small proportion (3.5% of whole sample) of middle and special schools were classified with secondary for the overall analysis. Half the secondary teachers who were awarded a first promotion had obtained it by their third or fourth year of teaching. A quarter of those receiving the first promotion had less than one-and-a-half years' experience. The typical middle 50 per cent were appointed between one-and-a-half and nine years after starting. For each rung up the ladder of promotion this variation in length of teaching characterized those who achieved higher status. The average experience at which these higher statuses were awarded to those among our secondary teachers holding such posts were: a head of department Grade A (now Scale 3) after seven years, a larger departmental headship (the present Scale 4) after 10 or 11 years, a very large departmental headship (present Scale 5) or a medium-sized deputy headship after about 13 years. Those who became deputy heads of large schools did so after

FIGURE 4.5: *Post-holders in secondary schools*

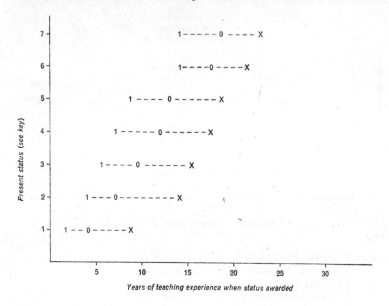

KEY

Status 1 Graded post I
,,   2 Graded post II, or Head of Department, A
,,   3 Graded post III, or Head of Department, B
,,   4 Head of Department, C—Deputy Head
,,   5 Head of Department, D, or Deputy Head (Medium Size School)
,,   6 Deputy Head (Large School)
,,   7 Head (Medium/Large School)

0 Median
X 75th Percentile
1 15th Percentile

having taught for about 17 years, and the relatively few who reached the pinnacle of headship of a medium-sized or large secondary school achieved this after about 19 years of teaching. In the primary schools, we looked at three factors that might have contributed to the variations among the profiles: the teacher's sex, the type of school in which she taught and her qualification. For the examination of the variations among post-holders in secondary schools we added the factor of subject specialism, as secondary teachers are concerned about comparative career prospects from one subject to another, yet this is a topic upon which very little information at a national level has been collected. *Sex* (Figure 4.6) The initial promotion of men and women in secondary schools was similar. Post-holders of either sex reached a first and then a second promotion at the same time—the first after three to four years, the second after seven. They then diverged: men who achieved the next status level did so three years earlier than their women colleagues. At the next two levels the difference was four-and-a-half years; at the penultimate level women had three years' more experience on appointment, while at the highest levels there were not enough women heads of large schools to compute a reliable median. Also while there was variation within each of the groups, it was about 50 per cent greater for women.

Many of the reasons put forward to explain the later promotion of secondary women would be those advanced to explain the same phenomenon among primary women. But how to account, then, for the fact that women who received the first and second promotion statuses did so no later than men? Did secondary women accumulate domestic commitments later than primary women? Or perhaps they chose to seek limited responsibility at school despite domestic commitments? Possibly other factors are at work, such as subject specialism, graduate status or less bias.

The women's profile is shortened, and there is no median calculated for the 'highest status'. That these statuses were available to women is shown by the fact that women do hold a few of these large headships. The reason may rest either with the supply of posts at this level (e.g are there more boys' schools than girls'?), or discrimination by appointing boards between men and women when selecting for those posts, or differences between men and women in demand for the posts. Reduced demand may have a major responsibility for the missing 'highest statuses' in the women's profile. Our check of 'responses to advertisements' showed that 164 men and seven women applied for four Group 13 headship vacancies, advertised by different LEAs and open to both men and women. For 133 schools (of Group 8 and over) that had headships advertised in the spring/summer of 1972—and these schools were spread across the country—there were 4,712 applications received from men, 276 from women. The sex ratio in applications in these two instances was more than 23 : 1 and 17 : 1 respectively.

It is said that the low demand for these posts by women is not because they do not want them but because they know they will not get them. Our other information—from interviews chiefly—suggests that men apply for promotion to a certain status many times more than women: in other words, they are rejected more often than woman and yet keep applying, which seems to indicate the greater urgency of men's demand for promotion.

FIGURE 4.6: *Post-holders, secondary, by sex*

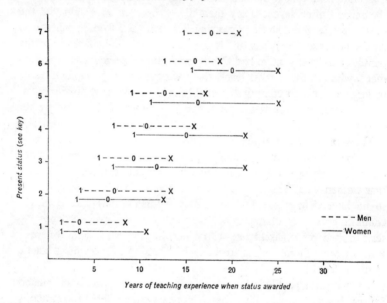

KEY

Status 1 Graded post I
  ,,   2 Graded post II, or Head of Department, A
  ,,   3 Graded post III, or Head of Department, B
  ,,   4 Head of Department, C—Deputy Head
  ,,   5 Head of Department, D, or Deputy Head (Medium Size School)
  ,,   6 Deputy Head (Large School)
  ,,   7 Head (Medium/Large School)
0 Median
X 75th Percentile
1 15th Percentile

Type of secondary school (Figure 4.7) The interpretation of these profiles is complicated, as present holders may have crossed from one school type to another. However, the general trend is quite clear—the promoted teachers in grammar and comprehensive schools advanced more quickly than those in modern schools. The interpretation of this trend is less clear for it is known that the latter contains proportionately more non-graduates, and the career profile of promoted non-graduates resembles the modern profile, certainly up to the deputy head stage.

The average length of experience when the promoted teachers in the three school types were awarded their respective posts can be seen in Figure 4.7. As always there were many teachers obtaining each promotion status earlier or later than the median times.

The teachers now holding promotion posts in comprehensive and grammar schools had closely similar career profiles, except that the former took one or two years longer in reaching the early promotion levels. One noticeable difference is that whereas three-quarters of those

FIGURE 4.7: *Post-holders among secondary teachers in different school types*

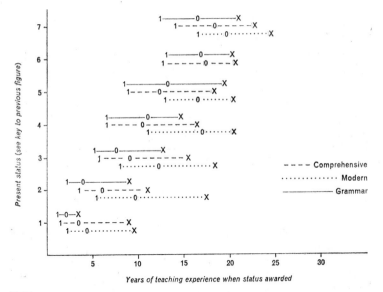

Years of teaching experience when status awarded

KEY

Status 1 Graded post I
   ,,   2 Graded post II, or Head of Department, A
   ,,   3 Graded post III, or Head of Department, B
   ,,   4 Head of Department, C—Deputy Head
   ,,   5 Head of Department, D, or Deputy Head (Medium Size School)
   ,,   6 Deputy Head (Large School)
   ,,   7 Head (Medium/Large School)

0 Median
X 75th Percentile
1 15th Percentile

who were awarded a graded post 1 (present equivalent Scale 2) in grammar schools received it before completing four years of teaching, for comprehensive and modern school teachers it was after 9 or 10 years' experience.

For the modern school teacher, progress was slower than for his colleagues in grammar or comprehensive schools. There seems no reason to assume that the demand for promotion was less in modern than in other types of school. Fewer status posts and more teachers searching for those that were available, probably delayed promotion for those now holding these posts.

Qualifications (Figure 4.8) The promoted teachers among 'ordinary' graduates in general lagged one or two years behind their good honours counterparts at each promotion stage up to deputy headship of a medium-sized school—when both groups had similar lengths of experience behind them. The ordinary graduates who were heads, however, achieved this status two years after the 'good honours' head.

The profile of the promoted non-graduate teachers generally reflects promotion two to four years later than was associated with comparable statuses for promoted graduates. Fifty per cent of the non-graduate deputy heads of large schools were appointed after 22 years of teaching experience, and at this level promotion virtually halted, for there were few non-graduates in our sample who held headship posts.

Subject specialism (Figures 4.9–4.14) At national or LEA level little information appears available comparing the promotion prospects and actual careers of teachers of different subjects. Nothing appears to have been published on what subjects are taught by non-graduates although, in 1970, this group comprised about two-thirds of the secondary school teacher population; and while the DES statistics list the degree subjects of graduate teachers, these are not necessarily the subjects taught by those teachers. Nor are there statistics relating subject taught to status held. Yet the relationship between subject taught and status held would have obvious interest to teachers, and if producing differential recruitment it would influence the shortage or surplus of various subject teachers. In practical common-sense terms, staffing problems will arise from encouraging the extension of a subject area if those who might be or are teaching the subject realize that their future career prospects will be limited in this area.

In the absence of official information, data were culled from our teacher questionnaires to probe the career profiles for those subject teachers who were reasonably well represented in our sample. This enabled some discussion of the relationship between promotion status and subject here and in other chapters.

In Figures 4.9 to 4.14 individual subject profiles can be inspected and compared easily where the profiles are on one graph. It was too difficult to present on one graph the 14 subjects with meaningful profiles. It is important to balance the rate of progress against the

FIGURE 4.8: *Post-holders among secondary graduates and non-graduates*

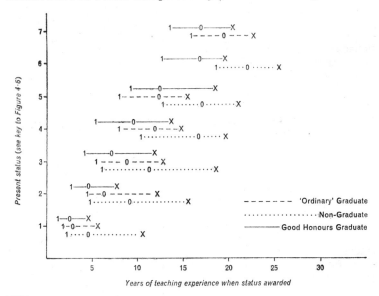

KEY

Status 1 Graded post I
    ,,   2 Graded post II, or Head of Department, A
    ,,   3 Graded post III, or Head of Department, B
    ,,   4 Head of Department, C—Deputy Head
    ,,   5 Head of Department, D, or Deputy Head (Medium Size School)
    ,,   6 Deputy Head (Large School)
    ,,   7 Head (Medium/Large School)

0 Median
X 75th Percentile
1 15th Percentile

accessibility to highest statuses. For example, while in our sample only teachers of history, English, maths and the natural sciences reached the highest statuses, the scientists were promoted earlier than those teaching the three other specialisms. Again, the physical education teacher who received a first promotion did so sooner than most other specialists, but ultimately was not likely to rise higher than a medium-sized departmental headship.

The median time to promotion at the different levels is provided in

FIGURES 4.9–4.14: *Post-holders among secondary subject specialists*

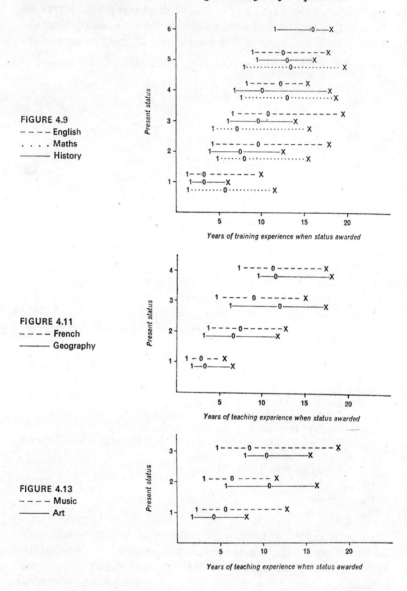

FIGURE 4.9
– – – – English
. . . . Maths
——— History

FIGURE 4.11
– – – – French
——— Geography

FIGURE 4.13
– – – – Music
——— Art

Status 1 Graded Post I
    ,,   2 Graded Post II or Head of Department A
    ,,   3 Graded Post III or Head of Department B
    ,,   4 Head of Department C, or Deputy Head (Small School)
    ,,   5 Head of Department D or Deputy Head (Medium Size School)

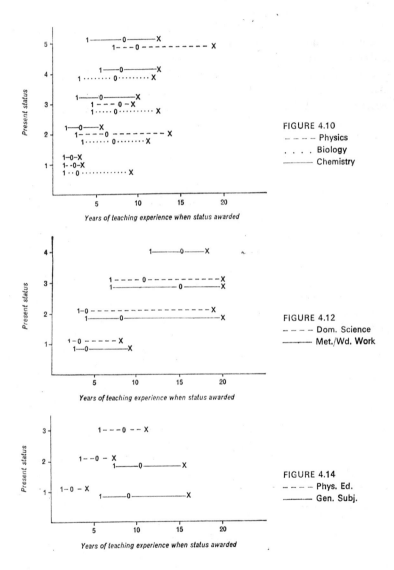

FIGURE 4.10
– – – – Physics
. . . . Biology
———— Chemistry

Years of teaching experience when status awarded

FIGURE 4.12
– – – – Dom. Science
———— Met./Wd. Work

Years of teaching experience when status awarded

FIGURE 4.14
– – – – Phys. Ed.
———— Gen. Subj.

Years of teaching experience when status awarded

Status 6 Head (Medium/Large School)
0 Median
X 75th Percentile
1 25th Percentile

Table 4.1. The median teaching experience for subject specialists who gained promotion to the different levels varies from subject to subject and level to level. It is summarized in Table 4.1. Table 4.1 gives a fair summary of which subject-teachers have reached the higher statuses in numbers sufficient to provide a reliable median score, but of course it shows only the general picture. Apart from history specialists other teachers, notably of English, maths and French, became heads of medium-sized or large secondary schools, and deputy headships were awarded to other specialists, chiefly needlework, biology and geography, in addition to those listed in Table 4.1.

One important aspect, however, can be seen only in the profiles, and that concerns the variations within each subject. Examples of striking items are:

(a) *First promotion status* When teachers of physics, chemistry and biology were awarded their promotion to graded post 1 (present Scale 2), it came after an average of two or three years; but whereas 75 per cent of the promoted teachers of the first two subjects were elevated by their fourth year of teaching, for biology it took up to nine years. Similar variations can be seen with English, maths and history specialists: 25 per cent of those receiving a first promotion did so by their second year, 50 per cent of promoted English and history specialists had four years or less experience, for maths it was six years and by the time 75 per cent of promoted history, maths and English teachers had been elevated one could see that it took only six years for historians but 10 to 12 years for teachers of English and maths. The teachers of 'general subjects' (non-specialist) fared worst of all— 25 per cent of those promoted, had been waiting over 17 years for that first step up.

(b) *Second promotion status* Teachers of chemistry and physical education resembled each other: of those teachers receiving a small departmental headship, 75 per cent were awarded that status within six or seven years (respectively) of beginning teaching. In general the range for other teachers was much greater. For example, a quarter of the physics teachers holding small departmental headships received them only after 14 years of teaching, and the period was longer still with maths and PE (15 years), art (16 years), English (18 years), domestic science (19 years) and metalwork/woodwork (20 years). The latter two are of no particular interest because while a quarter of these small departmental headships were awarded after 19 years of teaching, it is also true that another quarter were awarded before the third and fourth years. Patently those promoted early have more likelihood of catching the mainstream of career promotions. For many a late

TABLE 4.1: *Average length of experience when selected statuses* were first awarded to subject specialists*

Rank order of Subject	Average teaching exp. (yrs.) when awarded Status 1	Rank order of Subject	Average teaching exp. (yrs.) when awarded Status 2	Rank order of Subject	Average teaching exp. (yrs.) when awarded Status 5	Subject	Average teaching exp. (yrs.) when awarded Status 7**
Physical Education	2.1	Chemistry	3.0	Chemistry	8.8	History	16.1
Chemistry	2.1	Domestic Science	4.3	Physics	10.0		
Physics	2.3	Physical Education	5.3	English	13.3		
Biology	2.7	Physics	6.0	History	13.5		
Domestic Science	3.2	Music	6.5	Maths	14.0		
History	3.4	Geography	7.1				
French	3.5	History	7.5				
English	3.6	Metalwork/Woodwork	7.5				
Geography	3.8	Biology	7.7				
Metalwork/Woodwork	4.2	French	8.0				
Art	4.2	Maths	8.5				
Music	5.5	English	9.5				
Maths	6.0	General Subs	10.2				
General Subs	9.3	Art	10.8				

* Status 1 Graded Post I (Present Scale 2)   Status 2 Graded Post II/Head of Dept. A (Present Scale 3)
  Status 5 Head of Dept.D/Dep.Hd. med-sized school   Status 7 Head of med-sized/large school
** History was the only subject where a median value was regarded as meaningful (the few other subjects with holders at Status 7 containing less than 10 teachers). Further comparisons among subject specialisms may be inspected in the next chapter, where present distributions of posts is the theme rather than the career aspect of when posts were first awarded.

promotion may well be a service recognition. Several determinants are likely, as postulated by Start and Laundy (1973), notably professional competence and experience, and maturity with a strong but not domineering personality.

B. Changes over Time

There are many experienced teachers who believe that promotion comes more quickly now than in former years. Whether this is good or bad for the schools and the profession is a debatable point and one which is sometimes the subject of fierce argument in staffrooms. Earlier promotion could certainly encourage teacher mobility and if promotion was across and not within schools, the stability of the staff and hence the school would suffer as a result. In addition, older staff may resent the fact that they had to wait for promotion longer than younger colleagues. On the other hand, the prospect of comparatively early promotion should encourage young people to enter the profession even though the basic salary scale might be thought low, and should make a powerful antidote to possible wastage from the profession.

To gain objective data in this area we looked at the careers of those teachers with unbroken 'normal' careers who had entered the profession after 1956. We compared three quinquennial groups: teachers beginning their careers between 1956 and 1960, between 1961 and 1965, and between 1966 and 1970 respectively. A few statuses were selected and the average age at which each of the groups were awarded these statuses was compared. It should be recalled that there were virtually no entrants from colleges of education in 1962 as the two-year course of training was extended from 1961 onwards to a three-year course. In general, therefore, the mean age at which our 1956–60 group began teaching (about 21) was about six months younger than the 1961–65 group and a year younger than the 1966–70 group. Thus, if it were found that the later entry groups were promoted at younger ages than formerly, such a finding would be reinforced by the fact that these groups were actually older when first beginning teaching, i.e. they had been teaching for less time than their age (by comparison with the oldest entry group) would indicate.

Primary teachers—men and women For men, the 1956–60, 1961–65 and 1966–70 entry group achieved their first promotion to graded post 1 (now Scale 2) at 29, 28 and 25 years of age respectively. Appointments to head of department A (now Scale 3) came at 32, 27 and 26—the differences at both status levels being statistically significant. For women, the award ages for the three entry groups were not significantly different at those two promotion levels, although there seemed a definite similar trend for the younger teachers to receive the awards at an earlier age. Strangely enough, for women a deputy headship appeared to be awarded at a *later* age with each new entry group, but there was no discernible trend either way for men regarding this status. There were no women in the two later entry groups who held headships. None of the youngest male teachers held a large headship, but between the 1956–60 and 1961–65 periods the average age when this status was achieved by men fell by three-and-a-half years. In view of the age effect of the introduction of the three-year course, the younger group beginning teaching about a year after the oldest group, the fall in age of promotion at all five levels is somewhat greater than the figure suggests.

Secondary teachers—men and women There were too few teachers among the 1961–65 and 1966–70 groups who held any of the middle or higher statuses, so we were able to examine trends in the first (graded post 1) and second (small department head, A/B) promotion levels only.

The lowering of award age with each new entry group applied to both men and women (supplement Table G4.4). For men the first status promotion came for the 1956–60 entry at 27.5 years of age, for the 1961–65 entry at 26.5, and for the youngest entry group at just over 25. The second promotion was awarded respectively at 31.4, 28.5 and 26. The corresponding figures for women were: for first promotion—29.7, 26.5 and 24.8 years of age; for second promotion—33.6, 26.7 and 25.8. All four differences were statistically significant. It seems that men are obtaining the first promotion status two-and-a-half years earlier than they used to, and the second five-and-a-half years earlier; women now receive the first promotion five years earlier and the second eight years earlier. Over the last 15 years, the age of promotion in secondary schools has fallen and is considerably more marked for women than men. This conclusion should not be misunderstood. The figures and ages quoted comment on *when*, not *whether* promotion was awarded. As with primary teachers, these lowered ages of promotion over the 15-year span would, in fact, be lower still if the later age of beginning teaching (since 1962) were taken into account.

Secondary teachers—graduates and non-graduates The lowering of promotion age was true of both graduates and non-graduates, at least at the two early promotion levels that we examined, the average age at which graduates were awarded the first promotion status fell about two-and-a-half years over the 15 years from 27.5 to 26.4 to about 25, and about four years for non-graduates, from 28.7 to 26.6 to about 25. At the level of a small departmental headship, the graduate average age when promoted dropped from 31.6 to 28.2 to 25.5, the non-graduates from 32.3 to about 28 and then 26.6—roughly a six year reduction in both cases. All these changes were statistically significant.

The Promotion Routes Taken by Current Headteachers

All the analyses hitherto have been of cross-sections of the teacher population at the time of the survey in 1971/72. An alternative strategy would have been to undertake a longitudinal study and follow the progress of a particular group of teachers, say those who entered the profession in 1971. By the time they were fifty, say the year 2000, we would have gained a good insight into the promotion and careers of teachers. But time was not on our side—at least, not that amount of time. The next best thing was to start with a group at the same point in time and follow them not forwards but backwards. Since interest was in promotion rather than the lack of it, we looked at the current headteachers in our sample and tried to unravel the promotional routes by which they had achieved their headships. How many had been deputy heads? How many had been heads of departments and for how long? How many had held graded posts, and how many had bypassed one or more levels in their ascent to headship? The analysis from this approach was the basis of this part of the chapter.

A problem for this analysis is that there is some variation in remuneration and status among graded posts, more among heads of department, and heads and deputies in Group 1 and Group 14 schools are widely differentiated. Deputies of the larger schools could earn more than heads of the smaller schools. Heads of large departments in a large comprehensive school could be on a higher salary than deputy heads of small schools, and even perhaps the heads of the smallest schools. Thus while the nomenclature would suggest that the different statuses had discrete levels, financially they had broad bands with considerable overlap. Probably there was some overlap in prestige too, but that would be harder to establish. Hence it was possible, in theory, for the head of a large department to lose salary in a 'promotion' to the deputy headship of a small school. This will explain some but far from all the 'leapfrogging' we shall see in the following analyses.

To identify each level within every band would have led to an extremely complex branching diagram and subsequent analysis. Apart from the complexity, it was a practical impossibility to carry out, as the permutations of levels of head, by levels of deputy, department head and graded post outstripped the number of heads we had in the sample. Grouping thus became essential, and we returned to the broad classifications as these would be the simplest to follow. Hence the two main figures that follow (Figures 4.15 and 4.16) are over-simplified, though additional relevant detail, where important, is given in the text.

Primary headteachers

Five hundred and thirty-six headteachers completed the relevant sections of the questionnaire. In Figure 4.15 we see how many of the 536 primary headteachers had been deputies (264 or 49.3 per cent). Hence over half had not had experience as deputy headteacher. One hundred and seventy-three (32.3 per cent) had been deputies for between one and five years before promotion to head, and 91 (17.0 per cent) had had six or more years in that capacity.

Only 33 heads (6.2 per cent) had been heads of department. Nearly one fifth of these (7, or 1.3 per cent) had moved on to deputy position, while the other 26 (4.9 per cent) had been promoted directly to a headship. The low number of heads with head of department experience is undoubtedly due to primary school structure. The number and age of pupils would provide a high enough unit total for a head of department position in the very large schools only.

Sixty-one point four per cent (329) of our primary heads had been in graded posts. Ninety of them (16.8 per cent) were then promoted to head, more than 71 per cent having had three or more years' experience at the graded level. Two hundred and sixteen (40.3 per cent) went on to deputy first, then on to head. Twenty went to head via head of department, and three via head of department and deputy.

The important point that remains is that 156 heads were promoted direct from the level of qualified assistant teacher on the basic scale. Thus it would appear that 29.1 per cent of the primary heads in our sample had never been in a position of paid responsibility until they were promoted to headships. It must be reiterated at this juncture that we have not discriminated between the headship of a small school with a few teachers and one of a very large school with many staff. Nearly half this subgroup had fourteen or more years of service as an ungraded teacher, and nine out of ten of them had been more than five years in the classroom.

Obviously there are no fixed routes to a primary headship. and experience at any particular level did not appear to be essential.

FIGURE 4.15: *Pathways in the promotion of primary headteachers*

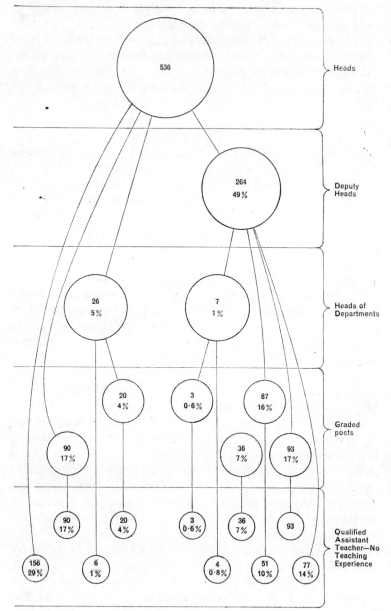

Only three (0.6 per cent) of our sample had held posts at all levels. Classroom experience in one form or another was obtained by them all. Promotion to head can occur from any level in the hierarchy, as evidenced by our sample, of whom 29.1 per cent were appointed from ungraded posts, 16.8 per cent from graded positions, 4.9 per cent from departmental head, and 49.3 per cent from deputy headships.

Secondary headteachers

Figure 4.16 shows the promotion routes of our sample of secondary headteachers.

Of the 139 secondary headteachers in our sample 73 (52.5 per cent) had not had experience as a deputy, 40 (28.8 per cent) had between one and five years, while the remaining 26 (18.7 per cent) had more than five years as a deputy. Only eight had been second masters/mistresses, suggesting either that this was not a popular route to headship or, much more likely, that there had been few positions available.

Of the 66 heads with experience as deputies, one had been a second master, leaving 65 who had come from being either heads of department (26 or 18.7 per cent), from graded positions (20 or 14.3 per cent) or direct from the ungraded level of qualified assistant teachers (19 or 13.7 per cent). Those who had been heads of department had had varied experience up to then. Three had taught for more than six years before being promoted direct to head of department. Four others had averaged three years' experience before receiving similar promotion. Nineteen had graded experience spread fairly evenly from two to six-plus years. The teachers without graded experience split into 14 with more than six years' teaching at the ungraded level, and five with between one and five years' qualified assistant teaching behind them before promotion to deputies. Eleven heads had taught for more than six years, and another eight for between one and five years before gaining graded status. One was lucky enough to have been appointed to a graded post on his first appointment to a school.

There were seven heads with experience as second masters, and four of these had served more than six years as department heads, three leapfrogging from ungraded posts after between one and three years at that level. One had spent five years as a qualified assistant and two years in a graded post before appointment to department head. The three who had not been department heads had all had twelve or more years' qualified assistant teaching, and one had had more than six years in a graded post prior to promotion to second master.

Sixty-six headteachers (47.5 per cent) had been neither deputies

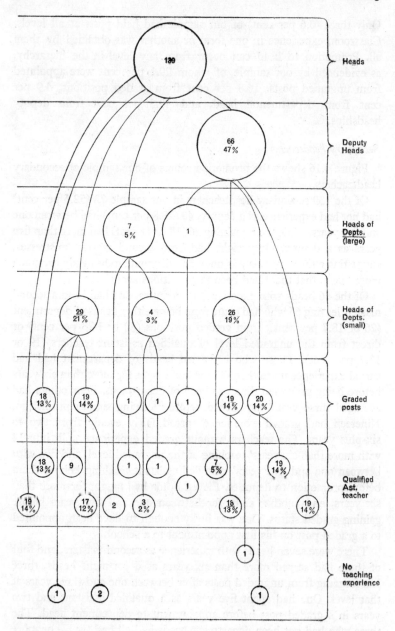

FIGURE 4.16: *Pathways in the promotion of secondary headteachers*

nor second masters. Thirty-seven had not been a head of department either, though 29 (20.9 per cent) had. Of the 37, 19 (13.7 per cent of all heads) had never held a graded post.

No one had managed to escape all contact with the classroom prior to being appointed head of a secondary school, though two had come close, with between one and three years only as an ungraded teacher. Of the remaining 17 in this category, two had had between four and six years' experience as a qualified assistant teacher before promotion to head, eight had had between seven and eleven years, and seven had had more than twelve years. Among the 19 heads who had not experienced any other promotion post until their headships there was a distinct trend for lengthy service in the ungraded ranks. Over three-quarters of them had had more than seven years' experience in the basic grade.

The 18 heads with graded experience in this group had had one to three years' (four), four to six years' (three) seven to eleven years' (four) and more than twelve years' (seven) experience at the ungraded level. Two-thirds of the heads who had had between one and five years in a graded post had completed at least seven years as an ungraded teacher, and only 50 per cent of those with six or more years at the graded level had exceeded six years without a promotion.

To summarize the secondary situation, of the 139 secondary heads in our sample, 47 per cent were appointed from deputy headships, 5 per cent from second master/mistress position, 21 per cent from head of departments, 13 per cent from graded posts and 14 per cent from the ranks of the ungraded teachers. Of this latter group, 15 heads (11 per cent) had taught for more than six years, and two (1.5 per cent) for three years or less. Five had bypassed the ungraded posts, taking a graded post on their first appointment to a school. Of these, two had gained their headship after experience as a deputy head, and the other three had arrived from head of department status. Again there was no exclusive route, heads being promoted from all ranks.

Patently the leap from deputy to head is equally frequent in both primary and secondary sectors. Second masterships are specific to secondary schools, so the major difference is the greater proportion of promotions from the levels of head of department in secondary and ungraded teacher in primary schools. Twice as many promotions from ungraded teacher to head occur in the primary school as in the secondary, but even so, 14 per cent of the secondary heads in our sample rose this way. All heads had at some time taught in the classroom.

Primary versus secondary pinnacles

TABLE 4.2: *Proportion of primary and secondary heads promoted from each status level*

	Deputy	Second Master	Head of Dept.	Graded Post	Ungraded Post	TOTAL
Primary	49	–	5	17	29	100
Secondary	47	5	21	13	14	100

General comment

Promotion to head can be from any of the lower levels within the career structure of the teaching profession, including the ungraded assistant teacher. This was also the case for all other promotion positions. All heads had had some experience of classroom teaching.

The impression that promotion now comes earlier than formerly seems justified and is reinforced when the later age of beginning teaching is taken into account. This is true at both primary and secondary levels, for both men and women, for both secondary graduates and non-graduates. However, the evidence derives from the first stages only in the teacher's career: our sample did not provide sufficient information to know whether it is applicable also to the higher statuses.

The reasons for the earlier promotion in more recent years are complex. Three with major effects could be: (a) proportionately more younger teachers within the profession now compared with earlier years; (b) deliberate national policy creating more status posts, as occurred after 1956 when the basis of unit total scoring changes; (c) the increasing demand by younger male teachers for early promotion, partly to further their careers and partly to keep pace with an increasing cost of living. Other reasons might well include deliberate 'manpower' policies affecting the relative balance of supply and demand, such as the sudden increase in demand for 'married women returners' in the 1960s, and the redeployment of staffing resources consequent upon school reorganization.

CHAPTER FIVE

The Distribution of Promotion Posts

A valid comparison of how the various promotion posts are distributed among the teachers in our sample can be made only if the total number of teachers in each group is taken into account. For example, if 50 out of 100 graduates hold headships and 100 out of 1,000 non-graduates do so, the figures of 50 and 100 are not strictly comparable.

Two-thirds of the headships are indeed held by non-graduates but a half of the graduates have obtained headships compared with only a tenth of the non-graduates. The way posts are distributed *within* a teacher group should perhaps form the basis of comparison between different teacher groups, and in the tables that follow, the number of teachers holding any status is always expressed as a percentage of the total number of teachers in the particular group.

The general picture

Combining data on primary and secondary teachers introduces considerable artificiality. Nevertheless this 'overall' impression is often what those outside the profession wish to gather. The combined data suggests that well over half the sample (57 per cent) held promotion status of some kind. Thirty-eight per cent existed on Scales 2 to 5, 8 per cent were deputy heads and $10\frac{1}{2}$ per cent were heads. Re-entrants (R group) tended to do better at the head and deputy head levels but a little worse in the middle levels; late entrants on the whole had less promotion at all levels ($1\frac{1}{2}$–$4\frac{1}{2}$%). The first comparison was between all primary and all secondary teachers. While the ranges of possible statuses are not common to both, Table 5.1 confirms the impression held that there are more ungraded primary than secondary teachers— in fact about twice as many. This must be balanced by the fact that 16 per cent of primary teachers held headships compared with 4.5 per cent of secondary teachers.

In order to understand better the issue of careers, we decided that it was the 'normal career' teacher sample whom we should study more closely, and in the following analyses the table and comments relate to the 'N' group of teachers unless specified otherwise.

To a large extent the higher proportion of 'promoted' secondary
teachers reflects the basic structural arrangements established by
Burnham, which decreed that older pupils will count for more points
when calculating a school's unit total, and then based the number and

TABLE 5.1: *Distribution of statuses among the whole sample: primary/
secondary*

		STATUS			
		Graded post/ Hd.Dept.			
SCHOOL TYPE	Ungraded	(Now Scale 2–5)	Deputy Head	Head	TOTAL
% of Primary (N = 3322)	56.2	17.7	10.0	16.1	100
% of Secondary (N = 3039)	28.6	60.8	6.1	4.5	100

X^2 Difference between primary and secondary distributions significant at
0.1% confidence level.

type of promoted statuses on these unit totals. As a result there are
fewer status position available in primary schools and the higher
promotion statuses below deputy head are not available in primary
schools. However, the prospective teacher, weighing up the pros and
cons of career prospects, should note that although the primary
teacher's likelihood of receiving a status below deputy head would
seem much less than a secondary teacher's, there are far more primary
schools than secondary schools whereby he can further his career
objective of a deputy headship or headship. Furthermore, relative
demand (hence competition) is different, as our data on application
rates showed that, *on average*, there were about twice as many applicants
for secondary as for primary headships—52 for a secondary, 27 for a
primary. However, the statuses of deputy or head in a primary school
(even in a large primary school) carry far less financial reward and
possibly less esteem than they do in most secondary schools.

The majority of teachers, having been selected and trained for one
of the two main school types, are subsequently concerned with opportunities in the different types of school within those two main fields.
(The advent of middle schools may well introduce a third career field
in the future.) Is there any difference in career prospects according to
the kind of primary or secondary school in which they teach?

(a) *School type: primary*

Three groups of primary teachers were studied: those teaching in (i) infant or infant and nursery schools; (ii) junior schools; and (iii) junior and infant schools. Table 5.2 shows how the promotion posts were distributed within each school type. Within the primary field all pupils are below thirteen years and count one-and-a-half points on the unit total, which alone determines the number and type of promotion posts available below deputy head. Size only then determines the differences between the three types of primary school, and as infant schools tend to be smaller they have proportionately fewer promotion posts than are found in junior/infant schools. Indeed, 'small schools' (below Group 4) are not permitted any promotion posts other than deputy head and head, while those below Group 2 usually have no deputy head post. Burnham had suggested that deputy heads *might* be appointed in large junior/infant schools within the Group 2 category, giving LEAs discretion about appointing deputy heads in other small schools; and since 1971 this general discretion applies to any school below Group 3.

TABLE 5.2: *Distribution of statuses: Primary (School types)*

	STATUS							
		Head of Graded Post I	Deputy Head Small/ Med.	Head Small/ Large	Deputy Head Large School	Head Med. School	Head Large School	
SCHOOL TYPE	Un-graded	A. (Now Sc. 2.)	(Now Sc. 3)	(<Gr. 4)	School (Gp. 4–6)	(<Gp. 4)	(Gp. 4–6)	TOTAL
% of Infant Teachers (N = 595)	58.8	9.7	0.7	6.2	5.9	9.1	9.6	100
% of Junior/ Infant Teachers (N = 1302)	54.5	13.5	3.6	3.4	6.5	11.1	7.4	100
% of Junior Teachers (N = 892)	54.1	18.9	5.8	1.3⁻	9.0	2.0	8.9	100

X^2 Difference in distribution among three primary school types significant at 0.1% confidence level.

The proportion of teachers who were not promoted was marginally higher in infant than either infant/junior or junior schools. But the proportion of promoted posts below deputy followed the predicted increase from infant to junior schools (10.4 per cent, 17.1 per cent, 24.7 per cent). There were fewer deputy heads in small infant/junior, as the smallest would not warrant them, and the similar scarcity in small junior schools reflected how few there were of such schools. (The latter reasons also explained the paucity of headships of these schools.) One oddity is the inbalance between the figures for headship and deputy headship of large infant schools. This is somewhat beyond the fluctuations explained by sampling errors which apply to the junior and junior/infant schools. Perhaps there were many unfilled deputy headships of large infant schools in 1971—we do not know. A noteworthy feature is the number holding headships of the more numerous smaller infant/junior schools. An important stepping stone is the experience of running a smaller school before proceeding to the greater responsibility of the larger headship.

The demand for infant headships was half that for other primary schools. For schools below Group 4, the average number of applicants for an infant headship was 13 and for other primary headships 26; for school groups of 4 and above, there was an average of 15 applications for infant headships and 32 for headships in junior or junior/infant schools.

(b) *School type: Secondary*

Of the three main types of secondary school, modern, comprehensive, grammar/technical, grammar schools usually have a pupil age-range of eleven to eighteen, but different comprehensive and modern schools may cater for either the eleven to eighteen or the eleven to sixteen age-range. As the number of pupils in various age bands within the secondary age-range determines the unit total of the school, any comparison of the distribution of promotion posts among the school types becomes much more complex than with primary schools.

Hence two analyses were undertaken, one for the eleven to sixteen and one for the eleven to eighteen schools. In both cases we wished to identify the difference in post distribution that was related to school type rather than school size. So the schools were first grouped by size and then within a size the school types were compared. Such a sub-dividing procedures often leaves too few teachers in certain categories to be compared; so care has to be taken in the interpretation.

i. *Pupil range 11–16* Table 5.3 shows the distribution of most of the promotion posts in modern and comprehensive schools, sub-divided into small and large schools (Small schools being those with less than 500 pupils.) The distributions were found to be significantly different.

TABLE 5.3: *Distribution of selected statuses. Secondary (pupil age range 11–16)—school type and size*

			SELECTED STATUSES*				
				Head of Graded Dept. Post I A. (Pres. Scale 2)	Head of Dept. B.C. (Pres. Scale 3)	Deputy (Pres. Scale 4)	Head below Group 9	Head below Group 7
SCHOOL SIZE (*Pupil roll*)	SCHOOL TYPE	*Un-graded*					
<500	% of Mod. (N = 249)	34.5	20.1	18.1	7.6	7.6	6.2
	% of Comp. (N = 64)	25.0	15.6	9.4	25.0	1.6	3.1
500– 800	% of Mod. (N = 83)	45.8	14.5	13.3	6.0	6.0	—
	% of Comp. (N = 70)	28.6	18.6	12.9	25.7	4.3	—

* The percentages will not add horizontally to 100 because the table does not include all statuses.

Comprehensive teachers held more promotion posts than their colleagues in equivalent sized modern schools (small 75 *v.* 65 per cent, large 71 *v.* 54 per cent). The major difference between the two school types is in the distribution of large departmental headships, both large and small comprehensive schools appearing to have far more. The unit totals of the comprehensives may well have been higher because they may have had more older pupils and/or more following academic courses. Perhaps LEAs were choosing to exercise their discretion regarding departmental headships by allowing more higher status department posts in comprehensive schools. The difference in the proportion of deputy headships may simply reflect the larger number of modern schools in the two relevant groups of school size. It suggests that the secondary teacher seeking a small deputy headship will find his chances of success greater in modern than in comprehensive schools (assuming that the demand for the post in both school types is the same).

Secondary modern teachers in the larger schools held fewer promotion posts at all levels than their colleagues in smaller schools. The increase in school roll and therefore school staff apparently did not justify a corresponding increase in the number of status posts. In comprehensive schools, the proportion of post-holders declined, but marginally (3.6 per cent), with increased size, so obviously the number of posts available was increased as pupil and staff members rose. Perhaps age and academic studies were more evident in the comprehensive.

ii. *Pupil range* 11-18 In moderate sized schools (500-800 pupils) with this age range, both grammar and comprehensive, about 75 per cent of the staff held promotion posts. In both the biggest, departmental headships (D and E, now called Scale 5) were awarded to a tenth of the teachers, but these statuses were rarely found in any of the modern schools with an eleven to eighteen range nor the eleven to sixteen age range schools. In seeking a big department headship a teacher was not well advised to look to a modern school, no matter what its size.

Very few of our teachers were in grammar or modern schools of the very large size so the comparison between the very large eleven to eighteen schools (those with over 800 pupils) and those of moderate size (between 500 and 800 pupils) virtually related to the comprehensives only. No significant differences were found in the way posts were distributed. The very large schools had, proportionally, fewer small departmental heads (Grade A) but nearly three times as many 'sub-departmental' statuses (graded posts II and III). It seemed that there was a limit to the number of head of department posts allowed—even in the largest schools—but the additional staff of the largest schools were rewarded with 'the next best' status.

For modern schools below Group 8, the average number of applicants for the headship was 67, and in the few larger schools 39. For comprehensive schools, the corresponding figures were 101 and 51; and for all grammar schools 62. There is much greater competition for headships in secondary than in primary schools, for not only are there fewer secondary schools, but indeed the average number of applications for those fewer secondary headships was higher (52, compared with 26 for primary school headships). Some indication of how intense this competition for secondary headships is can be seen from actual cases of individual schools, e.g. a comprehensive, Group 9—133 applications; comprehensive, Group 12—178; grammar, Group 9—149; grammar, Group 10—146; modern, Group 8—89; modern, Group 6—136. At the same time, one could find the other extreme, e.g. comprehensive, Group 12—18 applicants, comprehensive, Group 10—13, and comprehensive, Group 8—14. But such very small responses seemed thin on the ground.

Sex

Infant schools are staffed almost exclusively by women, and the distribution of posts in these schools can be seen in Table 5.2. The posts in the other primary schools are open to both sexes. There are some posts, usually in single sex schools, which are open exclusively to one sex of teacher, and this is very pertinent to the career structure. The distribution of the promotion posts in primary (non infant) and secondary schools is given in Tables 5.4 and 5.5. Men hold more of the higher statuses in both primary and secondary schools, with the trend being much more pronounced in primary schools than secondary. The proportion of non-promoted women was three times that of men in primary schools and twice that of secondary men. The proportion of men with headships in primary schools was seven times that for women, and in secondary schools nearly three times that of women.

TABLE 5.4: *Distribution of statuses among men and women—primary (excluding infant schools)*

					STATUS		
		Graded Head of				*Head*	
	Un-	*Post** (Now	*Dept.†* (Now	*Deputy*	Below	Gp. 4	
SEX	*graded*	Scale 2)	Scale 3)	*head*	Gp. 4	& over	TOTAL
% of Men (N = 696)	23.3	18.4	5.9	15.6	15.7	21.1	100
% of Women (N = 1435)	69.3	14.3	3.8	7.4	3.6	1.6	100

* Includes a few teachers now on Scale 3.
† Includes a few teachers now on Scale 4.
X^2 Difference in distributions between men and women significant at 0.1% confidence level.

Why are the posts so differently distributed among men and women? Hardly because of school type, for the difference is marked at both primary and secondary levels. It is not due to any difference in qualification, for a separate analysis which held the latter constant still left the sex difference relatively undisturbed. It is possible that the explanation for promotion posts being distributed unevenly and in favour of men is that there was discrimination by employers in favour of men. However, this seems unlikely to be true of departmental posts in a girls'

TABLE 5.5: Distribution of statuses among men and women—secondary

						STATUS						
	Un-graded	Gr.P. I. (Now Scale 2)	Gr.P. II HOD A (Now Scale 3)	Gr.P. III HOD. B/C (Now Scale 4)	HOD D/E (Now Scale 5)	Deputy Head Gps. Gp 7	Deputy Head Gps. 7,8	Gp 8	Head Gps. Gp 7	Head Gps. 7,8	Gp 8	TOTAL
Per cent of Men (N = 1596)	21.3	18.4	18.2	22.7	8.8	2.3	1.4	1.7	2.1	1.2	1.9	100
Per cent of Women (N = 1088)	42.3	18.8	15.8	13.1	2.2	1.5	1.2	3.3	0.9	0.3	0.6	100

X^2 Differences in distribution between men and women significant at 0.1% confidence level.

school, yet we found that men teachers in girls' schools still held proportionately more promotion posts than did the women teachers. Is it a question of shortage of interested and qualified teachers? Rather it was the old problem of supply and demand. Our analysis of the responses to advertised vacancies for headships (Table 5.6) supplied evidence for this explanation.

TABLE 5.6: *Applications for headships* advertised during Spring/Summer 1971*

SCHOOL TYPE	School Group	Total Number of Posts Advertised	Average Number of Applications from:	
			Men	*Women*
Junior and	0–3	148	20	6
Junior/Infant	above 3	227	28	4
Secondary	0–7	65	55	3
	8–11	88	46	3
	12–14	14	48	2

* All figures refer to vacancies open to both men and women.

For small primary schools the average number of applications for headships from men exceeded those from women by over three to one, with appointment rates of four to one (see Table 5.4). In larger primary schools seven men to every woman applied and the appointment ratio was thirteen to one. For secondary headships, well over 90 per cent of applications came from men, while the ratio of appointments favoured men by three to one. When the ratio of applications to the proportion of appointments is considered and allowance made for the differences in total numbers, the differences in promotion seem underwriteen largely by this 'demand' issue. The vacancies occurred in different geographical regions, and the tabled averages are based on LEA returns throughout the country.

Some may assert that women do not apply for headships because they believe that their applications will be rejected. Yet when we compare the number of applicants with the number of appointments, the rate of rejection for men is extremely high, yet they continue to apply. Where sex discrimination is not possible, for headships open to one sex only, our analysis showed that for junior and junior/infant schools the average number of applications from women for a headship open to women only was 11, the number from men for headships open to men only was 15. At the secondary level, headships open only to women drew an average of 15 applications, those open only to men an average of 59 applications.

We did not have sufficient data to comment definitively about the lower promotion posts, but the same trend seemed present with deputy headships, head of department posts and graded posts (present equivalents Scales 5, 4, 3, 2). The application rates did appear more even for vacancies at the lower level statuses, especially in primary schools. It is very difficult to check any link between application rates (demand) with actual distribution of these post-holders, for quite a large number of these lower status posts are not advertised, being awarded to someone already on the school staff. There is no doubt about the greater demand for higher statuses from men, and this may well be the chief factor determining the sex differences in the distribution of promotion posts.

Why men rather than women seek promotion is not implicit in or inferable from our data. Our general discussions with teachers, headteachers and LEAs and our own general acquaintance with the educational scene suggest that men seek promotion, particularly higher grades of promotion, because they believe such elevation brings additional money, greater esteem and wider responsibilities—all three of which may be less weighty sources of motivation in the life of the average woman teacher. Whereas a man may move his wife and children to take up a good promotional opportunity, the married woman rarely makes such a demand of her family. Hence for her the practicability of promotion lies in those posts which are within commutable distance of her present home.

Sex and school sex

Co-educational schools are usually larger than single-sex schools of the same age range, and the mixed schools would therefore have a greater supply of status posts. Would the ambitious teacher fare better in mixed schools, in schools containing pupils of their own sex, or in schools of the opposite sex? (Many men now teach in girls' schools, some women in boys'.) While limited resources prevented deeper analysis—e.g. allowing for the additional variable of school size among others—there were sufficient indications in the secondary school data for us to suggest tentative conclusions.

1. *Men in boys' schools and men in girls' schools*

While deputy headships and headships rarely came the way of men in girls' schools (though we did have a few instances) promotion prospects in girls' schools were better for almost all the remaining promotion posts. For example, about 34 per cent of the men in boys' schools were heads of departments, compared with over 50 per cent of the men in girls' schools.

2. *Men in boys' schools and men in mixed schools*

No significant difference was found in the overall distribution.

3. *Men in girls' schools and men in mixed schools*

No significant difference was found here either on the overall distributions, but closer inspection showed close similarities with (1) above. Proportionately more lower status posts, and particulary departmental headships, were being awarded to men in girls' schools than to men in mixed schools. One-fifth of the men teachers in mixed schools filled ungraded posts, as against only one twentieth of the men in girls' schools. Certainly, if deputy headships and headships were not the immediate main status objectives, serving in girls' schools (and possibly boys' schools) was a 'better bet' for men than serving in mixed schools.

4. *Women in girls' schools and women in mixed schools*

Women in girls' schools were awarded deputy headships and headships more than were women in mixed schools. About 70 per cent of the women in girls' schools held a promotion post, compared with 55 per cent in mixed schools. (There were too few women teaching in boys' schools to compare with either women in girls' schools or women in mixed schools.)

5. *Men in mixed schools and women in mixed schools*

The significantly different distributions for men and women already noted in secondary schools generally were reflected in the figures for mixed schools. This was to be expected because mixed schools formed the majority of our secondary schools.

6. *Men in girls' schools and women in girls' schools*

Seventy per cent of women held promotion posts compared with 95 per cent of the men. In this 'natural' field for women applicants, the appointment of men could reflect the higher drive for promotion in men, though the shortage of women with specialist subjects, e.g. mathematics, science, may well play a part.

Qualification

Over the whole sample of 'normal career' teachers, the distribution of statuses according to qualification was significantly different. Seventy per cent of the graduates held promotion statuses, 45 per cent of the non-graduates. This was due to differences among secondary rather than primary teachers. This is an interesting point, as it might have been thought that graduates in primary schools would monopolize promotion. In fact no *significant* difference was found between primary graduate and non-graduate in the way promotion statuses were distributed (see Table G5.4 in Appendix G for the details) but, if anything, the balance was tipped in the non-graduates' favour.

Among secondary teachers, the way in which the graduates and non-graduates differed significantly is of some consequence. Table 5.7 shows that within each main band of promotion (formerly graded post, head of department, deputy head and head) graduates were awarded proportionately more of the *higher level* posts than were non-graduates. In present-day terms one can reasonably interpret this as meaning that of the higher promotion scales (4 and 5) and the bigger deputy headships and headships, more were going to graduates than to non-graduates.

This trend was repeated within the graduates, as good honours graduates held proportionately more of the higher posts than 'ordinary' graduates (Table 5.8).

The majority of secondary graduates teach in either comprehensive or grammar schools, and because of their size, age range and academic courses it is in these rather than in modern schools that the higher statuses are found. Were graduates being awarded the higher statuses because of their degrees, or because they taught in comprehensive and grammar schools? There were too few teachers in the various sub-groups to test this, but an inspection of the data suggested that the school type (according to size) determined the number and range of statuses available, and within any school type, if there were higher statuses available these were more likely to go to graduates than to non-graduates.

The advantages of graduate status existed for both men and women, though they were somewhat less marked for the woman graduate. This may have reflected the smaller demand for posts from women.

Subject specialism

The teacher's subject specialism might have cut across the influence of qualifications on promotion distribution. A shortage or prestige subject

TABLE 5.7: *Distribution of statuses among secondary teachers: graduate and non-graduate*

QUALIFICATION	Un-graded (Now Scale 1)	Gr. Post I (now Scale 2)	Gr. Post II/Head of Dept. A (Now Scale 3)	Gr. Post III/Head of Dept. B,C (Now Scale 4)	Head of Dept. D, E (Now Scale 5)	Deputy Head		Head		TOTAL
						$<$Gp 9	Gp 9 and over	$<$Gp 7	Gp 7 and over	
% of Graduates (N = 1358)	27.0	13.2	14.7	22.1	11.0	2.5	3.0	1.8	4.7	100
% of Non-graduates (N = 1671)	30.0	23.4	20.0	15.6	2.0	4.7	1.4	2.1	0.8	100

X^2 Differences in distributions between graduate and non-graduate significant at 0.1% confidence level.

TABLE 5.8: *Distribution of statuses among secondary teachers: good honours and 'ordinary' graduates*

| | | | | STATUS | | Deputy Head | | Head | | |
	Un-graded (Now Scale 1)	Gr. Post I (Now Scale 2)	Gr. Post II/Head of Dept. A (Now Scale 3)	Gr. Post III/Head of Dept. B,C (Now Scale 4)	Head of Dept. D, E (Now Scale 5)	$<Gp\,9$	Gp 9 and over	$<Gp\,7$	Gp 7 and over	TOTAL
QUALIFICATION										
% of Good Hon. Grad. (N = 793)	27.2	11.1	13.8	21.6	12.5	2.0	4.7	1.6	5.5	100
(N of 'Ord' Grad. % = 575)	26.1	15.8	15.7	22.4	8.9	3.2	2.4	2.1	3.4	100

X^2 Difference in distributions between good honours and ordinary graduates significant at 1% confidence level.

might merit higher statuses regardless of the teacher's qualifications. All three 'Career types'—the normal, the re-entrant, and the late entrant —were pooled for the anlysis of subject specialism. This was necessary because breaking down the sample into subject sub-groups frequently produced very small numbers and little would be learned from this. The inclusion of 'R' and 'L' teachers would increase sample size and yet would not, as far as we could see, affect the distribution of posts according to subject specialism. Additionally, since this was a national survey of post distribution according to subject, it produced valuable data which should be maximized as it is not available from any other source.

'*Single subject' taught*: When completing questionnaires, teachers had noted the main subject they taught, as well as the main subject of their training and/or degree. There were 35 possible subjects listed, but as a preliminary inspection of data showed that certain subjects were being taught as a main subject by only a few teachers in the sample, e.g. Russian, psychology, statistics, these were combined with others, making a new total of 23 'subjects taught'. The questionnaire had allowed teachers to record up to three 'main subjects'. About two-thirds noted that they taught only one of over 23 main subjects, just over a third recorded two main subjects, and a few (7.6 per cent) recorded three. It was comparatively rare to find a second (or third) subject that would not be considered closely akin to the first subject mentioned, e.g. geography for first, and economics for second. The chief exceptions were associated with PE. Specialist PE teachers appeared to elect geography or history as their second subjects. Sometimes the history or geography teachers took PE or occasionally English. English teachers sometimes took PE. However, this seldom occurred with any teachers holding promotion posts.

It therefore seemed reasonable to regard the first-mentioned subject as the teacher's main subject in any subsequent analysis of the distribution of status posts according to subject taught.

Promotion differed widely among the subject specialisms. The first analysis shows the proportion of teachers in each subject who were promoted above the initial starting scale, and how the subjects were placed. Table 5.9 shows the proportion of teachers in each specialism who heald a promotion post, being listed in rank order from top to bottom. The second analysis, of the kind of promotion obtained, was drawn by selecting a few statuses of increasing prestige and indicating, again in rank order, the proportion of teachers within each subject specialism who held those statuses (Table 5.10, 11 and 12). The tables speak for themselves. The reader interested in any particular subject can see what are his chances of getting off the bottom rung (5.9) and can

TABLE 5.9: *Promoted teachers—per cent within subject specialism*[1]

SUBJECT	Per cent promoted	Per cent with over 5 years experience	Promoted with less than 5 years experience	Rank by promotion of the less experienced	Promotions as proportion of those with over 5 years experience	Rank by promotion as proportion of experience
Music	88.8	83.5	5.3	13	1.06	16
Physics	84.2	68.7	15.5	3	1.23	4
Chemistry	83.2	64.4	18.8	2	1.29	2
Latin/Greek	82.9	81.8	1.1	18	1.01	18
Sociology/Psychology/Education/'Others'	81.8	74.2	7.6	8	1.10	8
Drama	75.0	36.8	38.2	1	2.04	1
Geography	74.8	64.1	10.7	5	1.17	6
History ⎫	74.2	65.6	8.6	7	1.13	7
German ⎭	74.2	67.9	6.3	10	1.09	10
Maths	74.1	69.5	4.6	15	1.07	14
Woodwork/Metalwork/Craft/Engineering	72.5	70.5	2.0	17	1.07	14
English	70.6	65.2	5.4	12	1.08	13
French	68.9	62.5	6.4	9	1.10	8
Shorthand/Typing/Business Studies/Commerce	68.2	62.5	5.7	11	1.09	10
Needlework/Embroidery	67.8	64.7	3.1	16	1.05	17
Art	67.1	67.6	−0.5	20	0.99	20
General Science	65.7	69.5	−3.8	22	0.95	21
Physical Education	64.9	51.5	13.4	4	1.26	3
General subjects	63.2	80.1	−16.9	23	0.79	23
Religious education	61.7	61.9	−0.2	19	1.00	19
Domestic science	61.6	56.6	5.0	14	1.09	10
Biology	60.0	63.5	−3.5	21	0.94	22
Welsh/Russian/Spanish	58.8	50.0	8.8	6	1.18	5

[1] There were a few deputy heads (13 out of 189) who were virtually non-teaching and were therefore excluded from this analysis. It is likely that their original teaching subject was spread among the specialists, and had they been included the relative 'placings' of the subjects would not have been altered much, either in Table 5.11 or in the deputy head column of Table 5.12.

follow the probability of promotion to the higher levels by reading from Table 5.10 through to Table 5.12.

Simple ranking and promotion percentages can be deceptive, as two subjects equal on these might comprise one set of teachers with vast experience and, on the other hand, a group with an average of two or three years teaching behind them. We have therefore included in Table 5.9 the percentage of teachers in each subject who had five or more years' experience (the median for those obtaining first promotion was between three and four years and three quarters had been promoted by nine years). Presumably after five years' teaching every teacher has had enough experience to be considered for promotion, and this permits a fairer comparison. The longer the experience the more promotion chances would have come along. Hence music, with 83.5 per cent of its teachers having five or more years experience, had 88.8 per cent promoted and comes top of the simple ranking (Column 1). What is the relationship between those eligible (by experience) for initial promotion and those promoted? Who has more promotion or less promotion than would be expected from their 'eligibility' by experience? The percentage of teachers promoted over and above those with at least five years' experience gives a rough estimate of chances of rapid promotion, and these figures appear in the third column of Table 5.9. We can then calculate promotions as a proportion of those with five years' experience or more (fifth column), and rank these proportions as a general indication of promotion chance in each subject (sixth column). This shows the position more truly. For example, although nearly nine out of ten music teachers occupy promoted posts, a relatively small number of music teachers get rapid promotion compared with other subjects.

The top five subjects now become drama (where almost two-thirds have less than five years' experience, perhaps because it is a relatively new and burgeoning subject), chemistry, physics, PE (youth again the factor, as almost half have less than five years' experience) and geography. The three science subjects are about the same in terms of experience—two-thirds with more than five years' experience and two-thirds promoted. The 'relegation' subjects in descending order are RE, art, biology, general science (all low on promotion) and general subjects (low on promotion and high on experience).

Tables 5.10, 5.11 and 5.12 show the comparable figures for particular positions occupied—respectively graded post 1 (now Scale 2), head of department and head or deputy head.

From Table 5.10 it can be seen that drama and PE are the 'best bets' for initial promotion to a graded (Scale 2) post. As the median age for such promotion was three to five years, we took five or more years' experience as the criterion for eligibility, and worked out the percentage of those promoted as a proportion of those eligible (second column) and then ranked them (third column). The order does not change all

TABLE 5.10: *Percentage of teachers of subject specialisms who held graded post status*

	STATUS—GRADED POST I (now Scale 2)		
SUBJECT	Per cent promoted	Promoted/ Eligible	New rank
1. Drama	35.0	.95	1
2. Physical Education	31.2	.61	2
3. Sociology/Psychology/ Education/'Others'	30.3	.41	5
4. General Subjects	28.5	.36	7
5. Music	27.7	.33	10
6. Needlework	27.1	.42	4
7. Woodwork/Metalwork	26.9	.38	6
8. Welsh/Russian/Spanish	23.5	.47	3
9. Geography	22.0	.34	9
10. Art	20.4	.30	11
11. Domestic Science	20.3	.36	7
12. General Sciences	17.9	.26	12
13. German	16.0	.24	13
14. English	15.9	.24	13
15. History	15.1	.23	15
16. Physics	14.7	.21	16
17. Maths	14.5	.21	16
18. Chemistry	13.5	.21	16
19. Biology	12.6	.20	19
19. French	12.6	.20	19
21. Religious Education	11.8	.19	21
22. Shorthand Typing	9.1	.15	22
23. Latin/Greek	2.9	.04	23

★ 5 or more years' experience is used as our measure of 'eligibility'.

that drastically, with three of the original top five remaining, and nine of the top ten. The biggest drop was music, primarily because of the seniority of its teachers in relation to their frequency of promotion. Attention is drawn to Latin and Greek—last by any method. This is something to which we will refer later.

Table 5.11 provides the picture for head of department appointments (currently Scales 3, 4 and 5). First, the raw percentage of promotions

TABLE 5.11: *Percentages of subject specialists holding head of department status*

Head of Dept. A: (small departments) (Now Scale 3)				Head of Dept. B, C: (moderate size departments) (Now Scale 4)				Head of Dept. D, E: (large departments) (Now Scale 5)			
SUBJECT	Per cent pro-moted	Pro-moted/ Elig-ible*	Rank	SUBJECT	Per cent pro-moted	Pro-moted/ Elig-ible	Rank	SUBJECT	Per cent pro-moted	Pro-moted/ Elig-ible	Rank
1. Music	23.6	43	6	1. Int/GK	37.1	56	3	1. Physics	16.8	71	2
2. German	22.6	90	2	2. Music	26.4	49	6	2. Chem	15.6	113	1
3. Gen. Sci.	19.4	37	9	3. Chem.	25.0	68	1	3. English	10.6	30	4
4. Art	18.4	43	6	4. Sh. Typ.	22.7	45	9	4. Maths	10.2	15	9
5. Sh. Typ.	18.2	36	10	5. Physics	20.0	46	8	5. French	8.2	29	6
6. Dom. Sci.	15.9	45	5	6. Geog.	19.6	43	11	6. Geog.	7.5	26	7
7. Sociol.	15.2	34	11	7. History	18.8	40	14	7. History	7.1	24	8
8. Drama	15.0	95	1	8. Biology	18.5	50	5	8. W/R/S**	5.9	71	2
9. RE	14.7	39	8	9. Art	18.4	43	11	9. Biology	5.2	30	4
10. W/R/S**	11.7	47	4	10. RE	17.7	46	8	10. Wood/Met	4.6	13	10
11. PE	11.4	58	3	11. French	16.9	38	15	11. Lat/Gk	2.9	7	12
12. History	11.3	24	14	12. German	16.2	65	2	11. RE	2.9	12	11
13. Wood/Met	10.9	24	14	13. Dom. Sci.	16.0	45	10	13. Gen. Sci.	1.5	4	15
14. Chem.	10.4	28	12	14. Maths	15.9	30	19	14. Dom. Sci.	1.4	6	13
15. Lat/Gk	8.6	13	20	15. Sociol.	15.1	33	16	Music	1.4	4	13
16. Geog.	8.0	17	17	16. Wood/Met	14.5	32	17	16. Art	1.3	6	16
17. Maths	7.7	15	19	17. English	13.8	29	20	17. Gen. Sub.	1.0	2	17
18. Physics	7.4	17	17	18. Gen. Sci.	11.9	23	21				
19. Biology	6.7	18	16	19. W/R/S**	11.8	47	7				
20. English	6.4	13	20	20. PE	10.9	55	4				
21. Gen. Sub.	5.7	10	23	21. Need/k	8.5	43	11				
22. French	5.5	12	22	22. Drama	5.0	32	17				
23. Need'k	5.1	26	13	23. Gen. Sub.	4.7	8	22				

* 'Eligibility' Scale 3 : 5 or more years, Scale 4 : 10 or more years, Scale 5 : 15 or more years

** W/R/S   Welsh, Russian and Spanish (combined)

are given in rank order. The median age for promotion to head of department A was seven years, to B 10–11 years, and C 13 years. Hence in deciding our approximate criteria of eligibility, the percentages of teachers with experience equal to or greater than five years, 10 years and 15 years were taken respectively for the three status levels. The rank was then adjusted to show which departments had the highest proportion of promotions compared with those 'eligible'. As before, music dropped and drama rose in ranking, the respective maturity and youth of the teachers of these two subjects affecting the number of these teachers 'eligible' for promotion. Teachers of subjects such as Welsh, Russian and Spanish did well at the level of department head—mainly because of their scarcity value, it would seem. With the removal of Latin as a university entrance requirement, the size of classics departments might have fallen, leaving a number of moderately senior positions but few promotion vacancies. The upsurge of interest in drama and movement might well be the cause of the success story of these young teachers at the lower promotion levels. In the biggest departments chemistry and physics are joined by the rarity languages Welsh, Russian and Spanish, teachers of all these being at least twice as successful in obtaining department headships, as their colleagues of equal experience in other subjects.

Subjects success at the levels of deputy head and headteacher can be traced from Table 5.12. The raw and relative rankings can be seen to coincide much more at the level of headteacher. The classicist does very well at deputy level but does not appear to be well represented among the heads. Teachers of general subjects had a chequered career, successful at graded post level, in the doldrums at the department head level, then a moment of glory at deputy, only to slump out of the picture among the heads. Probably the category is too broad to produce a simple picture and within the area there are constant but different trends. If a headship is the target, then *for teachers of equal experience* the best chances of achieving that goal lie with history, physics, French and maths. The teacher of certain subjects will have to balance high probability of rapid promotion to low or moderate levels in the structure against the equally high probability of staying at those levels. Teachers of other subjects can perceive reasonable probability of both speed and ascent. Subjects do matter, though there is no certainty that the future pattern will remain the same.

Age

A reasonable hypothesis is that age, experience and promotion would be linked. This was found to be generally the case. The older the age-group of the teachers, the more the higher statuses were awarded in both primary and secondary schools.

The trend for fewer and fewer teachers to remain ungraded as age advanced stopped with those over fifty-five. Proportionately more of the

TABLE 5.12: *Percentages of subject specialists holding headship and deputy headship status*

Deputy Head				Head			
SUBJECT	Per cent Pro- moted	Pro- moted/ Elig- ible*	Rank	SUBJECT	Per cent Pro- moted	Pro- moted/ Elig- ible*	Rank
1. Lat/Gk	17.1	58	1	1. History	9.1	31	1
2. Gen. Sub.	14.5	35	2	2. Physics	6.3	27	2
3. Need'k	10.1	29	4	3. French	5.4	19	3
4. English	9.5	27	5	4. Maths	4.3	16	4
5. Sh. Typ.	9.1	21	11	5. English	3.5	10	6
6. Geography	7.9	27	5	6. Geography	2.3	7	8
7. Gen. Science ⎱	7.5	20	12	7. Biology	2.2	13	5
History ⎰	7.5	26	8	8. Art	2.0	9	7
9. Maths	7.1	27	5	9. Music	1.4	4	11
10. French	6.6	23	9	10. Chem. ⎱	1.0	7	8
11. Biology	5.2	34	3	Wood/Met ⎰	1.0	3	12
12. German	3.2	18	13	12. PE	0.5	6	10
13. Chemistry	3.1	22	10				
14. RE	2.9	12	14				
15. Dom. Sci.	2.2	9	15				
16. Art	2.0	9	15				
17. Wood/Met	1.6	5	18				
18. Music	1.4	4	20				
19. Physics	1.1	5	18				
20. PE	0.5	6	17				

* 'Eligibility' 15 years' experience or over.

oldest teachers in primary and secondary schools were ungraded than occurred with colleagues five and ten years younger. If a teacher in any school had not received some form of promotion by the age of about fifty-five, his chances of gaining even a small promotion after that age rapidly declined. In primary schools the proportion of teachers who were appointed heads of large schools increased with age until about fifty, after which it declined, suggesting that first appointment to a large headship became in general less likely after fifty. In secondary schools the large departmental headships (now Scales 4 and 5) were awarded to proportionately fewer teachers over forty than was the case with teachers between thirty-five and forty. Promotion to supervise a large department became less likely after forty, and scarce after fifty. The number of primary teachers in the age groups after thirty fluctuated. The number of secondary teachers in the age groups after thirty showed a continuous fall, there being, for example, less than half the number of teachers between fifty and fifty-four years old as there were between thirty and thirty-four (Tables G5.6, G5.7 in the supplement). Why, as they grow older, do secondary teachers appear to leave school-teaching relatively more than primary teachers? Is this because of general dissatisfaction with secondary teaching? Perhaps there are more opportunities for secondary teachers in other fields of education (administration, college, university, advisory) or outside education. Perhaps it is related to the realization that a watershed occurs at age forty, i.e. statuses below deputy head become relatively more remote after the age of forty.

Career groups: normal (N), re-entrant (R) and late entrant (L)

It was mentioned earlier that whereas 57 per cent of our 'normal' teachers hold a promotion post of some kind, the figures for re-entrants and late entrants were respectively 60 per cent and 49 per cent (roughly). However, this is misleading without bearing in mind that for any given age they have been teaching for differing lengths of time. We therefore divided each of the three groups into four 'teaching experience' sub-groups: (1) less than five years' teaching; (2) 5–9 years; (3) 10–14 years; and (4) over 14 years. The 'career type' groups with the same lengths of teaching experience were then compared and are summarized in Table 5:13.

TABLE 5.13: *Career type (N, R, L): proportion of teachers in each type who held promotion status (primary plus secondary)*

CAREER TYPE	Promoted teachers within career type, with teaching experience of:			
	5 years	5–9 years	10–14 years	14 years
Per cent of N (normal)	20.2	62.1	75.4	83.8
Per cent of R (re-entrants)	19.0	27.8	46.4	76.9
Per cent of L (late entrants)	11.5	52.6	83.9	89.0

(a) *Less than five years' teaching experience.* At this early stage of their varying careers the groups differed significantly. About 20 per cent of the normal and re-entrant groups held promotion posts, whereas only 12 per cent of late entrants did so. The difference arose from the secondary rather than the primary sector.

(b) *Between five and nine years' experience.* The three career groups again differed significantly: 62 per cent of the 'normals' were promoted, 53 per cent of the late entrants, and only 28 per cent of the re-entrants. The higher status posts were going to 'normals' rather than late entrants, and the re-entrants were generally falling behind now. The re-entrants' setback was seen more with primary teachers than with their secondary counterparts, and in fact the secondary re-entrants were keeping pace with 'normals' where higher statuses were concerned.

(c) *Between 10 and 14 years' experience.* The overall situation showed that 84 per cent of late entrants were promoted, 75 per cent of normal, and 46 per cent of re-entrants, the latter being significantly 'disadvantaged'. These differences were also more pronounced for primary than for secondary teachers. This length of experience brought more of the higher promotion levels within reach, and these began to be awarded to normals, followed by re-entrants edging out late entrants. The lower promotion posts, however, were now going to late entrants, normals and re-entrants, in that order.

(d) *Over 14 years' experience.* Ambitious teachers with this amount of experience would hope to have been awarded one of the higher rather than lower statuses. In fact 89 per cent of the late entrants had now been promoted, 84 per cent of the normals, and 77 per cent of the re-entrants. The promoted teachers among the re-entrants and normals were awarded relatively more of the high status posts than were the late entrants, and the latter more of the low promotion posts. An interesting point is that with the secondary group the re-entrants held proportionately more headship posts than did normal career teachers. Is a period out of the school in educational administration or commerce, business, or industry regarded as an asset in a secondary head?

Career groups: career types within sex

The comparison just made concerned the total sample of each career type. Another kind of comparison may be made by sex:

(a) *Women—normal and re-entrant.* There has been over the last 15 years a definite policy of drawing back to the classroom women who had left to raise families. Many of those who did not leave or who returned fairly quickly might well regard themselves as true 'career teachers'. Their concern with their careers would be as deep as any man's. Re-entrant women colleagues with long absences may be seen as returning to teaching for a supplementary income to escape domestic boredom, or for genuine interest in the work. The 'career woman' may feel she is more entitled than the re-entrant to the higher statuses of the career she has chosen, and as the number of re-entrants increases, she may wonder if her prospects of progressing in that chosen career are diminishing.

As far as the distribution of statuses gives any clue to the answer, it would appear that at the primary level the significant difference between the groups works in the 'normal' woman's favour. At the 10–14 years' experience range 46 per cent of the normals were promoted and 29 per cent of the re-entrants. After 14 years' experience 66 per cent of the normals were promoted, compared with 44 per cent of the re-entrants. Headships and deputy headships among women were mostly held by the 'normal' career teacher.

Promotion posts at the secondary level were not distributed *significantly* differently between the two career types. Probably subject specialisms were more important than career type. Re-entrants held proportionately more graded post 1 statuses than did normals, but this weighting was reversed for later promotion, restored at deputy head level, and reversed again for headships.

There were very few women late entrants in the sample apart from those with less than five years' experience, and at this stage all the career types had only 5 to 10 per cent of teachers with a promotion post. (b) *Men—normals, re-entrants and late entrants.* The only experience stage with more than a sprinkling of either men late entrants or men re-entrants was the over-14 years' range. This was probably a mixture of those coming from industry and those who resumed or began a teaching career after the last war. There were significant differences at both primary and secondary levels. At primary level, the most striking feature was the four-fifths of experienced re-entrant men compared with three-fifths 'normal' men who were heads (half in large schools). And one-third of the late entrants were deputy heads compared with less than one-sixth of the 'normals'. Over a quarter of secondary re-entrants were heads. In general the normal career teacher in this group with 14 years' experience had no overall advantage over re-entrants. In fact there were proportionately twice as many re-entrants promoted to headships as were 'normal' teachers (29.4 and 15.1 per cent respectively). However, both groups did significantly better than late entrants with the same experience.

CHAPTER SIX

Characteristics of Promoted Teachers

In our questionnaire to teachers we asked promoted teachers if their present status had been (a) awarded internally at their school without a formal application, (b) awarded internally but formally applied for, or (c) accompanied by a move from another school. The analysis revealed a highly significant difference between the primary and secondary sectors (Table 6.1). During re-organization, increases in status were granted internally and without application to teachers involved in the enlargement or amalgamation of schools, but this would not explain all the informal internal promotion, because the high rate of recommendation for internal promotion was found in all three types of secondary school. In both primary and secondary schools, even a few heads had, without formal application, been appointed to the headship of the school in which they were already teaching. Perhaps the teacher, usually a deputy head, had been acting head because of some specific school circumstance, and was subsequently recommended as the new head.

TABLE 6.1: *Type of promotion (teachers of all career types)*

| | | TYPE OF PROMOTION | | | TOTAL No. |
| | | Internal | Internal | | OF PROMO- |
SCHOOL TYPE		Informal	Formal	External	TIONS
Primary	N	350	271	707	1328
	%	26.4	20.4	53.2	100
Secondary	N	832	225	537	1594
	%	52.2	14.1	33.7	100

X^2 Difference in distributions between Primary and Secondary significant at 0.1% confidence level.

(a) *Primary schools*

At the lower levels of promotion, about three-quarters of the promoted teachers were awarded their posts internally, half on 'recommendation', about a quarter after formal application. The remaining quarter involved appointment from another school. At the deputy head level, over half the promotions were internal—21 per cent 'recommended', 33 per cent after formal application—and 46 per cent of the deputy heads came from other schools. Over 10 per cent of the heads had been teaching at their schools before gaining the headship, and a quarter of these were 'recommended'. In general, infant promotions occurred less frequently by recommendation than in junior and junior/infant schools, but the promotions to deputy head involved internal applicants relatively more often than in the other school types.

(b) *Secondary schools*

Three-quarters of all promotions at the first promotion level were made internally, 64 per cent without formal application. Similar proportions prevailed at old graded post II (usually a position of second in department). Successful applicants for the headship of medium-sized departments were roughly 55 per cent internal recommendation, 16 per cent internal formal application, and 29 per cent external. At the large department stage (now Scale 5), internal promotion still accounted for 60 per cent of the promotions, 42 per cent by recommendation. Fifty-five per cent of those who are now deputy heads were teaching at the school prior to their present appointment, and half of these did not apply formally for their posts. Finally, out of 97 heads in this secondary analysis, 74 were external applicants and 23 internal.

In all three types of secondary school there was a high level (65 per cent) of promotions going to internal candidates, but the proportion of these resulting from formal application was significantly less in the grammar schools (9 per cent formal applications against 15 per cent and 16 per cent respectively in modern and comprehensive schools). This balance between formal and informal internal promotions seemed to vary with status level.

This evidence supports the impression held by many teachers that many promotion appointments are filled internally at school without an open advertisement. Another concern is the advertised appointments which teachers feel are 'fixed' in favour of internal candidates and where the appointment procedure is a superfluous formality, involving an unnecessary waste of time, money and energy both for the school and the unsuccessful candidates. To look at this, one should compare the proportions of internal and external promotions following formal application. Presumably these posts were advertised locally or nationally and the appointment procedure employed. From Table 6.1 it can be calculated that out of the 1740 formal promotions (the combined internal formal and external, primary and secondary) about 28 per cent went to candidates already teaching at the school, and 72 per cent to external applicants, these proportions being roughly the same in both secondary and primary schools. Whether these proportions are reasonable cannot be evaluated. We do not know the proportion of applicants who were internal. It may reflect a 'rigging' element in appointments, or a reward for loyalty to one's school, or a case of selecting 'the devil you know', or the genuine result of choosing the best man for the job. Certainly all these explanations were represented among the people we interviewed. Whichever explanation holds true in an individual situation, it is only to be expected that the applicants concerned might tend to approve or protest according to their success or failure.

Variety of teaching experience

Loyalty or width of experience—which is the most important? To some teachers long service in a school appears to promote school and pupil stability and mark a teacher's sense of loyalty, while frequent moves among schools denotes a shallow approach to the job and personal instability. To others, long service in a school appears to produce stagnation of thought, while movement breeds versatility and flexibility, and an open-minded approach. A relevant question would seem to be which of the two counts more for promotion? Variety of experience ought to include the kind of schools as well as the number, but restricted resources compelled us to limit the analysis to the relationship between promotion status and the number of schools in which the teacher had taught for at least a full term, and included only 'normal career' teachers, not re-entrants or late entrants to the profession.

The largest number of schools served by any one teacher was 20, but the average was about three. Table 6.2 gives the reader an indication of how many teachers served in more or less than this average, but it should be remembered that this table ignores the age of teacher, his length of service and the level of appointment. About half the sample had taught in only one or two schools and about one-tenth in more than five. Primary teachers had moved round much more than had secondary teachers. Just over an eighth of secondary teachers had taught in five or more schools, but nearly a quarter of primary teachers had—perhaps because their average length of service was greater.

Promoted teachers and variety of experience (Table 6.3)

Over half (57%) of the appointments to head of department position were to teachers with experience in two or three schools. First appointments to deputy head were mainly (46%) teachers with experience in three or four schools and the range two to five schools accounted for over three-quarters of such appointments. Teachers with backgrounds in four or five schools provided 47 per cent of heads, with almost

TABLE 6.2: *Number of schools in which served*

		Number of Schools					
SCHOOL TYPE		1	2	3	4	5	5+
Per cent of Primary Teachers (N = 2764)		26.6	19.8	16.3	14.1	9.5	13.7
Per cent of Secondary Teachers (N = 2631)		29.7	26.5	18.6	11.4	5.6	8.2
Per cent of all Teachers (P and S) (N = 5395)		28.1	23.0	17.5	12.8	7.6	11.0

X^2 Difference between Primary and Secondary significant at 0.1% confidence level.

another third coming from teachers with yet more varied experience. As a counter to this trend, of all the teachers who had taught in four or more schools, over a quarter held no promotion post at all.

TABLE 6.3: *Number of schools in which served: post holders (primary and secondary)*

		NUMBER OF SCHOOLS					
STATUS	N	1	2	3	4	5	5+
% of all Ungraded (New Scale 1)	2313	48.0	21.2	12.4	7.5	4.3	6.6
% of all Hds. of Dept. (New Scales 3–4)	941	11.4	30.5	26.6	15.1	7.4	9.0
% of Deputy Heads	440	4.8	18.2	22.0	24.1	11.8	19.1
% of Heads	543	1.1	5.2	15.5	24.5	22.4	31.3

X^2 Difference in number of schools among statuses significant at 0.1% confidence level.

While increased status was generally connected with number of teaching appointments, there came a brief plateau, usually within the two to five schools range, after which the number of appointments ceased to be an advantage and might even begin to hinder progress.

(a) *Primary and Secondary* In Table 6.4 you can see that the average number of schools increases with status but by negligible or diminishing amounts. It also shows that primary teachers had served in more schools than secondary teachers of similar status. Internal promotion would reduce the average number of schools in which appointees served. Internal promotion to any particular status level occurred more at lower promotion levels than at higher and also, as we have seen, more at the secondary than the primary level. This might account for some of the significantly increased mobility among appointees to the lower status posts in primary school. The overall relationship between number of appointments and status was similar for both secondary and primary, suggesting that this relationship is relatively independent of the factor of internal promotion.

TABLE 6.4: *Mean number of schools in which served: post holders and school type*

		SCHOOL TYPE				
		Primary			Secondary	
STATUS	No.	Mean	SD*	No.	Mean	SD*
Ungraded	1581	2.4	2.1	784	1.7	1.7
Graded post (Now Scale 2)	415	3.1	2.2	492	2.5	1.7
Head of Dept. A (Now Scale 3)	110	3.5	1.9	248	2.9	1.6
Head of Dept. D/E (Now Sc. 5)	—	—	—	163	3.1	1.3
Deputy Head	204	4.1	2.7	150	3.9	1.7
Small Headship (Prim.Gp. 0, 1) (Sec. GP. 7)	74	4.8	4.1	42	5.4	3.9
Med./Large Headship (Prim. Gps. 4 and over) (Sec. Gp. 7 and over)	240	4.9	2.3	61	4.5	1.4

t-test: Differences between primary and secondary for ungraded status and graded post, both significant at 0.1% confidence level; for head of dept. A, at 1.0% confidence level.
*SD Standard Deviation

School type (secondary) Two-thirds of all grammar school teachers had taught in only one or two schools, compared with 59 per cent in modern schools and 52 per cent in comprehensive schools. Just over a

quarter of modern and comprehensive teachers had served in four or
more schools, compared with 16 per cent of grammar teachers. However, the differences were at the lower promotion levels only, because
teachers appointed to deputy and head statuses had taught in roughly
the same number of schools, regardless of school type.

(b) *Sex*   Seventeen per cent of primary men had taught in only one
school, and 30 per cent of primary women. For secondary teachers
these proportions were 27 per cent and 33 per cent. At the other end,
65 per cent of primary men had taught in three schools or more, and
49 per cent of primary women. For secondary teachers the proportions
were 45 per cent of men, 43 per cent of women. Whether these
differences produced differential promotion was too difficult to extract
from the data definitively; too many other variables such as experience
and school type intervened, and the number of teachers in each of the
sub-categories would have been too small for respectable analysis. The
best summary of the general position, covering all schools, is that
although men had moved school more often than women, this variety
of experience counted less for them where promotion was concerned
than it did for women.

Length of experience of current status holders

The career profiles in Chapter Four were based on the length of the
teacher's experience when *first appointed* to a particular post. The
following analysis describes the attributes of present status holders in
the sample irrespective of how long they have been in that status post.
The first of those attributes is current length of experience including
all the years at the present level.

Promoted teachers and length of teaching experience

(a) *Primary and secondary*   Table 6.5 sets out the length of teaching
experience for each status such that primary and secondary teachers
can be compared. The length of experience of teachers at each level
varied widely. The variation appeared marginally greater in primary
schools. The primary teacher had, in general, taught longer (one to
five years) than his secondary colleague on a similar promotion level.
Not unexpectedly, the average length of experience of the present
incumbents of promotion appointments increased with their responsibility. The standard deviation is remarkably steady and indicates
considerably skewed distribution at the lowest and highest appointments. The fairly regular progress at primary compares with the
plateaus at head of department and head/deputy head in secondary

schools. The long experience of heads and deputy heads of small secondary schools is associated with the fact that most of these were secondary modern schools. Perhaps these teachers had not made bids for promotion into bigger, comprehensive schools.

TABLE 6.5: *Mean length of teaching experience (years): post holders and school type*

| | SCHOOL TYPE | | | | | |
| | Primary | | | Secondary | | |
STATUS	No.	Mean	S.D.*	No.	Mean	S.D.*
Ungraded	1554	7.5	8.4	786	4.4	5.9
Graded post (Now Scale 2)	407	12.7	9.3	492	9.2	7.3
Head of Dept. A (Now Scale 3)	109	14.9	9.3	252	14.1	9.0
Head of Dept. B (Now Scale 4)	—	—	—	235	14.2	7.9
Head of Dept. C (Now Scale 4)	—	—	—	191	15.3	7.2
Head of Dept.D/E (Now Scale 5)	—	—	—	165	16.7	7.8
Deputy head (Pr.Gps. 4 & over) (Sec.Gps. 7, 8)	201	18.5	8.8	35	23.2	8.0
Deputy head (Sec. Gps. 9 & over)	—	—	—	63	21.3	7.9
Head (Pr. Gps. 0, 1; Sec. Gp.7)	70	21.5	8.5	43	26.1	7.4
Head (Pr. Gps. 4 and over) (Sec. Gps. 9 and over)	235	24.5	7.4	61	23.3	7.1

t-tests Differences between primary and secondary in mean length of teaching experience: ungraded, graded post and small deputy head—significant at 0.1% confidence level; small headship—1.0% level.
*SD Standard Deviation

School type (secondary) The trend was for teachers in secondary modern schools to have taught longer than teachers of similar status in the other types of school; e.g. at the old graded post 1 level, now designated Scale 2, teachers in grammar, comprehensive and modern schools had taught for seven, nine and 10 years respectively; in small departments, now Scale 3, the corresponding lengths of experience were 10, 12 and 16 years.

(b) *Sex* Except for graded post 1 (now Scale 2) in secondary schools, where the sexes had taught for an equal length of time, men had taught for less time than women at corresponding status levels in both primary and secondary schools. The average length of experience at lower promotion levels (formerly graded post) was about 10 years for men and 12 for women; at head of department level for men 14, 16 for women; at deputy head level 18 and 22; and at head level 22 and 27. Experience hierarchies, each higher status having on average more experience than the one below it, existed for both sexes in both types of school. In addition, at any particular promotion level the range in length of experience was greater for women.

(c) *Qualification* At almost all status levels graduates had had less experience than non-graduates.

(d) *Subject specialism* As there would have been too few teachers in each group if we had analysed all 23 subjects separately, we arbitrarily classified the subjects into three 'areas': arts, science and cultural/ practical. The picture proved a complex one. For example, at the graded post level which is now Scale 2, the length of experience was similar at eight or nine years for all three subject groups. All three had the same length of experience, about 13 or 14 years, at the small departmental level. Heads of medium-sized science departments seemed to have less experience than the departmental head in the other two subject groups. Among the heads of large departments, the Arts and Science teachers had taught for 16 years compared with the 23 years of the cultural/practical teachers.

(e) *Career type* There were too few teachers in the re-entrants and late entrants groups to make a detailed analysis of all status levels for men, women, graduates, etc. The analysis that was attempted and inspection of data suggested that late entrants had roughly the same lengths of teaching experience as 'normal' teachers at corresponding status levels, but re-entrants at these levels had been teaching longer than either. This seemed to apply to both sexes in both primary and secondary schools. The explanation cannot therefore lie with sex or school type differences. Perhaps re-entrants are less ambitious, or more settled, and are thus more content than are 'normals' or late entrants to keep the status they have.

Age

In general, the mean age of the teachers following a 'normal' career mirrors the length of their teaching experience. There are, however, two exceptions—graduates, and teachers who have been out of teaching for less than five years, and who therefore are not classed as re-entrants but included in the general analysis. Both groups will have grown older without accruing corresponding teaching experience.

Age increases with promotion level. Women are older than men at the same level in both primary and secondary schools. For the lower appointments (below deputy head) age is inversely related to age of children taught. For example, for a given level the age of the teacher decreases from infant to infant/junior to junior, while at secondary school the decrease is from modern to comprehensive to grammar. However, at deputy head and head levels no consistent pattern exists. Among the three subject groups, arts, science and cultural/practical, the differences are small and erratic across levels.

Attendance at courses

About four-fifths of our interviewed teachers told us that they believed attendance at courses helped promotion. Some felt that attendance indicated a teacher's keenness to keep himself up-to-date. Others thought that many teachers who attended courses did so to catch an inspector's eye, being more interested in promotion than keeping up-to-date.

Experienced teachers would not necessarily have been able to recall with accuracy the number of courses attended since beginning their careers or prior to each promotion. We compromised by asking how many courses had been attended during the previous five years (1966–71), and defined a course as lasting for at least five days' full-time study or the equivalent (say, one evening a week for a term).

(a) *General Survey of course attendance* Table 6.6 refers to the whole sample of teachers, including the three career types. The rest of the analysis concerned only the 'normal'. The mean number of courses attended between 1966 and 1971 was 1.6 for primary teachers and 1.3 for secondary. The largest number recorded for a primary teacher was 25, and for a secondary 14. Men had attended more courses than women, in both primary and secondary schools. Secondary modern teachers had attended more than had comprehensive teachers, and both more than grammar teachers. Non-graduates had attended more than graduates. Teachers at higher status levels had attended more than those at lower levels. Teachers with more experience had attended just as many as less experienced teachers. These last two findings imply that senior teachers (in terms of either years or status or both) are keeping themselves aware of educational development just as much as, if not more than, younger and junior teachers. On the other hand, only 4.4 per cent of secondary and 7.1 per cent of primary teachers had averaged one course per year in the 1966–71 period, and over 40 per cent had not attended a single course.

(b) *Promoted teachers and course attendance* The mean number of courses attended by our current post holders during 1966–1971 is as

TABLE 6.6: *Courses attended during period 1969–1971 (all career types included)*

	NUMBER OF COURSES							
SCHOOL TYPE	0	1	2	3	4	5	6	6†
Per cent of Primary Teachers (N = 3005)	40.4	21.6	15.9	9.7	5.3	3.0	1.9	2.2
Per cent of Secondary Teachers (N = 2792)	43.5	23.4	16.0	8.2	4.5	2.0	1.3	1.1

shown in Table 6.7. For both primary and secondary teachers it seemed that higher status was associated with more course attendance.

TABLE 6.7: *Mean number of courses attended between 1966–1971 by post holders in primary and secondary schools (normal career type)*

PRIMARY				SECONDARY			
Present post	N	Mean	SD	Present post	N	Mean	SD
Ungraded	1316	1.0	1.5	Ungraded	673	0.7	1.1
Graded Post	353	1.5	1.5	Graded Post	698	1.3	1.7
Head of Dept.	94	2.5	2.5	Head of Dept. (A/C)	629	1.5	1.6
Deputy Head	268	2.4	2.6	Head of Dept. (D/E)	161	1.8	1.8
Head	423	2.8	3.4	Deputy Head	149	1.8	1.7
				Head	41	1.6	1.9

Analysis of variance: differences in mean number of courses significant at 0.1% confidence level for both primary and secondary post holders.

However, the association was difficult to interpret as the level now held might have been achieved prior to 1966. The direct relevance of attendance and promotion is obscured. More relevant was an analysis relating course attendance to present status of those teachers who entered the profession between 1963 and 1967. We had to accept that the higher promotion levels would be largely excluded from this analysis.

A positive association was found between status and course attendance for men in primary schools, women in primary schools, all teaches in junior/infant schools and teachers in comprehensive schools. No association was found for secondary men or secondary women, for teachers in secondary modern or grammar schools, and for secondary graduates or non-graduates. Why the trend existed in primary and comprehensive schools but not in grammars or secondary moderns remains unanswered. Among the promoted teachers we cannot infer cause and effect, for promotion may result from course attendance, but it may be that increased course attendance was the result of being promoted. Probably both are involved—attendance at courses could help promotion, and the promoted status imposes a greater obligation to attend courses, which in turn may bring further promotion, and so on.

Secondary—change of subject

Many secondary teachers have been aware of the possibility, already discussed, that promotion may be restricted by virtue of the subject one teaches. Such awareness may induce teachers to change their teaching subject. We wished to know how many teachers were now teaching the subject they had studied in initial training or for a degree. We also wanted to see if there was any association between change of subject and promotion prospects. To help this analysis we merged the original 35 subjects into 12 'subject groups', trying as far as possible to keep 'similar' subjects together. Thus for example, French, German, etc. became 'modern languages' and chemistry, physics, etc. became 'sciences'. Even so some very surprising results emerged.

(a) *General survey* Over a quarter (25.7 per cent) of our secondary teachers were teaching a different subject group from the one they had studied in initial training or for degree. The findings closely parallel earlier figures (Start, 1968) indicating that 72.4 per cent of secondary teachers were teaching subjects studied at main or subsidiary level at college. This classification of main and subsidiary would parallel the subject group employed in this study. Only 15 per cent of primary teachers laid claim to emphasising the main or subsidiary level subject in school, however.

The changes were not confined to subjects like education, sociology and psychology, which do not fit 'naturally' into a school curriculum. Ninety per cent of the 'students' who had changed now taught a variety of other subjects, including arts/crafts, sciences, environmental studies, English and maths. Many of the teachers who had studied these latter 'curriculum' subjects were teaching other subjects as main subjects. The only subject groups where more than 85 per cent of teachers were teaching what they had initially studied were modern languages and business studies.

These changes of subject occurred with men and women about equally, but far more non-graduates than graduates had changed

(31.7 per cent compared with 18.2 per cent). Some of this non-graduate change arises because non-graduates teach 'general subjects' much more often than do graduates, and 'general subjects' is by definition not a subject recorded as 'specialism studied'. Even so, there was still as large a proportion of 'specialist' non-graduates as of graduates who had changed from their 'genuine' subject of initial study.

The question 'are teachers teaching what they studied?' is related to our perspective of a career in teaching, i.e. finding out if such changes altered promotion prospects. It may also be of some importance to training colleges and to economists of education to know that these changes occur. An alternative method of considering the data, from the perspective of an educator, parent or child, is to answer the question 'Have teachers studied what they now teach?' Our evidence suggests that a large proportion of teachers, varying from nine per cent to 45 per cent according to subject, were teaching a subject they had not studied in initial training or for a degree. We also learned that 11 per cent of all secondary teachers were still teaching the specific subject for which they had been trained since beginning their career.

(b) *Promoted teachers* Teachers in Table 6.8 can be seen in three groups: the unpromoted, the promoted (graded and head of department), and deputy head. The unpromoted group must contain a large number of teachers who will not have had much time to change. Even so, between one in five and one in four of these unpromoted teachers have changed subject specialism. The promoted pattern differs between graduate and non-graduate. In the former the proportion changed drops to one in seven or eight, whereas for the non-graduates it increases to one in three. Subject stability appears to favour the promotion of graduates, but selective change could improve the promotion chances of non-graduates. However, the fact remains that, apart from deputy headships, the great majority of promoted teachers were teachers who had *not* changed subject.

The deputy head position is an enigma, for change of subject does seem to have exerted more influence here than at other levels. Over half of all deputy heads had changed their subject group. As far as we could tell from the data, the change was not towards any subject in particular. Explanations are not obvious. It may be that, with their reduced teaching loads, deputies have tended to take whatever subjects were short-staffed at particular times.

Evening lecturing (secondary)

We wondered if lecturing in evening schools or institutes was associated with a teacher's career prospects. Nearly half of the secondary sample recorded that they had undertaken this work at some time. Among those 'normal career' teachers below the status of head, 38 per cent had lectured in evening classes for more than a year, 15 per cent had spent one or two years in this evening work, about 14 per cent had

TABLE 6.8: *Proportions of post holders teaching subjects not studied in initial training or for a degree (Secondary)*

		Teachers not teaching subject studied		
STATUS	N	Grad.	Non-grad.	All Sec.
Per cent of Ungraded teachers	844	21.7	24.8	23.5
Per cent of Graded posts	867	16.1	33.3	26.9
Per cent of Heads of Dept. A/B	545	16.8	31.3	25.9
Per cent of Heads of Dept. C	210	12.7	33.8	19.5
Per cent of Heads of Dept. D/E	181	12.8	34.7	16.6
Per cent of Deputy Heads	139	39.7	63.2	52.5
Per cent of TOTAL	2786	18.2	31.7	25.7

spent three to five years, and nearly nine per cent had lectured in the evenings for six years or more.

Promoted teachers and years of evening lecturing

It is very difficult to unravel the age effect in interpreting this aspect, especially at the lower promotion levels. In general, higher status accompanied more years in evening lecturing. At the intermediate and higher promotion levels (now Scales 3, 4, 5) between 50 and 60 per cent of secondary teachers had lectured in evening institutes for a period of time, and about three-quarters of deputy heads had done so. This compares with 20 per cent who had lectured but were still unpromoted. The majority of those who had lectured in the evenings had done so for about four years, but there were a substantial number of teachers of high status (about 20 per cent) who had lectured for more than five years, and no doubt quite a few of these were still currently involved in evening work at the time they received the questionnaire.

It is not clear in what way evening lecturing might have influenced a teacher's career. Perhaps the lecturing was a result of promotion, as some principals of evening institutes might invite teachers of high rather than low status to take evening classes. On the other hand a teacher of a lower status level (usually implying less salary) might be more likely to seek an opportunity for evening work. However, even when promoted a teacher would be reluctant to forgo this extra income. If evening lecturing does help achieve higher status, it could be considered as adding another contributory factor to a teacher's career prospects. *Qualification* Non-graduates spent more years in evening work than graduates of similar status. The association between evening work and higher status still held for graduates, but it was much more pronounced with non-graduates. The financial explanation is stronger still here, as a non-graduate is paid less than a graduate of similar experience, and the number and range of high status positions are more limited for him. He may therefore take on evening work to bring in more money. Most of the technical, handicraft and art areas are taught by non-graduates, and these subjects are commonly found in further education institutes. There may be a subject effect coming into play too.

Mobility

The questionnaire to teachers included items on the teachers' mobility, and we analysed (a) the number of home moves which were a direct result of the teacher's seeking promotion and (b) the numbers of LEAs in which the teacher had served. Employers might consider service with several LEAs a sign of wide experience, or of unsettled relations with administration. Many home moves might reflect a less parochial outlook or an instability of temperament.

(a) *Number of home moves* ('normal career' teachers)

It was stressed that the teacher should record only those moves that were the direct result of his or her search for promotion. Moves made because another member of the family had changed jobs were explicitly excluded. Over the whole sample, three-quarters of the teachers had not moved home for this reason at all. Secondary teachers had moved significantly more often than had primary teachers, as shown in Table 6.9. The largest number of moves recorded by any teacher was 14.

Promoted teachers and number of home moves

The 10 per cent of the ungraded teachers who had moved home in their search to widen their experience presumably had moved 'laterally'. At the first stage of promotion, 16 per cent had moved once and four per cent twice. Nearly a quarter of those who were departmental heads had moved once, 11 per cent twice, and six per cent three or more times. Deputy heads appear to have moved less—15 per cent

TABLE 6.9: *Number of home moves in search of promotion*

| SCHOOL TYPE | N | Number of home moves | | | |
		0	1	2	3 or more
Per cent of Primary Teachers	2532	83.3	10.6	3.7	2.4
Per cent of Secondary Teachers	2533	68.3	18.4	7.5	3.8
Per cent of all teachers (Pr. and Sec.)	5065	75.7	14.5	5.7	4.1

X^2 Difference in distributions between primary and secondary significant at 0.1% confidence level.

once, 7 per cent twice and six per cent three or more times. Heads had moved most of all—23 per cent of them once, 15 per cent twice and another 15 per cent three times or more.

As a large proportion of lower (and even upper) level promotions are internal to schools, any association between promotion and home moves must be coming from the externally appointed candidates. If the internally promoted teachers had been excluded from this particular analysis, the average number of home moves at each promotion level would have been considerably higher and perhaps the relation stronger. Naturally the absence of a home move does not necessarily mean that there was an internal promotion—merely that the promotion was in a school within commutable distance from the teacher's current home. On balance, though half the teachers who reached high status did so without a home move, the other half had to accept one or more moves before obtaining a headship.

The association between home moves and increased status existed for both primary and secondary teachers. However, the secondary teacher who sought promotion moved more often than a primary teacher of comparable status. Grammar and comprehensive school teachers had moved home for promotion reasons more often than had teachers in modern schools. Graduates had moved home more than non-graduates.

Men moved home when seeking promotion significantly more often than women did. This was true for primary teachers at all status levels, and for secondary teachers at all levels except deputy head. These data confirm the view that family ties restricted women in this respect more than they did men. This has a major negative impact on the careers of women teachers by limiting the posts for which they will apply.

(b) *Number of LEAs in which served*

Our question to teachers about service with LEAs was not tied to the search for promotion (as was our question on home moves). The largest number of LEAs in which any teacher in the sample had served was eight. About half the sample had served in just one LEA, just under a third in two LEAs, about 13 per cent in three, and about seven per cent in four or more. As can be seen from Table 6.10, primary and secondary schools were very similar in all these respects.

TABLE 6.10: *Number of LEAs in which served*

		Number of LEAs			
SCHOOL TYPE	N	1	2	3	4 or more
Per cent of Primary Teachers	2848	50.0	29.4	12.7	7.9
Per cent of Secondary Teachers	2676	50.5	28.8	13.9	6.8
Per cent of all teachers (Pr. and Sec.)	5524	50.3	29.1	13.2	7.4

Promoted teachers and number of LEAs

There was a very significant association between promotion levels and the number of LEAs in which teachers had served. As the teacher's status rose, so did his experience of different LEAs. Among the ungraded teachers, 37 per cent had served in more than one LEA. Through the initial stages of promotion the figure rose from 50 per cent to 63 per cent. Some 64 per cent of deputy heads had had experience with more than one authority, and about 70 per cent of heads. And whereas only a twentieth of the unpromoted teachers had been with four or more LEAs, a sixth of the heads had. No doubt there had simply not been much time for the young, therefore unpromoted, teacher to sample many LEAs. Despite this, movement among different LEAs does seem to be part of the ambitious teacher's lot. But this will not arise if the teacher happens to be in an area which operates a promotion system for its own teacher employees or which does not advertise promotion posts beyond its own authority area.

i. *Primary and Secondary* The association of status with number of LEAs applied to both primary and secondary teachers separately. Primary teachers, however, seemed to move around more than secondary teachers at the lower levels of promotion, but the position was reversed where high status was concerned.

ii. *Sex* Women had served with more LEAs than men, and this was true of both primary and secondary teachers, and at many of the status levels. Perhaps the greater LEAs experience of women than men was the natural consequence of their moving to different areas when their husband or family moved jobs.

(c) *Differences in LEA and home mobility*

The two questions on mobility (LEA and home) were couched differently. The LEA inquiry was unrestricted, whereas the home question asked for moves undertaken in the pursuit of promotion. The differences can be seen in Table 6.11.

TABLE 6.11: *LEA and home mobility of teachers*

	PERCENTAGE OF TEACHERS WITH AT LEAST ONE MOVE	
STATUS	*LEA*	*Home*
Ungraded	37	10
Graded	50	22
Head of Dept.	63	41
Deputy Head	64	28
Head	70	53

Patently there have been many more moves than those specifically in pursuit of promotion, or else many teachers live on or near the borders of LEAs.

CHAPTER SEVEN

Teachers' Views on Factors that Favour Promotion

In the previous sections, evidence about the way promotion posts were distributed was derived from the biographical details provided by our sample of teachers. However, some influences affecting careers may be too subtle to probe through a general survey of biographical data. To learn what these more subtle influences were, or at least what teachers believed them to be, we included in the questionnaire items that asked the teacher what he *believed* to be the chief factors influencing promotion. This information was supplemented by the data subsequently collected via depth interviews with teachers.

Our asking for teachers' views on what affected promotion was prompted by much more than a desire to know about any factors that were not easily identifiable. We thought it important to know what teachers believed about promotion, because it was their beliefs that probably determined their attitudes to this issue and also contributed to any general satisfaction or dissatisfaction with their job. We wanted to compare the teachers' opinions about promotion prospects with what we were able to establish as the facts about prospects.

In addition to asking teachers what they thought *did* influence promotion, we asked them what *ought* to influence promotion.

We shall look first at what teachers in the sample believed to be factors that favoured promotion, and then at how far these opinions coincided with objective findings. In the next chapter the teachers' ideal situation will be examined. All these anlayses concerned the views of our 'normal career' teachers only.

The teacher questionnaire listed 31 possible factors in promotion. These were arrived at after our original consultations with various interested parties, and after perusing many of the documents, press articles, letters, etc., that were available. To have asked teachers to rank the factors in order of influence would have made the questionnaire too tiresome. To have left it to individual respondents to tick as many as they wished would have led to inconsistencies across the sample. Yet to have asked for *one* chief factor might have limited the teacher too severely. We compromised and asked the teacher to identify *five* factors to be pinpointed, and the great majority of respondents did so. It was reasonable for some teachers to select fewer than five factors simply because they did not feel strongly on the issue. We did not ask teachers to rank the five choices. We believed that if the choices from all teachers were summed for each subject, a comparison of these totals would show us clearly which were, in the teachers' opinions, the most significant of the 31 possibles. To help the comparison, the total 'votes' given to any factor by a group of teachers were expressed as a percentage of the group of teachers studied. We were able to rank order the factors for the whole sample, for any group of teachers, and could thus compare the ways in which different groups stressed one factor more than another.

The whole sample

The factors selected by more than 10 per cent of our sampled teachers are listed in Table 7.1. Comparisons made later between different groups of teachers will be confined in the main to the 'top ten' of each group.

Teachers obviously disagreed quite markedly on what they thought favoured promotion. There is not one single factor that even half the

TABLE 7.1: *Teachers' opinions on factors that favour promotion—all teachers (primary plus secondary)*

RANK ORDER	Factor	Per cent of sample choosing factor (N = 5794)
1.	Being a graduate	41.7
2.	Specialism in shortage subject	41.3
3.	Social contacts	39.6
4.	Conformity with advisers	29.0
5.	Good relations with head	27.6
6.	Length of teaching experience	24.6
7.	Course attendance	21.5
8.	Variety of schools	19.8
9.	Extra-curricular work	19.7
10.	Familiarity with new ideas	19.6
11.	Subject specialism	16.3
12.	Strong personality	14.7
13.	'Youth' (younger than 40)	14.4
14.	Being male	12.8
15.	Participation in innovations	12.6
16.	Willingness to move area	12.1
17.	Success with examination pupils	11.5
18.	Long service in one school	10.9

school sector and which affected them more directly. The most simple explanation is that primary specialisms like music and French, and also remedial work, 'new' mathematics, modern methods, etc. are both increasing and in short supply.

TABLE 7.2: *Teachers' opinions on factors favouring promotions by school type*

	PRIMARY (N = 3021)			SECONDARY (N = 2773)	
Rank	Factor	Per cent of Teachers	Rank	Factor	Per cent of Teachers
1.	Social contacts	45.3	1.	Being a graduate	58.1
2.	Specialism in shortage subject	34.2	2.	Specialism in shortage subject	49.0
3.	Conformity with advisers	33.6	3.	Social contacts	33.0
4.	Course attendance	26.9	4.	Good relations with head	31.3
5.	Being a graduate	26.7	5.	Conformity with advisers	24.1
6.	Length of teaching experience	26.1	6.	Length of teaching experience	22.9
7.	Familiarity with new ideas	24.2	7.	Variety of schools	21.1
8.	Good relations with head	24.2	8.	Extra-curricular work	20.7
9.	Extra-curricular work	18.8	9.	Success with exam. pupils	18.7
10.	Variety of schools	18.6	10.	Course attendance	15.5

Secondary

The high placing given to good relations with the head may reflect the large amount of internal promotion that occurs in the secondary sector, but it is then strange to find variety of schools placed fairly high also.

Primary and Secondary compared

Secondary teachers seemed to concentrate their selections on fewer items than primary teachers. The two top secondary choices have relatively far more votes than the two top primary choices, and first choice for secondary teachers was selected by a majority of the group— nearly 60 per cent.

Both sets of teachers were obviously concerned about the unmeasured factors like social contacts (over a third of the teachers) and conformity with advisers (a quarter to a third). Both considered length of experience an important factor that helped prospects. Secondary teachers placed greater stress than did primary colleagues on being a graduate, specialism in a shortage subject, good relations with the head, and variety of schools; and less stress on course attendance, familiarity with new ideas, conformity with advisers, social contacts, and length of teaching experience. Success with examination pupils appeared in secondary's top ten only. The demise of the eleven-plus probably removed this sole mention of pupil learning from the primary teachers' opinions.

(a) *Primary: school type* (Table G7.1 in the supplement—see P.1.7 above). Infant teachers and teachers in junior or junior/infant schools did not differ radically from each other. Proportionately more junior and junior/infant teachers than infant teachers selected being a graduate (nearly 30 per cent compared with 20 per cent) and specialism in a shortage subject (37 per cent compared with 31 per cent); while relatively more infant teachers voted for familiarity with new ideas (29 per cent infants compared with 24 per cent for the other types).

(b) *Secondary: school type* (Table G7.2 in the supplement). The following factors revealed significant disparities between secondary school types:

Being a graduate—comprehensive 63.8%, modern 58.9%, grammar 47.6%

Social contacts—modern 39.6%, comprehensive 33.8%, grammar 21.5%.

Length of experience—grammar 28.3%, modern 21.8%, comprehensive 20.5%

Variety of schools—grammar 27.9%, modern 20.3%, comprehensive 19.7%

Conformity with advisers—modern 28.1%, comprehensive 22.3%, grammar 20.8%

Specialism in shortage subject—grammar 54.3%, comprehensive 51.1%, modern 46.3%.

Course attendance—modern 17.0%, comprehensive 14.3%, grammar 12.7%.

The majority of grammar teachers are graduates, so a degree in itself confers no greater advantage on one grammar teacher than another. Modern, and especially comprehensive teachers obviously see their situations differently. Social contacts were selected by relatively few grammar teachers, perhaps believing that promotion for them depends on what you know rather than whom you know—a premise obviously less accepted by comprehensive teachers and even less by modern teachers. The greater importance seen by grammar teachers in professional rather than social factors as aids to promotion is confirmed by the fact that they laid much greater stress than did other teachers on professional experience, both in length and width.

2. *Sex* (Appendix G, Table G7.3)

It is better here to treat the primary and secondary sectors separately.

(a) *Sex—primary teachers* (Table 7.3)

Men and women Both men and women placed strong emphasis on contacts and conforming. Significantly more men than women chose as favourable factors: being a graduate, variety of schools, familiarity with new ideas, conformity with advisers, and course attendance; while women rather than men emphasized specialism in a shortage subject. One difference not shown up by the above list: 16.5 per cent of primary women believed that being a man was a favourable factor in obtaining promotion and placed it 12th in rank. The men placed this factor 19th with a vote of 6.0 per cent. Teachers in the woman's world of infant schools had ranked it 17th with 11.2 per cent, so the primary women's placing of 12th was determined by women in the junior and junior/infant schools.

Men No common factor was chosen by a majority of the primary men, and only three factors by over a third: social contacts, conformity with advisers, and being a graduate. The newcomer to the list is participation in innovations. Extra-curricular work was the eleventh choice, with 19.1 per cent of the men voting for it. The top placings of social contacts and conformity with advisers manifest the primary men's belief that non-professional factors help promotion more than do professional.

Women A new factor here, though well down the list, is subject specialism—again an oddity as this might be considered a factor related to secondary work more than to primary. Inspection showed that this factor was chosen by both infant and junior/infant teachers in roughly the same proportions, so its emergence as ninth for primary women is not caused by any special stress by the women in infant schools.

(b) *Sex—secondary teachers* (Table 7.4)

Men and Women Although the votes from men and women contain nine factors out of the top ten in common, and the top four have identical rank, there were several significant differences. Relatively more men than women believed the following to favour promotion: variety of schools, being a graduate, conformity with advisers, specialism in a shortage subject, and social contacts. More women than men thought being a man and length of experience were favourable factors. Of interest are some other figures: course attendance, which was placed 10th with 17.8 per cent, came 16th with women with 12.4 per cent; and women placed long service in one school 11th with 14.4 per cent, while

TABLE 7.3: *Factors that favour promotion: views of men and women (primary)*

	MEN (N = 763)			WOMEN (N = 2255)	
Rank	Factor	Per cent of Teachers	Rank	Factor	Per cent of Teachers
1.	Social contacts	43.5	1.	Social contacts	43.3
2.	Conformity with advisers	35.8	2.	Specialism in a shortage subject	35.2
3.	Being a graduate	33.2	3.	Conformity with advisers	30.2
4.	Course attendance	29.8	4.	Length of teaching experience	27.2
5.	Specialism in a shortage subject	29.6	5.	Course attendance	24.9
6.	Familiarity with new ideas	26.5	6.	Good relations with head	24.3
7.	Length of teaching experience	23.6	7.	Being a graduate	23.6
8.	Good relations with head	22.3	8.	Familiarity with new ideas	21.2
9.	Variety of schools	22.1	9.	Subject specialism	17.8
10.	Participation in innovations	19.5	10.	Variety of schools	17.0

men relegated this to 18th, with 8.4 per cent. Finally, men placed willingness to move area 11th, with a 16.1 per cent vote, and for women this came 17th with only 11.2 per cent. This supports the view offered earlier that mobility is seen as an aid towards promotion for men. But one wonders why women would not have mentioned it more. Is moving for promotion so far beyond the realm of reality for most (married) women that it is not even considered?

Men Being a graduate was seen by secondary men as the most important factor favouring promotion. We can reasonably presume from the earlier figures that it is the men in modern and comprehensive rather than grammar schools who believe this. The second factor, specialism in a shortage subject, also was way ahead of other favourable factors.

Women. Being a graduate and specialism in a shortage subject were the top two factors with women as with men, all other factors being voted for by less than a third of the secondary women. A new factor here was being a male, and this was higher in the list and rated more votes (20.2 per cent) than was the case with primary women (16.5 per cent).

TABLE 7.4: *Factors that favour promotion: views of men and women (secondary)*

	MEN (N = 1625)			WOMEN (N = 1147)	
Rank	Factor	Per cent of Teachers	Rank	Factor	Per cent of Teachers
1.	Being a graduate	62.6	1.	Being a graduate	51.6
2.	Specialism in a shortage subject	51.0	2.	Specialism in a shortage subject	46.3
3.	Social contacts	35.1	3.	Social contacts	30.8
4.	Good relations with head	32.6	4.	Good relations with head	29.6
5.	Conformity with advisers	26.0	5.	Length of teaching experience	25.4
6.	Variety of schools	25.0	6.	Extra-curricular work	22.3
7.	Length of teaching experience	21.2	7.	Conformity with advisers	21.4
8.	Extra-curricular work	19.6	8.	Being male	20.2
9.	Success with exam. pupils	18.8	9.	Success with exam. pupils	18.7
10.	Course attendance	17.8	10.	Variety of schools	15.4

3. *Secondary Teachers—Qualifications* (Table G7.4 in the supplement)

Was the choice of factors different for graduates and non-graduates? The general answer was—very much so. Good honours graduates, ordinary graduates and non-graduates all placed being a graduate and specialism in a shortage subject as their top two factors favouring promotion way ahead of all other factors, but the non-graduate regarded being a graduate as of supreme importance, giving this a 63.8 per cent vote compared with 51.4 per cent from both types of graduate. The chief significant differences were:

Being a graduate: non-graduate 63.8%, ordinary and good honours graduate 51.4%.

Specialism in shortage subject: good hons. graduate 52.9%, ordinary graduate 50.5%, non-graduate 46.4%.
Social contacts: non-graduate 38.8%, ordinary graduate 31.5%, good hons. graduate 23.5%.
Conformity with advisers: non-graduate 28.2%, ordinary graduate 22.4%, good hons. graduate 17.1%.
Variety of schools: ordinary graduate 25.4%, good hons. graduate 22.5%, non-graduate 18.5%.
Course attendance: non-graduate 18.7%, ordinary graduatd 14.8%, good hons. graduate 9.7%.

Other marked disparities involved willingness to move area (placed higher by graduates), strong personality (again considered a favourable factor more by graduates than non-graduates), participation in innovation (ordinary graduates placing this higher), familiarity with new ideas (ranked higher by non-graduates), and ability to control pupils— regarded as a favourable factor by 15.4 per cent of good honours graduates, 13.2 per cent of ordinary graduates, and only 8.5 per cent of non-graduates. An odd voting this, perhaps reflecting the graduate from a grammar school faced with non-academic children in a comprehensive or secondary modern school.

We wondered if the qualification and school type lists showed any correspondences, and found that lists from the non-graduates and the modern school teachers mirrored each other closely. Some of the grammar school items appeared to reflect the good honours graduate list (e.g. social contacts and participation in innovation) and other items seemed to coincide more with the views of ordinary graduates (conformity with advisers, familiarity with new ideas, ability to control pupils, and being a male). The factors of strong personality and long service in one school seemed to be regarded in the same way by both the grammar teacher and the non-graduate teacher.

4. *Age groups*

It would be surprising if younger and older teachers held the same views on what influenced promotion, and we did indeed find many differences. With the older teachers, views were probably based more on experience than hearsay. The teachers were classified into four age groups: less than 30 years old, 30–39, 40 to 49, and over 49.

(a) *Age groups—primary teachers*

The opinions of the primary age groups are shown in Table 7.5. Some points to note are: (1) Length of experience was ranked high by

TABLE 7.5: *Factors favouring promotion: views of age groups (primary)*

	<30 Years old (N = 1149)	Per cent of Teachers		30–39 (N = 624)	Per cent of Teachers		40–49 (N = 646)	Per cent of Teachers		Over 49 (N = 538)	Per cent of Teachers
Rank	Factor		Rank	Factor		Rank	Factor		Rank	Factor	
1.	Social contacts	45.5	1.	Social contacts	43.1	1.	Social contacts	40.9	1.	Social contacts	41.6
2.	Length of teaching experience	40.1	2.	Conformity with advisers	34.6	2.	Conformity with advisers	30.7	2.	Conformity with advisers	29.4
3.	Specialism in shortage subjects	38.4	3.	Specialism in shortage subjects	34.3	3.	Specialism in shortage subjects	28.8	3.	Specialism in shortage subjects	28.8
4.	Conformity with advisers	31.4	4.	Course attendance	29.6	4.	Course attendance	27.7	4.	'Youth' (<40 years)	25.7
5.	Being a graduate	30.1	5.	Familiarity with new ideas	27.9	5.	Familiarity with new ideas	25.2	5.	Course attendance	23.4
6.	Good relations with head	29.5	6.	Being a graduate	25.3	6.	Being a graduate	24.3	6.	Familiarity with new ideas	23.2
7.	Course attendance	23.8	7.	Good relations with head	23.7	7.	Good relations with head	20.6	7.	Being a graduate	20.6
8.	Familiarity with new ideas	17.6	8.	Length of teaching experience	22.0	8.	Variety of schools	20.6	8.	Extra-curricular work	19.9
9.	Long service in one school	16.3	9.	Variety of schools	20.4	9.	Strong personality	18.1	9.	Subject specialism	19.5
10.	Being a male	16.3	10.	Extra-curricular work	18.3	10.	Participation in innovation	17.6	10.	Variety of schools	19.1

the youngest teachers, lower by the 30–39 group, and disappeared altogether for the older teachers. (2) The reverse notion occurred where 'youth' (being under 40) appeared on the oldest teachers' list but not on the lists of the younger teachers. (3) Good relations with the head were seen by all three lower ages as favouring promotion, while the over-49s discounted it. Had the older teachers found the factor of no help, or were they unwilling to recognize such in their own case? Perhaps the older teachers *were* heads and believed they did not let their relations with colleagues influence their staff's prospects? (4) After 30, the age groups showed remarkable unanimity of ranking, as if their views on promotion factors had been settled after the first five or six years. Often the same factors commanded a smaller percentage as the teacher's age increased, perhaps suggesting a growing lack of interest in or satisfaction with promotion, or a growing diversity of factors thought to be useful. It seemed that the older the teacher became, the less favourable were considered the following factors in promotion: social contacts, length of teaching experience, specialism in shortage subjects, being a graduate, good relations with the head, being a male, taking part in civic work; and from 30 on, the decline in importance applied also to conformity with advisers, course attendance, and familiarity with new ideas. The only factors that were thought to become more favourable as teachers grew older were being a local person and being young!

(b) *Age groups—secondary teachers*

From Table 7.6 there seemed to be fewer clear trends in the views of the secondary age groups compared with primary teachers. Across the age groups several factors varied up and down in placing and in voting percentages, while some stayed relatively steady. The chief differences were that young teachers believed length of experience and exam success to be important, while older teachers disregarded these factors; good relations with the head were considered less favourable as a help in promotion as the teachers grew older; older teachers thought youth important.

5. *Present Post*

Teachers suggested factors that they felt influenced the rather broad distinction between promotion and non-promotion. Perhaps the factors favouring promotion varied according to the level or promotion being considered. We therefore analysed opinions in terms of a teacher's present promotion level. This analysis might be based on increasing

TABLE 7.6: Factors favouring promotion: views of age groups (secondary)

	<30 Years old (N = 1100)			30–39 (N = 736)			40–49 (N = 502)			Over 49 (N = 380)		
	Rank	Factor	Per cent of Teachers	Rank	Factor	Per cent of Teachers	Rank	Factor	Per cent of Teachers	Rank	Factor	Per cent of Teachers
	1.	Being a graduate	58.0	1.	Being a graduate	64.7	1.	Being a graduate	52.6	1.	Specialism in shortage subject	54.5
	2.	Specialism in shortage subject	46.7	2.	Specialism in shortage subject	47.7	2.	Specialism in shortage subject	52.2	2.	Being a graduate	52.9
	3.	Good relations with head	36.6	3.	Social contacts	34.1	3.	Social contacts	35.1	3.	Social contacts	29.2
	4.	Length of teaching experience	34.8	4.	Good relations with head	31.8	4.	Variety of schools	27.5	4.	'Youth' (<40 years)	24.2
	5.	Social contacts	34.0	5.	Conformity with advisers	24.0	5.	Good relations with head	25.3	5.	Extra-curricular work	23.9
	6.	Conformity with advisers	25.1	6.	Variety of schools	23.8	6.	Conformity with advisers	24.9	6.	Good relations with head	23.2
	7.	Success with exam. pupils	21.5	7.	Extra-curricular work	20.1	7.	'Youth' (<40 years)	20.7	7.	Conformity with advisers	21.3
	8.	Extra-curricular work	20.3	8.	Course attendance	18.9	8.	Extra-curricular work	19.5	8.	Participation in innovation	18.9
	9.	Variety of schools	17.3	9.	Familiarity with new ideas	18.5	9.	Course attendance	16.1	9.	Variety of schools	18.7
	10.	Long service in one school	14.9	10.	Success with exam. pupils	18.2	10.	Willingness to move area	15.7	10.	Course attendance	17.4

personal experience rather than hearsay. Of particular interest are the views of heads, being formed from a combination of their experiences as applicants and their experiences as 'employers'.

(a) *Present post: primary* (Table 7.7)

Length of experience was considered important as a promotion factor by the ungraded and lower promotion levels, though heads did place a little stress on it; it was variety of experience rather than length that heads rated highly. The promoted teachers believed that familiarity with new ideas helped promotion, while unpromoted teachers were less convinced of this, and the latter especially discounted participation in innovation (only 9.1 per cent of them selected this). The same trend occurred with course attendance, holders of higher status selecting this factor relatively more frequently than holders of lower status. Deputies and heads both regarded being younger than 40 an important factor that favoured promotion, while the ungraded and lower status-holders, who would include the younger teachers, did not. All statuses rated being a graduate quite favourably.

The heads, though rating social contacts highly, nevertheless were far less convinced of the importance of this factor than were other teachers, and the same was true of specialism in a shortage subject. Perhaps more significant, they placed good relations with the head low down on their list (16.0 per cent). Of course heads may have deliberately 'played down' this particular factor because it might be thought to suggest abuse of their role as 'employer'; but it is just as feasible that, from their vantage point as employer, they knew from this experience that the factor was not as favourable to promotion as non-heads believed. The one factor that heads rated as much more favourable than did non-heads was variety of experience.

Between a third and a half of primary teachers at each status level thought social contacts and conformity with advisers favoured promotion. These were two of the three most favourable factors. For all promoted teachers, conformity with advisers was closely accompanied by course attendance, familiarity with new ideas, and specialism in a shortage subject.

(b) *Present post: secondary* (Table 7.8)

All the secondary status groups placed being a graduate and specialism in a shortage subject first and second respectively in their lists, and they felt far more strongly about both factors favouring promotion than did primary colleagues of comparable status. Also all secondary status

TABLE 7.7: *Factors favouring promotion: views of post-holders (primary)*

	UNGRADED (N = 1582)		GRADED POST/HEAD OF DEPT. (N = 526)		DEPUTY HEAD (N = 300)		HEAD (N = 387)	
Rank Factor		Per cent of Teachers	Rank Factor	Per cent of Teachers	Rank Factor	Per cent of Teachers	Rank Factor	Per cent of Teachers
1. Social Contacts		49.1	1. Social contacts	45.8	1. Social contacts	46.0	1. Conformity with advisers	33.3
2. Specialism in shortage subject		38.1	2. Specialism in shortage subject	37.5	2. Conformity with advisers	37.7	2. Social contacts	33.3
3. Conformity with advisers		34.1	3. Conformity with advisers	34.2	3. Course attendance	31.7	3. Course attendance	31.8
4. Length of teaching experience		31.4	4. Familiarity with new ideas	32.7	4. Familiarity with new ideas	31.3	4. Familiarity with new ideas	30.0
5. Being a graduate		27.2	5. Being a graduate	31.7	5. Specialism in shortage subject	30.3	5. Specialism in shortage subject	28.9
6. Course attendance		25.0	6. Course attendance	28.3	6. Being a graduate	24.0	6. Variety of schools	28.7
7. Good relations with head		24.0	7. Good relations with head	25.7	7. 'Youth' (<40 years)	24.0	7. Being a graduate	26.1
8. Familiarity with new ideas		19.0	8. Subject specialism	23.8	8. Good relations with head	23.7	8. 'Youth' (<40 years)	21.2
9. Extra-curricular work		17.1	9. Length of teaching experience	23.6	9. Extra-curricular work	23.3	9. Length of teaching experience	20.7
10. Subject specialism		16.8	10. Extra-curricular work	22.4	10. Participation in innovation	22.7	10. Participation in innovation	20.7
					11. Variety of schools	21.0		

TABLE 7.8: *Factors favouring promotion: views of post-holders (secondary)*

	UNGRADED (N = 802)			GRADED POST (N = 783)			HEAD OF DEPT. (N = 853)			DEPUTY HEAD (N = 152)			HEAD (N = 83)		
Rank	Factor	Per cent of Teachers		Factor	Per cent of Teachers		Factor	Per cent of Teachers		Factor	Per cent of Teachers		Factor	Per cent of Teachers		
1.	Being a graduate	56.4		Being a graduate	59.3		Being a graduate	58.5		Being a graduate	63.2		Being a graduate	54.2		
2.	Specialism in shortage sub.	43.8		Specialism in shortage sub.	50.7		Specialism in shortage sub.	52.3		Specialism in shortage sub.	53.3		Specialism in shortage sub.	44.5		
3.	Good relations with head	35.4		Social contacts	37.2		Social contacts	33.4		Variety of schools	25.7		Variety of schools	32.5		
4.	Length of teaching exp.	35.2		Good relations with head	34.5		Good relations with head	29.7		Social contacts	25.0		Course attendance	20.5		
5.	Social contacts	33.5		Conformity with advisers	24.6		Variety of schools	25.3		Familiarity with new ideas	24.3		'Youth' (<40 years)	20.5		
6.	Conformity with advisers	25.9		Extra-curric. work	22.6		Conformity with advisers	24.0		Good relations with head	23.7		Subject specialism	19.3		
7.	Success with exam. pupils	20.3		Variety of schools	21.8		Extra-curric. work	21.3		Course attendance	20.4		Ability to control pupils	19.3		
8.	Extra-curric. work	20.0		Length of teaching exp.	20.9		Subject specialism	17.4		'Youth' (<40 years)	19.1		Familiarity with new ideas	19.3		
9.	Long service in one school	16.1		Success with exam. pupils	19.3		Success with exam. pupils	17.1		Subject specialism	19.1		Social contacts	19.3		
10.	Being a male	15.8		Course attendance	17.0		Participation in innovation	17.0		Conformity with advisers	17.8		Length of tchg. experience / Willingness to move area	18.1 / 18.1		

groups rated social contacts relatively less important than was the case with primary teachers.

Within the secondary sector, the chief differences noted were: (1) teachers of lower rather than higher status thought promotion was helped by length of teaching experience, good relations with the heads, social contacts, conformity with advisers, extra-curricular work, and long service in one school. (2) Deputy heads felt especially strongly that being a graduate was a favourable factor. (3) Only deputy heads and heads placed course attendance, and familiarity with new ideas reasonably high on their lists; and it was only among deputy heads and heads that ability to control pupils was a favourable factor (17.1 per cent and 19.3 per cent respectively). (4) As status advanced, so did belief that being younger than 40 helped promotion. Conformity was seen as an aid by first level promoted teachers most, but with increasing status its value fell until it did not appear among the top ten of the heads' list. Success with exam pupils faded from a 7th for ungraded (young?) teachers to a 9th for holders of graded posts and heads of departments, and out of the reckoning for deputy heads and heads.

The opinions of heads were not unlike those of deputy heads but they placed more emphasis than deputies on variety of schools and length of teaching experience, and less on social contacts, being a graduate, specialism in a shortage subject, and good relations with the head.

Teachers' opinions and the facts

Having reviewed what various groups of teachers believed as factors that favoured promotion, it is appropriate at this point to see how far the teacher opinions measure up to the facts as far as they are known.

The measurable factors

Whatever the effect that the unmeasured and ill-defined factors like 'social contacts' may have had on promotion, for the more concrete factors a comparison between teachers' views and our findings is presented in summary form in Table 7.9.

Findings on some other factors may be reported briefly

(a) *Extra-curricular work*—ranked 9th (19.1 per cent) in the survey. At our interviews with a sub-sample of teachers we asked if the teacher believed extra-curricular activities (running school clubs and societies, arranging school visits, etc.) helped promotion, and stressed that the answer should be based on experience and observation. Of 135 teachers interviewed, 93 (69 per cent) thought it helped, a view shared by half the heads and three quarters of other teachers. These teachers reported experiences to support the main sample's relatively high ranking for this factor.

(b) *Participation in innovation*—ranked 15th (12.6 per cent) in the survey. 104 (77 per cent) of the teachers interviewed felt that this factor helped promotion. The heads and others held similar views. The main sample's ranking is lower than the interview data would imply.

(c) *Willingness to move home* (16th with 12.1 per cent) was estimated by the question 'number of home moves in search of promotion' in the factual survey. While more moves were associated with higher status, 40 per cent of teachers who had *not* moved had been promoted. Willingness to move home was by no means an essential factor in promotion, and the low ranking based on teachers' opinions was supported. Since the survey, the rise in land and house prices will have affected this factor. The relation between number of homes and higher status might be reduced in areas where housing costs are highest because local teachers, who did not need to move home, would have had more opportunity to secure the vacancies available. The relation might be enhanced where housing costs are lower, because of the potential exodus of teachers from high priced areas.

(d) *Having taught in area where post advertised* (23rd). This was indirectly measured via the factual questionnaire. Although the higher statuses were going to teachers with experience in more than one LEA, one quarter of all promoted teachers had taught in only one LEA. Hence the teachers' low ranking of the factor of having taught in the area where posts are advertised was only partly justified.

(e) *Experience outside education* was ranked 28th out of 31 opinion factors. Yet our late entrants (many of whom probably came from industry or from domestic commitments) appeared in general to have held their own compared with 'normal' career teachers with the same teaching experience. Without allowing for teaching experience differences, late entrants held a sufficient proportion of various status levels to conclude that experience outside education was neither help nor hindrance to the advancement of a career. Fact and opinion agreed.

(f) *Being a woman and being a parent* were the 30th and 31st ranked out of 31 factors favouring promotion. We had no data on the effect that being a parent may have had in promotion prospects. Our evidence showed women were promoted later and less often than men. Equally marked, however, was women's lower apparent demand for promotion teachers regard as a chief factor favouring promotion. A few of the most-chosen factors are not easily measurable, e.g. social contacts (third), conformity with the views of inspectors and advisers (fourth), familiarity with new ideas (10th and (12th). It is also of interest to see what teachers think count for little, i.e. the factors omitted from the list, such as concern for the development of individual pupils, ability to control pupils, good relationships with staff, being a parent, being a 'local lad/lass', non-teaching experience and—perhaps a cynical omission, considering the question was about promotion to posts of responsibility—administrative ability. Again, several of these omitted factors would be difficult to measure objectively.

The appearance of 'success with examination pupils' is an ambivalent point. It may be a partial recognition that one criterion should be children's learning. Or it may be a pragmatic recognition of the contribution external examinations and courses make to the school's unit total, with all that implies for promotion posts.

1. *Primary and secondary teachers*

When comparing the top ten selections of different teacher groups, one must bear in mind not only the rank order allocated but also the percentage of 'votes' given a factor. For example, Table 7.2 shows that both primary and secondary teachers believed 'specialism in a shortage subject' to be a very important factor favouring promotion, and accordingly placed it second. Yet secondary teachers felt much more strongly about it than did primary teachers (49 per cent compared with 34 per cent).

'Social contacts' can reasonably be taken to mean being known by the 'right people', and refers to the usefulness of mixing socially with those who may have a direct or indirect personal influence on an appointment. Alternatively, some teachers may be referring to those professional and semi-social contacts who may be thought to carry professional weight as referees on an application form.

Primary

An oddity in the primary list is *specialism in a shortage subject,* for such specialisms are not thought to be common practice in primary schools. Of course the original question did not specify factors favouring promotion in 'your' school, and its feasible that primary teachers might have been commenting on their view of the profession as a whole. It is more likely that teachers would base their selections on the kind of experiences and situations with which they were familiar in their own

TABLE 7.9: *Measured factors that favour promotion: teachers' views versus survey findings*

FACTOR	Teachers' ranking	Per cent of Teachers selecting factor	SURVEY FINDINGS
Being a graduate	1st	41.7	Primary teachers—no difference between graduate and non-graduate. Secondary—higher statuses went to graduate, lower to non-graduate.
Specialism in shortage subject	2nd	41.3	Not a measured factor but linked to subject specialism and therefore probably very important in fact as well as opinion.
Length of teaching experience	6th	24.6	Generally favourable factor, but relatively more important at lower status levels.
Course attendance	7th	21.5	Generally favourable factor, and applies more to primary teachers.
Variety of schools	8th	19.8	Partly favourable; up to 4/5 schools important, after 4/5 schools variety no advantage and may even hinder promotion.
Subject specialism	11th	16.3	Very important factor, but depends on promotion level; some subjects help for high status but hinder for low, others favour low status with little prospects of high.
Being younger than 40	13th	14.4	Generally favourable factor: less chance of high status for primary teachers over 50 and secondary over 40.
Being a male	14th	12.6	Men promoted relatively much more than women, but much greater demand for promotion from men.
Being a local person	19th	9.4	Very important factor at lower status levels because of much internal promotion within schools (informal and formal).

posts. The latter came close to explaining the former, but the issue is far too complex for such a facile inference. Here much more detailed study is warranted.

(g) Finally, one extremely important measured factor should not be overlooked—*school type*. Our analyses found that teachers in different school types varied considerably in the ranking they gave to factors favouring promotion. Usually primary differed from secondary, and the three secondary groups differed from each other. Almost certainly this reflected the teachers' opinion that promotion factors differed with type of school and that even the common factors favoured one type more than another. This would seem a perfectly justifiable opinion to hold—we found that school type was indeed a crucial factor in promotion prospects.

Non measurable (ill defined) factors

Of these factors, teachers regarded as the most influential: social contacts (3rd with 39.6 per cent), conformity with advisers (4th with 29.0 per cent), good relations with the head (5th with 27.6 per cent) and familiarity with new ideas (which came 10th with 19.6 per cent and which may have been reflected in course attendance, already dealt with). The experiences of the teachers we interviewed enabled us to comment on two of these 'most favourable' factors: social contact and good relations with the head.

Social Contacts. Out of 135 respondents interviewed, 101 (75 per cent) said they believed 'contacts' helped promotion, and the kind of contacts mentioned included Freemason, Church, Sports Club, Political organizations, Professional associations, Councillor, Social Club and 'knew the Head'. Yet the overwhelming majority of the 101 who held this view had had no personal experience of it, nor could (or would?) quote specific examples they knew of.

'I have had no personal experience of this but have heard people talk' (from a Group 4 Head); 'I have no experience of this but think it does happen' (Group 8 Head); 'It undoubtedly does, but I have had no experience of it' (Head of Department); 'I think if you know the right people it can sometimes influence things. No experience of it—just an impression' (Ungraded teacher); 'No experience of it, but I suspect it does happen' (Ungraded teacher).

Even when instances were specified, the account was rarely nearer than third-hand, i.e. our interviewee had heard another teacher talking about a third teacher's promotion. Only a few teachers could quote at first or second hand:

'I think I got the job because I knew the church and vicar very well' (Head of Dept. Domestic Science); 'My husband was told quite definitely that if he had been a Mason he would have got his headship by now'.

Most but not all of those who believed that contacts helped promotion disapproved. Occasionally the teacher's prospects were thought to have suffered from the social contact.

'As a member of a political organization and also as a strong union official, I have often been a thorn in the flesh of the Authority and I feel this has worked against my own interests' (Group 4 Head).

Reliable evidence on this extremely sensitive matter would be extremely difficult to come by. On the whole what *evidence* existed for social contact as a factor favouring promotion was extremely thin. While most teachers thought social contacts helped, it was almost always somebody else who had had those contacts—and this from a random albeit small (135) sample of interviewed teachers of different grades and schools throughout the country.

Good relations with the head. In our 135 interviews with teachers we asked the teacher's views of the head's role in promotion, and while this did not specifically entail the topic of relations with the head, many teachers wove this into their answers. There were one or two cases where it was believed a head had impeded another teacher's progress, but these may have had to do more with the head's estimate of the teacher's ability than with any personal antagonism. The overwhelming majority of teachers commented that the heads they had served under in the past had been fair and impartial.

'I don't think it right for a head to exercise his powers to restrict promotion, and in my experience, apart from one isolated case, I have never found that heads restricted promotion possibilities to their staff' (Head Group 6). 'One can see if there were a personality clash, a situation could develop to the detriment of the prospective candidate . . . but in my own experience this has not happened' (Deputy Head). 'Other staff I know of in the area—their heads have not helped, but ours is very fair and always gives a tremendous amount of help to staff who are leaving' (Graded post teacher).

Conformity with advisers. In our study there was no direct evidence to which we could turn to substantiate or reject the teachers' very high ranking of this factor. Would it be stretching credibility too far to suggest that, as many of the courses for teachers are arranged by advisers, and course attendance was a factor found to favour promotion, the teachers' general impression that conforming with an adviser's views (or at least conveying the appearance of doing so) could help promotion was reasonably justified?

CHAPTER EIGHT

Teachers' Views: Factors that Ought to Favour Promotion

What do teachers feel ought to help promotion? Does the 'ideal' vary with the different teacher groups? And how far does the ideal vary from reality? These questions are looked at in this chapter. All tables refer to normal career teachers only, and the method of obtaining the data was outlined in the previous chapter.

The whole sample

In Table 8.1 the factors that teachers believed should favour promotion are shown in order of the size of their 'vote' across the whole sample of normal career teachers. Of the 31 possible factors, only 13 were selected by more than 10 per cent of the sample. As in the previous chapter, all 13 are presented here, but in analyses of the views of different teacher groups only the 'top ten' will usually be quoted.

TABLE 8.1: *Factors that ought to favour promotion—views of all teachers (primary and secondary)*

Rank	Factor	Per cent of teachers (N = 5794)
1.	Flexibility in teaching methods	50.1
2.	Familiarity with new ideas	43.8
3.	Ability to control pupils	43.1
4.	Concern for pupil welfare	41.7
5.	Variety of Schools	34.1
6.	Length of experience	32.0
7.	Good relations with staff	28.9
8.	Subject specialism	28.4
9.	Administrative ability	26.7
10.	Extra-curricular work	19.1
11.	Strong personality	15.4
12.	Course attendance	12.8
13.	Outside experience	11.1

Teachers were more agreed on what *ought* to favour promotion than on what they *thought* favoured promotion. Thirteen factors of the 31 received more than 10 per cent of the votes compared with the 19 factors noted in the previous chapter. Even so, no factor, apart from flexibility in teaching methods (50.1 per cent) was selected by more than half the teachers. While familiarity with new ideas was considered important, actual attendance at courses was well down the list of desirable factors. Good relations with staff had become important but not good relations with head. There was a stress on the teaching process, flexibility of method, new ideas, and a broadly expressed 'concern for pupil welfare'. Only a quarter thought administrative ability ought to count very much. Experience outside education was seen by a tenth as a valuable asset.

Flexibility and new ideas echoed the primacy of the current concern for the teaching process. Ability to control pupils and concern for pupil welfare were both ranked high, suggesting that a valuable quality in a teacher (or at least in one seeking promotion) should be the ability to treat pupils with a firmness combined with solicitude. Notable by its absence was any reference to whether or not children learned, unless that was subsumed in the 'welfare' category.

Of the nine factors considered as desirable promotion qualities by over a quarter of the sampled teachers, only three can currently be measured directly. The others rely on subjective judgements. For their wishes on promotion to be translated into action, teachers would have to accept either that promotion would depend on judgement rather than fact, or insist that attempts should be made to devise acceptable objective measures of such qualities as flexibility, concern, control, good relations, etc.

1. *Primary and secondary teachers*

Table 8.2 lists the priorities that primary and secondary teachers place on promotion attributes. The first number indicates the rank in that group of teachers, the second the rank awarded by the other group. For example, in the Primary column Rank 5.1—Ability to control pupils—is the fifth for primary and first for secondary teachers; 1.5 in the Secondary column indicates it is first for secondary and fifth for primary teachers—instant comparison!

Primary teachers

Half the primary teachers believed that the promoted teacher should have flexible teaching methods. Familiarity with new ideas was the next most important attribute. Then there was a drop of 10 per cent to concern for pupils, and five others commanded support from more than a quarter of the teachers. The low ranking of administrative ability perhaps reflects a desire to promote on grounds of proven teaching capacity rather than anticipated responsibilities.

TABLE 8.2: *Factors that ought to favour promotion—views of primary and secondary teachers*

PRIMARY (N = 3021)			SECONDARY (N = 2773)		
Rank	Factor	Per cent of Teachers	Rank	Factor	Per cent of Teachers
1.2	Flexibility in teaching methods	54.5	1.5	Ability to control pupils	48.5
2.5	Familiarity with new ideas	49.0	2.1	Flexibility in teaching methods	45.4
3.3	Concern for pupil welfare	39.4	3.3	Concern for pupil welfare	44.1
4.7	Variety of schools	39.1	4.9	Subject specialism	39.8
5.1	Ability to control pupils	38.2	5.2	Familiarity with new ideas	38.2
6.9	Good relations with staff	33.6	6.7	Length of teaching experience	30.8
7.6	Length of teaching experience	33.1	7.4	Variety of schools	28.6
8.8	Administrative ability	25.7	8.8	Administrative ability	27.8
9.4	Subject specialism	17.9	9.6	Good relations with staff	23.8
10.10	Extra-curricular work	16.2	10.10	Extra-curricular work	22.3

Only two of the most desirable qualities are usually quantified, the number of schools in which taught, and the number of years of experience. One intriguing placing is the relatively high ranking given to subject specialism. Primary teachers would, it seems, like to see more specialists getting promotion, and one wonders if this implies that, contrary to the 'experts' who advocate the benefits of generalization, the teachers actually in the primary classrooms would like to see more specialist teaching in their schools.

Secondary teachers

No factor was agreed on by the majority of secondary teachers, but ten commanded support from over a fifth of the secondary sample.

Control was the top priority. The next four suggested that the promoted teacher should be flexible, up-to-date, have a recognized subject expertise and a general social concern for the child. Forty per cent of secondary teachers felt subject specialism should be a major factor in promotion, yet perhaps there would be disagreement on whether specific subjects merited high status. Teachers in all types of secondary school ranked success with examination pupils (12th with 12.6. per cent) as of relatively low priority among factors that ought to help promotion, preferring the more general concept of teaching success, 'pupil welfare'.

Primary and secondary teachers compared

The ten most desirable factors in promoted teachers are identified for both primary and secondary teachers, but the support given to each factor varied. The significant differences found were as follows: primary teachers placed much greater stress than secondary teachers on variety of school, flexibility in teaching method, familiarity with new ideas and good relations with staff. Secondary teachers rather than primary regarded subject specialism, ability to control pupils and extra-curricular work as desirable promotion factors. While familiarity with new ideas was a high priority for both teacher groups, the factors that might be expected to be associated with this—course attendance and participation in innovations—were ranked relatively low by both groups: course attendance: primary 11th (15.1 per cent), secondary 14th (10.4 per cent); and participation in innovations: primary 15th (7.2 per cent), secondary 15th (10.2 per cent). The specific issue of pupil learning was not listed within the top ten most desirable criteria by either group.

(a) *Primary: school type* (Table G8.1 in supplement—see p. 14. above)

Infant teachers differed from teachers in junior, and junior/infant schools on two issues. Proportionately fewer of them considered that ability to control pupils ought to be a factor favouring promotion (infant teachers: sixth with 33.5 per cent; other primary teachers: third with 41.2 per cent); and far fewer thought extra-curricular work should count (infant teachers: 12th with 8.6 per cent, other primary teachers: 20th with 19.1 per cent).

(b) *Secondary: school type* (Table G8.2 in supplement)

Although the teachers in all three types of secondary school ranked success with exam pupils as a factor of relatively low priority for promotion, grammar teachers rated it highest: Grammar 11th (18.5 per cent), Comprehensive 13th (13.4 per cent), Modern 14th (10.4 per cent). Three other factors revealed significant differences—administrative ability: Comprehensive fifth (30.4 per cent), Grammar seventh (26.2 per cent), Modern eighth (23.9 per cent); length of teaching experience: Modern sixth (33.9 per cent), Grammar sixth (29.2 per cent), Comprehensive eighth (28.5 per cent); concern for pupil welfare —Comprehensive second (47.0 per cent), Grammar third (41.8 per cent), Modern third (41.1 per cent). Ability to control pupils was ranked first in all three groups but was considered most important by teachers in Secondary Modern schools (52 per cent with 46 per cent for second choice), then Comprehensive (48 per cent with 47 per cent next) and lastly Grammar schools (46 per cent with 43 per cent next).

Sex (Table G8.3 in supplement)

The different priorities of men and women are better understood when primary and secondary teachers are studied separately.

(a) Sex-primary teachers (Table 8.3)

Both men and women regarded flexibility in method, familiarity with new ideas and length of experience as paramount. Both sexes thought promotion should be given to people who were open to new ideas but who had had solid experience. The significant differences were found where proportionately more men than women valued administrative ability, course attendance (women placed this 11th with 13.7 per cent) and extra-curricular work. Men placed strong personality 11th with 19.3 per cent, while women ranked this factor 12th with only 12.3 per cent. Women's ranking for subject specialism does not signal a difference; 17.8 per cent of men voted similarly, placing it 12th. Class control had a 2 per cent and 2 rank elevation by men, but this was within sampling fluctuation.

(b) Sex—secondary teachers (Table 8.4)

While the first five factors were the same for both sexes, men moved class control top of the list and placed a higher valuation on subject specialism. Both are significant differences. Compared with primary teachers, subject specialism replaces length of service, losing 11.9 per cent and 12.8 per cent of teachers' support. Class control becomes more of an issue, gaining 9.9 per cent of male votes and 6.6 per cent of women's votes. Though valued, flexibility and new ideas did not get much support by either sex, as happened with primary teachers. On

TABLE 8.3: *Factors that ought to favour promotion—views of men and women (primary)*

	MEN (N = 763)			WOMEN (N = 2255)	
Rank	Factor	Per cent of primary men	Rank	Factor	Per cent of primary women
1.1	Flexibility in teaching methods	55.0	1.1	Flexibility in teaching methods	56.4
2.2	Familiarity with new ideas	53.2	2.2	Familiarity with new ideas	49.4
3.3	Length of teaching experience	43.9	3.3	Length of teaching experience	42.3
4.6	Ability to control pupils	40.9	4.5	Concern for pupil welfare	41.4
5.4	Concern for pupil welfare	38.4	5.6	Variety of schools	41.3
6.5	Variety of schools	38.0	6.4	Ability to control pupils	38.8
7.8	Administrative ability	34.3	7.8	Good relations with staff	34.9
8.7	Good relations with staff	34.1	8.7	Administrative ability	24.0
9.10	Extra-curricular work	23.1	9.12	Subject specialism	19.3
10	Course attendance	21.1	10.9	Extra-curricular work	14.8

the other hand, pupil welfare raised a higher percentage (4.5 per cent) of the vote. As with primary teachers, proportionately more men than women thought administrative ability ought to be a factor helping promotion. Twenty-three per cent of men in both primary and secondary sectors wanted extra-curricular work to count for promotion, but secondary women wanted it much more (21.3 per cent) than primary women did (14.8 per cent).

Secondary—qualifications (Table G8.4 in supplement)

Teachers holding different qualifications did not differ much in what they wanted most to favour promotion. The chief significant differences were: length of teaching experience—non-graduate 34.3 per cent (sixth), ordinary graduate 29.3 per cent (seventh), good honours graduate 25.0 per cent (eighth); ability to control pupils—non-graudate 52.5 per cent (first), ordinary graduate 45.6 per cent (second), good honours graduate 42.6 per cent (third); administrative ability—

good honours graduate 31.2 per cent (sixth), ordinary graduate 29.3 per cent (eight), non-graduate 23.7 per cent (eighth).

Lower down the rankings was one expected difference: success with examination pupils (good graduates placing this 11th with 16.6 per

TABLE 8.4: *Factors that ought to favour promotion—views of men and women (secondary)*

	MEN (N = 1625)			WOMEN (N = 1147)	
Rank	Factor	Per cent of sec. men	Rank	Factor	Per cent of sec. women
1.3	Ability to control pupils	50.7	1.2	Flexibility in teaching methods	46.6
2.1	Flexibility in teaching methods	44.6	2.3	Concern for pupil welfare	45.9
3.2	Concern for pupil welfare	42.9	3.1	Ability to control pupils	45.4
4.5	Subject specialism	41.8	4.5	Familiarity with new ideas	38.8
5.4	Familiarity with new ideas	37.7	5.4	Subject specialism	37.1
6.9	Administrative ability	31.3	6.7	Length of teaching experience	30.4
7.6	Length of teaching experience	31.1	7.8	Variety of schools	30.4
8.7	Variety of schools	27.3	8.9	Good relations with staff	23.9
9.8	Good relations with staff	23.7	9.6	Administrative ability	22.8
10.10	Extra-curricular work	23.0	10.10	Extra-curricular work	21.3

cent, ordinary graduates 12th with 15.2 per cent and non-graduates 14th with 9.7 per cent); and one intriguing difference—participation in innovations was valued higher as a promotion factor by good honours graduates (13th with 15.3 per cent) than by ordinary graduates (13th with 10.8 per cent) or by non-graduates (15th with only 7.4 per cent). Notable by its absence even from the graduates' list was the factor of being a graduate. Possibly teachers believe that academic qualification ought to be disregarded when promotion posts are to be filled. Perhaps non-graduates have this view, while for graduates it is not consciously a promotion issue. Subject specialism, however, was placed high by most secondary teacher groups.

Age groups (Table G8.5. in supplement)

Teachers of different age groups wanted promotion to depend on different qualities.

(a) *Age groups—primary* (Table G8.6 in supplement)

Intensity of view decreased with age, but eight issues were considered important by all four groups. Course attendance and strong personality, rated nine and ten by senior teachers, were less important for the young teachers. In turn, their valuation of subject specialism and extra-curricular activity was not reflected among their older colleagues. Among the consistent eight, flexibility and new ideas fell in value with age, whereas teaching experience and class control rose. The other four were consistent across the three older groups, though two, good staff relations and administrative ability, were thought less important for the youngest teachers.

(b) *Age-groups—secondary* (Table G8.7 in supplement)

Fifty per cent of teachers over 29 years of age thought that class control ought to be an ingredient for promotion, and no other item at any age group gathered as high a percentage of the vote. In fact, for the oldest group class control was a clear 13.4 per cent above concern for pupil welfare, placed second. As age increased, relatively more teachers believed that promotion should depend on ability to control pupils, and length of experience. Older teachers gave less weight to extra-curricular work, subject specialism and familiarity with new ideas. Administrative ability and good relations with staff were rated less important by the youngest than by other teachers. Participation in innovations was rated low by all groups.

Present Post

Promoted and unpromoted teachers' opinions about what ought to favour promotion might differ. We therefore analysed the primary and secondary teachers' views in terms of the status they held. The views of the head were of particular interest because if, as is often believed, he plays a large role in promotion procedures for other teachers, his opinion of what ought to favour promotion would have considerable influence over the opportunities open to those at a lower level.

(a) *Present post—primary* (Table G8.8 in supplement)

Three consistent opinion groups can be seen—very important: flexibility and new ideas; important: variety of schools, concern for welfare, teaching experience and good relations and, for deputies and heads, administrative ability; of questionable importance: specialism, extra-curricular activities, strong personality and course attendance. Head teachers' views countered the trend for more importance to be attached to length of teaching and good relations with increasing status level, and also countered the trend for less importance to be attached to variety of schools and concern for pupil welfare with increasing status level.

Looking at the views of heads, one finds that eight qualities were considered by over a third of them to be valuable assets to look for in a teacher seeking promotion. Two attributes thought desirable by over half the primary heads were flexibility in teaching methods and familiarity with new ideas. Noticeable by its absence was any suggestion that promotion should be linked with a teacher's ability to produce children's learning.

(b) *Present post—secondary* (Table G8.9 in supplement)

Class control is the most universally recognised of promotion assets by all promoted secondary teachers. This alone takes 50 per cent of the votes of any teacher group. Neither head nor deputy head valued subject specialism or length of teaching experience as highly as other teachers. The importance attached to flexibility by unpromoted teachers was echoed less and less through the promotion levels. The value put upon administrative ability increased steadily to deputy heads, but then fell four ranks and 14 per cent for heads. Good relations with staff were increasingly valued at ascending levels of promotion.

Secondary head teachers appeared to believe that promotion should go to teachers who, above all, could maintain a high standard of discipline. They should have a concern for the general welfare of children, be able to adapt their teaching to varying circumstances, and keep themselves aware of new ideas. Subject specialism was valued by nearly a third of the heads, but success with examination pupils was not one of their priorities.

Factors favouring promotion: 'What does' versus 'What ought to'

A summary is given here of how the sample as a whole believed the reality matched up to their ideal. Since, as we have seen, different groups of teachers valued different factors, the summary is necessarily a simplification.

1. Factors which ought to favour promotion *a great deal* and are believed to do so:
   (a) *Fully:* (i) length of teaching experience.
   (b) *To a limited extent only:* (i) familiarity with new ideas; (iii) variety of schools; (iv) subject specialism.
   (c) *Hardly at all:* (i) flexibility in teaching methods; (ii) ability to control pupils; (iii) concern for pupil welfare; (iv) good relations with staff; (v) administrative ability.

2. Factors which ought to favour promotion to *a limited extent,* and are believed:
   (a) *to do so:* (i) extra-curricular work; (ii) strong personality.
   (b) *to have very little effect:* (i) outside experience.
   (c) *to have too much effect:* (i) course attendance.

3. Factors which ought *not* to influence promotion at all and are believed:
   (a) *do not:* (i) being married; (ii) being a parent; (iii) being a woman; (iv) being a local teacher; (v) experience in non-school education; (vi) civic work; (vii) having local teaching experience.
   (b) *to have a moderate effect:* (i) being younger than 40; (ii) being a male; (iii) participation in innovations; (iv) willingness to move area; (v) success with examination pupils; (vi) long service in one school.
   (c) *to have a great effect:* (i) being a graduate; (ii) specialism in a shortage subject; (iii) social contacts; (iv) conformity with advisers; (v) good relations with head.

Did the teachers' preferred factors differ from those found to be operating in the survey? This is a difficult question to answer because six of the top ten 'ought' qualities were ill-defined and thus not reliably measured. Of the quantifiable factors, variety of experience, length of experience and subject specialism were thought desirable by over a quarter of our sampled teachers, and were all in operation in practice. Graduate status and course attendance were found to favour promotion more than teachers felt they warranted. The survey found that being a local candidate was a very favourable factor in promotion, yet teachers thought it was a trivial attribute, nor did they think it ought to be a factor in promotion. This was the only factor where the fact was at variance with both the preferences and the beliefs of teachers.

SECTION III
Appointment Procedures

CHAPTER NINE

LEA Policies

Teachers criticise the widely differing promotion procedures they have encountered. Yet for advertised posts there seems to be a standard basic procedure—the post is advertised, a short-list of applicants is prepared, these candidates are interviewed and one is appointed. How do the variations reported by teachers arise, and are teachers perhaps exaggerating their extent?

Data for this chapter were drawn from the experiences of teachers and heads, but mainly from the descriptions of appointment procedures given us by the teachers' employers, the LEAs. A questionnaire[1] was sent to 164 LEAs in England and Wales, and the LEA data derive from the 155 returned questionnaires. Further details were collected from confidential interviews with the Education Officers of a subsample of 20 LEAs (including counties and county boroughs in different regions).

The general setting

Before reporting this analysis of LEA policies, the reader should be aware of vital aspects of the setting within which appointment procedures operate:

1. Maintained schools may be 'county' or 'voluntary': the former are maintained entirely by public funds, while many of the latter are maintained the latter partly by public funds and partly by funds from a religious denomination or similar body. The difference lies largely in their origin. Voluntary schools are subdivided into Controlled, Aided and Special Agreement schools, and in general the degree of independence of public funds and of autonomous functioning increases from Controlled through Aided to Special Agreement.

2. By statute, all schools must be managed/governed by means of instruments and rules/articles. (Primary schools must be 'managed by rules', and secondary 'governed by articles'.) The instrument specifies the structure and composition of the body that will perform the managing/governing function, and the rules/articles specify the duties and powers of that body.

---

[1] Reproduced in Appendix B of the supplement—see p. 14 above.

3. (a) For a county primary school, the instrument and rules are to be by order of the LEA.

(b) For a voluntary primary school, the instrument is by order of the DES, and the rules by order of the LEA.

(c) For a county secondary school, the instrument is by order of the LEA, and the articles are by order of the LEA and approved by the DES.

(d) For a voluntary secondary school, the instrument and articles are to be by order of the DES, after consultation with the Foundation and the LEA.

4. Although the DES offers 'Model Instruments and Articles' to guide LEAs, the implementation of the statutory obligation to provide managing/governing bodies is anything but uniform. Some authorities have one managing/governing body per school, others group several schools under one body, others group primary but not secondary. The structure of a managing or governing body may vary if the school is county or voluntary, the latter having a set proportion of governors nominated by the denominational organization concerned.

5. Executive authority for the provision of schools in a community is invested in the elected members of the local authority (LEA). This power is frequently delegated to the Education Committee of the council concerned but it is nevertheless the Authority as such that retains the ultimate influence. While this committee will include co-opted members experienced in education, the great majority will be elected members of the council. Their interests may influence the selection of school governors/managers, as these appointments are the responsibility of the committee. Often council or committee members are themselves selected. Managers and governors need have no professional experience or interest in education, although many authorities attempt to ensure that they do.

The LEA employs professional education staff (the most senior usually with a title like Chief Education Officer) as *administrative officers* whose duties are to carry out the policy laid down by the executive authority. This is the basis for the distinction so many teachers make between the 'laymen' (elected to the central education committee or nominated to the local board of managers/governors) and the professionals (the administrators with educational experience and, of course, the teachers themselves).

6. One of the powers usually delegated to the managers/governors is that of appointing teaching staff, with the proviso that appointments need to be ratified by the LEA. In practice this delegation takes many

forms. The managing/governing body can be the full education committee serving simultaneously as a recommending and a ratifying authority. A subcommittee of the education committee may be entrusted with both tasks. Sometimes a managing/governing body may select an appointing panel from among its members, or it may even delegate the responsibility to its Chairman alone. The appointing managers or governors are expected to consult the professional employees of the LEA, e.g. the Education Officer or his representative, as well as the head of the school. But the extent of consultation varies not only between different LEAs but also for different schools.

7. Finally, some large LEAs delegate responsibility for arranging staff appointments to the executive authoities in 'Excepted Districts' and 'Divisional Areas' within the LEA, and this adds further variations to the total scene. (These Excepted Districts and Divisional Areas will have disappeared in 1974 under the reorganized system of local authorities.)

When one adds to the permutations of the interactions between these procedural factors the personalities and attitudes of the appointing boards, together these are bound to bring about the large variations that teachers report concerning their personal experience.

For this chapter, LEAs were asked about their *general policies*, and these will apply generally to all county schools and most controlled schools.

Other types of school exercise greater autonomy, and may diverge considerably from the 'usual' practice.

A. Advertising Vacancies for Promotion Posts

We already know that many promotions are made internally at the school. For many others successful applicants are already employed by the authority advertising the post. Are posts advertised locally only, or were the applicants competing against others drawn from different regions ? Were the promotion posts open or closed ?

(1) *Open and Restricted Advertising* (Table 9.1)

While the general rule was open advertisement, primary school vacancies were more (9–15 per cent) restricted to teachers already serving with the LEA. With the primary schools, county boroughs more than county councils restricted advertisements to local applicants. Whether the vacancy in question was open or restricted, some LEAs stipulated that it was desirable (13–15 per cent) or essential (10 per cent) that applicants for primary promotion posts should have taught at some time in the authority advertising the post. Only three or four per cent made the same stipulation for secondary vacancies.

TABLE 9.1: *Proportion of LEAs with restricted and open vacancies**

| | PRIMARY | | | SECONDARY | | |
| | *Per cent of LEAs with vacancies open to applicants from:* | | | *Per cent of LEAs with vacancies open to applicants from:* | | |
STATUS VACANT	Within school	Within locality	Any region	Within school	Within locality	Any region
Graded post (now Sc. 2–4)	6.5	18.7	74.2	2.6	6.5	89.7
Head of Dept. (now Sc. 3–5)	3.9	14.2	81.3	1.3	3.2	94.2
Deputy Head	1.9	15.5	81.9	2.6	4.5	91.6
Head	—	12.9	86.5	—	3.2	95.5

* Percentages in all tables in this chapter are based on a total of 155. Where the percentages do not add to 100%, the balance is made up of LEAs who gave indeterminate or no answer to the item in question.

These LEA figures for promotions from within schools are much lower and favour primary more than those based on the replies of sampled teachers. Because of the stratified sampling it is unlikely that the teachers were concentrated in LEAs with this as a policy. A more likely explanation is that policies advocated by LEAs are not necessarily fully implemented in practice.

(2) *Placement of Advertisements* (Tables G 9.1, G 9.2 in supplement).

The chief placements for advertisements were the bulletin circulated locally within LEAs, and the educational press, e.g. *Times Educational Supplement* (TES), *Teachers World* (TW), and journals of the professional associations.

(a) *Educational press.* Between 90 and 95 per cent of the LEAs advertised secondary vacancies at any promotion level in the educational press. For primary posts the figure fell to 87 per cent for headships and to 73 per cent for lower level promotions. County boroughs used the educational press much less than counties.

(b) *Local LEA bulletin.* For all secondary promotion vacancies the local bulletin was used by about three-quarters of the LEAs, and by a slightly higher proportion (80–84 per cent) for primary posts. County boroughs used the bulletin much more than county LEAs.

(c) *National press.* About a quarter of the LEAs placed secondary advertisements in the national press (e.g. *Times, Guardian, Telegraph*). The proportion dropped to 15 per cent for lower level primary appointments.

(d) *Local press.* Between a quarter and a third of all LEAs advertised both primary and secondary promotion posts in their local press. County boroughs favoured this method more than did county authorities.

(e) *Other outlets.* Between 50 and 60 per cent of LEAs placed promotion advertisements in other, chiefly denominational, journals, and presumably such posts were mainly in voluntary schools. County boroughs used these journal outlets for secondary appointments much more than county LEAs.

We analysed the 1172 advertisements appearing in the *Times Educational Supplement* of 2nd and 9th April 1971 (Appendix E). Panel advertisements (those which stand out most) were used more for comprehensive appointments (26 per cent) than grammar, technical, modern, junior or junior/infant (11–12 per cent), with infant appointments bringing up the rear (seven per cent). Ordinary column advertisements can either be single or grouped (i.e. more than one vacancy advertised together). More of the infant column advertisements were grouped (58 per cent) than single (36 per cent), and the same is true for comprehensives (50 per cent *v.* 24 per cent). Junior and junior/infants tended the other way, more individual (47 per cent) than grouped (41 per cent); whilst the modern, grammar and technical advertisements marginally favoured grouping (46–49 *v.* 40–42 per cent). It seems that some comprehensive advertisements got maximum display (panel) and others minimum (grouped column). As regards level of post, proportionally more graded posts obtained panel display (25 per cent secondary, 22 per cent primary) than head of department (16 per cent and 15 per cent), than deputy head (eight per cent, zero per cent). The panel display for headship vacancies then rose to 30 per cent for secondary and 15 per cent for primary. Among the column advertisements the deputy heads showed an interesting difference between the school systems, as for primary the individual and group values were 55 per cent and 45 per cent respectively, whilst for secondary they were 69 per cent and 23 per cent. Only 17 per cent of secondary headships were announced in group advertisements, compared with 49 per cent of primary. However, vacancies for heads of department in primary schools had more visibility than similar secondary posts: primary individual 38 per cent, group 47 per cent; secondary 30 per cent and 55 per cent respectively. Hence marked differences in style of advertisement existed.

B. Application Procedures

The advertisement usually provides a little information about the post and invites applicants to apply sometimes by letter, sometimes by form, sometimes by both. It may also promise to forward further details about the post.

1. *Application forms*

About 95 per cent of LEAs required applicants for headships to complete an application form, for vacancies below headships the figure fell to 90 per cent. For all secondary posts, county boroughs requested forms more than did county councils.

The content of such forms is obviously important, and we asked LEAs to provide a specimen copy of their application form. Several authorities apparently issued different forms according to the type of school or level of post, but the majority used a general standard application form. An analysis on this type of form has, as far as we know, not been undertaken before. It appears as Appendix D in the supplement—see page 1.4 above.

2. *Letters of application*

Letters of application, as distinct from forms, were required for primary posts by a third of the LEAs, with two to three per cent more for secondary posts; e.g. for lower status posts 32 per cent primary, 34 per cent secondary; for deputy headships 36 per cent/39 per cent; for headships, 39 per cent/41 per cent.

3. *Application form and/or Letter of application*

Between 55 per cent and 60 per cent of LEAs required applicants to submit a form and made no stipulation about a letter; three to seven per cent asked for a letter but no form. Both a letter and a form were required by about a quarter for lower status posts and nearly 40 per cent for headship vacancies.

4. *Acknowledgement of Applications*

Ninety per cent of LEAs said they acknowledged applications for headship posts, and 85 per cent did so for other posts. The county LEAs acknowledged much less than did the boroughs.

5. Testimonials

Between a third and a half of authorities requested applicants to send any open testimonials, with a greater tendency among county councils than county boroughs. Table 9.2 shows the position with regard to secondary headship vacancies, and this was typical of all promotion posts in both primary and secondary schools.

TABLE 9.2: *Proportion of LEAs requesting testimonials from applicants for secondary headships*

| LEA | No. of testimonials requested | | | |
	None	1	2	3 or more
Per cent of County Councils (N = 60)	48.3	10.0	30.0	10.0
Per cent of County Boroughs (N = 95)	63.2	12.6	13.7	4.2

6. Referees

In primary schools referees' names were asked for by 84 per cent of LEAs where lower status posts were advertised, and by 93 per cent for headship vacancies. The corresponding figures for secondary school vacancies were 87 and 95 per cent. The average number of referees requested was two, with county boroughs tending to ask for fewer referees than did county councils. The position for all statuses in both primary and secondary schools is typified in the figures for secondary head appointment applications shown in Table 9.3.

TABLE 9.3: *Proportion of LEAs requesting referees from applicants for secondary headships*

| LEA | No. of referees to be quoted | | | |
	None	1	2	3 or more
Per cent of County Councils (N = 60)	3.3	3.3	70.0	21.7
Per cent of County Boroughs (N = 95)	3.2	0.0	81.1	13.6

Little distinction was made between vacancies for an initial ungraded appointment, the first promotion post or a large headship.

7. *Testimonials and/or References*

Over a quarter of LEAs asked for two or more referees *and* two or more testimonials. In Table 9.4 some of the possible combinations are shown for a primary headship vacancy, though these figures are typical of all promotion vacancies in primary and secondary sectors.

TABLE 9.4: *Proportion of LEAs requesting testimonials and/or referees from applicants for primary headship posts*

		Requests from applicants for		
LEA	*No testimonial & no referees*	*No testimonial & 2 referees*	*1 Testimonial & 2 referees*	*2 or more testimonials & 2 or more referees*
Per cent of County Councils (N = 60)	5.0	38.3	8.3	36.7
Per cent of County Boroughs (N = 95)	2.1	60.0	11.6	18.9

C. Short-listing

1. *Processing of Applications*

Seventeen per cent of advertisements for non-headship vacancies in primary schools required applicants to reply to the head; the equivalent figure for the secondary sector was 69 per cent. This does not imply that primary heads had less involvement with initial stages of short-listing than did secondary heads, for the primary heads might still have had access to all the applications sent direct to the 'office'.

2. *Short-listing the candidates*

The requirements for a headship vacancy are drawn up by the education office, for lower appointments by the head, both after consultation with the school governors and educational advisors.

Two examples of shortlisting quoted from our interviews with LEA officers will illustrate the variations in degree and kind. They also indicate the roles played by managers/governors, heads and the 'office'.

LEA No. 1.

Primary posts below head—Divisional Executive Committee short list; professional officer gives facts, not asked for opinion; managers play no part; head consulted.

Primary head—short-listing by joint committee (12 County Education Committee, 6 Divisional Education Committee, 6 managers); Director or representative offers evidence, otherwise not consulted.

Secondary posts below head—governors short-list, head normally consulted, professional officers give facts, no advice.

Secondary head—short listing by joint committee (6 County Education Committee, 6 Divisional Education Committee, 12 Governors); professional officers offer evidence, not opinion.

LEA No. 2.

Primary posts below head—all forms to head; head and advisors prepare short list, possibly helped by Chief Inspector.

Primary head—all forms to Chief Inspector; he and Chairman of Managers prepare short list.

Secondary posts below deputy head—all forms to head; head and chairman of governors prepare short list.

Secondary deputy head—all forms to office; head and Chief Inspector prepare short list.

Secondary head—short list by Chief Inspector, Chairman of Governors and sometimes Director.

Half of all short lists to be internal applicants.

The initial handling of applications could involve any of the following: staffing officers, Assistant or Chief Education officers, advisory staff and Divisional Education Officer, heads, managers, governors, education committees, education sub-committees. Some authorities minimized the participation of managers and governors, while some (fewer) actively encouraged their interest. Overall the shortlisting process is extraordinarily varied, with no group universally dominant, though the approaches to primary and secondary appointments do seem to differ.

From the LEA questionnaire we were able to deduce whether or not the head of the school was involved in short-listing for posts below headship. From Table 9.5 it would seem that just over a third of LEAs have joint decision-making on short-listing at all levels of secondary and primary promotion appointments. The essential difference is exclusivity—more secondary heads have sole responsibility and fewer are totally excluded.

It is noteworthy that over a quarter of the LEAs allowed secondary heads to play no part in selecting the short list for their deputies, and over a third allowed primary heads no part. County councils gave heads in both types of school greater responsibility, 37 per cent of councils allowed the primary head full responsibility for short-listing, compared with 14 per cent of county boroughs. The corresponding secondary figures were 55 per cent and 20 per cent. In giving the head no say at

TABLE 9.5: *LEA description of involvement of heads on short-listing procedure*

| | PRIMARY | | | SECONDARY | | |
| | Per cent of LEAs in which head: | | | Per cent of LEAs in which head: | | |
STATUS OF VACANCY	is solely responsible	is involved with LEA etc.	plays no part	is solely responsible	is involved with LEA etc.	plays no part
Head of Dept.*	28.4	37.4	27.7	45.8	38.1	10.3
Deputy head	22.6	36.8	34.8	33.5	34.2	26.5

* Figures for lower status posts similar to head of department.

all, whereas primary heads were treated by councils and boroughs similarly, boroughs 'denied' secondary heads much more than did councils.

To give a head sole responsibility for short-listing does not necessarily promote justice for applicants. From their knowledge of the school, the LEA and their general experience in education, the professional staff at the education office could well make a positive contribution in sifting the possibles and probables from among the applicants. To *deny* the head any say whatever in the procedure would seem less defensible. What is very difficult to understand is the position of certain LEAs where none of the professionals—neither educational administrators nor the head—were permitted a viewpoint. There, the laymen, either in the central committee or at local management level assumed entire responsibility for short-listing. As many LEA officers and teachers put it to us, the short-listing stage is where the stress is laid on assessing applicants' professional competence (academic qualifications and past experience). The judicious 'weeding-out' of the possibles and probables is of the utmost importance. If the processing procedure adopted produces an unsatisfactory short-list, the interview stage is rendered that much less effective. The great variety in short-listing procedures almost certainly produces inequalities in the treatment of applications and must contribute to the notion widely held among teachers that justice does not prevail. Our impression from several sources is that the inter-relationships between heads, managers/governors, committees and officers are extraordinarily varied in kind and degree, and yet are inextricably tied to the whole procedure by which teachers are promoted.

D. Confidential Reports

The request for 'confidentials' sometimes occurs during short-listing, but more often between the short-listing and interview stages. Discussion of these arouses strong feelings, yet we found that teachers were frequently confused about what was meant by a confidential report. For the sake of clarity in this section a few definitions are proffered.

Testimonial   This is an open document possessed by an applicant and hence its contents are known to him.

Reference   Though usually a written communication, the reference for the candidate's professional competence and character may be a conversation between referee and employer in direct personal contact or over the telephone. The applicant in nominating the referee has given his permission for this confidential dialogue, whether written or spoken, and he does not expect and is not entitled to know what is said of him.

Informal confidences   Sometimes the head of the school or an adviser in the authority to which the applicant applies will contact informally the applicant's present head or adviser to seek information of the applicant's character, competence, etc. Often the applicant knows this will happen, but he may not have actually given permission for it to occur.

'Confidentials'   When a teacher applies for a post with another LEA, that prospective employer requests the teacher's present LEA to forward a confidential report on the teacher. This report, formally requested and formally communicated, is referred to as a 'confidential'. For many teachers 'confidentials' are shrouded in mystery, a situation that makes for maximum rumour founded on minimum knowledge. Our comments cannot be definitive, but they are based on what 155 LEAs told us in questionnaires and/or interviews.

1. *Why have 'confidentials'?*   As normal practice with external applicants, the prospective LEA requests from the previous LEA a confidential report either on all applicants or just those who have been short-listed. It checks that an applicant is a 'bona-fide' candidate, i.e. fulfils

the professional conditions for qualified status and the non-professional conditions relating to moral or medical infirmity. By this inquiry the LEA is implementing a statutory obligation which is accepted by the teachers' organisations themselves as intended to protect their professional status. The 'confidential' also tries to discover an applicant's suitability for the post, and here the LEA is concerned with the more local matter of appointing to its schools those whom it conceives are the most suitable teaching staff.

The 'bona-fide' nature of an internal application should not be an issue, but the suitability of the applicant for a particular post may need a 'confidential', although this time the sources of information are internal to the LEA. The 'confidential' prepared on an internal applicant is almost certainly the same document basically as would be sent to another LEA were the same applicant to apply for a post outside his own LEA.

Many teachers ask, why have testimonials, references and LEA confidentials? Testimonials are not always specific to a particular job, are not confidential, and the prospective employer has no proof of their origin. Applicants choose referees. These will tend to present a positive picture and may not be in a position to comment on what the LEA regards as the essential points it needs to know. Some applicants are at a disadvantage if they have few referees 'of standing' compared with those quoted by other applicants. It is nevertheless accepted that references can be of great value, particularly in separating candidates with fairly equal paper qualifications.

However, the LEAs believe that 'confidentials' compiled from direct knowledge of an applicant's capabilities and qualities in his professional work, are the most reliable guide. Thus it is crucial that such reports should be compiled with fairness and accuracy. Some LEAs go to great lengths to ensure this, but inevitably the variation in compilation must allow injustices to be 'seen', even if not actually occurring.

Essentially, 'confidentials' represent the *normal employment practice* of obtaining a reference from a previous employer. In a minority of other occupations the prospective employer may accept the candidate's wish that his present employer is not contacted, but the teacher is not allowed this veto. LEAs explain that this procedure of automatically approaching the previous employer is in the public interest because the teacher is to be employed as a public servant. Nearly 70 per cent of the teachers we interviewed said that, when applying for posts, they had no objection if a prospective employer went beyond the reference offered in order to seek confidential information about their professional character and capabilities. Even so, the very existence of these 'confidentials' frequently generates heat among some interested parties.

2. *Who requests the confidentials?*   Officially the prospective LEA requests the confidential. Where the office handles the processing, the office makes a direct request to the employing LEA for confidentials. Where the head of the school handles the processing, he asks the office to get them for him, or occasionally he has authority to write for them himself. The system automatically builds up a 'library' of confidentials on an LEA's own teachers.

Where the teacher quotes his own LEA as a referee he is in fact volunteering a 'confidential'. Then the prospective LEA observes its normal procedure, as it would have contacted the applicant's present LEA even if it had not been specifically quoted as a referee!

3. *Who writes the 'confidentials'?*   Though officially from the Chief Education Officer (or equivalent), the raising of a 'confidential' is usually delegated to a subordinate officer (e.g. Assistant Education Officer in charge of schools). He may actually compile the report himself, but more often will refer the matter to his staff of advisers, inspectors and ultimately, if the applicant is not the head, to the head of the school where the applicant teaches. (As an applicant often offers his present head as a referee, this frequently means that the prospective employer will receive duplicated information, i.e. the reference and the 'confidential'). The authority's own records of the teacher may be consulted, especially if the details required by the prospective authority are documented data, like salary, degree status or dates of employment.

Some examples of methods used, as quoted to us by interviewed LEAs, will illustrate:

LEA No. 1: AEO prepares confidentials on basis of information provided by advisory staff; AEO feels he knows a lot about the teachers.

LEA No. 2: For heads leaving—Senior adviser drafts report and CEO ratifies. For other teachers, head asked for comments and can send direct to prospective employer or ask CEO for advice. If teacher known to adviser, adviser compiles report and sends direct to requesting LEA.

LEA No. 3: Report prepared by local inspectorate, must be approved by Director or Deputy Director.

LEA No. 4: Heads leaving—AEO drafts reports, sends to Director for approval. Others—report requested from head and possibly modified by 'office'.
(With some LEAs, it was expected that when a head helped with short-listing junior appointments, he might ask his senior staff for their views.)

Sometimes the head's views are sought, sometimes they are not. Sometimes the advisers are involved, sometimes they are not. Sometimes the AEO or senior administrator takes a part, sometimes he does not. How can a confidential from an adviser in LEA 'X' be compared with one from an AEO in LEA 'Y' or with one from a head in LEA 'Z'? The usual request for a confidential listed nothing more specific than a comment on *suitability* for the 'post being advertised'. But as the 'post being advertised' is rarely described in a specific and itemised way, the subsequent assessment of suitability is rendered virtually meaningless.

Only one of our 20 interviewed authorities, when supplying confidentials, commented on a set list of features: teaching ability, attitude to pupil and staff, extra-curricular work, any special work done in school, courses attended and (very insistent on this) application of knowledge in practice, personality, and health record. Whether these traits were measured accurately is another matter. A system which relies on global subjective assessments, from a variety of assessors, with no criteria other than 'suitability', inevitably must lack comparability if not utility.

Rarely were confidentials the work of one person. At least more than one opinion went to their compilation. The potential contributors, CEO, AEO, advisers, heads, inspectors, should be able to give the fullest picture. But sometimes all their opinions were not sought. Sometimes they knew 'show' or difficult schools better than others. Albeit the system rests on the integrity of the assessors (and many teachers and some LEA officials were not convinced of a uniform integrity.)

Whilst the confidential may be for the public interest, it certainly does not follow that it works against the interest of individual teachers. A complimentary confidential can usefully counteract a diffident teacher's modesty. At the same time, the confidential may contain estimated features of the applicant's professional character and competence, believed to be relevant to the post applied for, that may be injurious to his prospects. Some LEAs told us that they have instituted the practice of regular up-datings of records so that an early injurious comment should not remain on a teacher's record permanently. This sound procedure increases both the credibility of confidentials and their fairness to teachers.

Confidentials may be statutory. They may be in the public interest and protect LEAs, schools and teachers. But the manner in which they are compiled leaves much to be desired.

However compiled, the short-list of candidates are now interviewed— the next stage of the appointments procedure.

E. Interviewing Candidates

More than any other aspect of promotion procedures, the interviewing process produces the 'horror stories' that abound in the press and in staffroom banter. Before surveying, in the next chapter, the experiences of our sample of teachers, we discuss in this section the policies and practices of LEAs.

1. *The purpose of the interview.*

Officially the rationale of the interview is that all candidates have passed the 'paper' tests and now are being assessed by the interview panel on their personal and professional capacities. The interviewing panel must appoint the applicant whose abilities and character, as far as they can judge, are most suited to the position to be filled. However, the criteria for suitability might be seen differently by the elected members (political), school governors (teacher as an employee) and local individuals (specific community needs). Because of these different points of view, the layman's approach and his assessments are believed by some teachers to be just as valid as the professional's.

2. *How many candidates are interviewed?*

The *usual* numbers invited by LEAs for interview (assuming there were a sufficient number of suitable short-listed candidates) were as shown in Table 9.6. There was a tendency to short-list and interview more candidates in secondary than in primary schools for the same type of appointment. More candidates were short-listed for senior posts than for junior levels. These findings may have been related to the differential demand for posts found earlier, but the figures probably are independent of this factor, as LEAs were answering about general policy.

For some senior posts an LEA may practise 'double-interviewing', i.e. interview a dozen or so 'long-listed' applicants at a first-stage interview and then invite a 'short-list' of these to return for a second-stage interview, but this was not a common practice.

3. *What form does the interview take?*

The majority of interviews consisted of formally appearing before a panel of interviewers for a given period of time. Quite often candidates could look around the school before the interview. LEAs stressed that practice varied with the school and post level, and an interesting variation involved the school staff, especially the head of the department concerned, chatting informally to applicants prior to the formal interview and then to give the head their opinion of the various candidates. Sometimes prior to the formal interview the candidates met the head informally, and he described the school, answered their queries and generally helped them relax.

TABLE 9.6: *Proportion of LEAs and number of candidates usually invited for interview*

| | PRIMARY | | | | SECONDARY | | | |
| | Per cent of LEAs where candidates invited for interview numbered: | | | | Per cent of LEAs where candidates invited for interview numbered: | | | |
STATUS OF VACANCY	3	4	5	6 or more	3	4	5	6 or more
Graded post	25.8	27.7	15.5	13.5	21.9	33.0	17.5	13.5
Head of dept.	16.8	34.2	16.8	18.7	12.3	34.2	23.2	18.7
Deputy head	9.0	28.4	25.8	27.1	5.8	22.6	28.4	33.5
Head	5.8	19.4	27.7	42.6	3.2	12.3	26.5	53.5

The formal interview varied a great deal, but one or two basic procedures prevailed. The Chairman of managers/governors, as formal chairman of the discussion, invited panel members in turn to ask the candidate one or more questions. If professional advisers were present, they might be invited to do so also. Alternatively, just prior to his interview each candidate was handed a paper on which was written one or two questions (or topics) related to education, and at the interview he was asked to comment on these. The merits of candidates might be debated after each candidate had been seen in turn, or after all had been seen. Only the managers/governors may vote when the decision on appointment is taken, and it is the managing/governing body that officially recommends an appointment, not the head or an adviser or a professional administrator. This recommendation is passed for approval to the executive authority, which is, for practical purposes, the LEA's education committee. The latter may, for particular appointments, bypass the managing/governing body and both recommend and appoint.

In practice, managers/governors and executive committees lean on the professional advice of the head or 'office', but the extent depends entirely on the policy and relationships existing in the LEA and in the locality where the post is vacant.

4. *Who are the interviewing panel?*

(a) *The head.* A small proportion of LEAs (four to five per cent) exclude the primary head teacher from interviews relating to vacancies at his school.

(b) *Other teaching staff.* At interviews for head of department or lower level posts in primary schools, two or three per cent of LEAs encouraged the additional presence of the school's deputy head, while seven or eight per cent said this was a common practice in their secondary schools. Where the vacant post was of junior status, the head of the department concerned attended the interviews in 16 per cent of the LEAs. (These figures concern actual attendance at the formal interview; the LEAs could not specify the extent to which the other senior staff might be involved in informally appraising candidates prior to their interview proper.)

(c) *The Education Officer* (or representative). Table 9.7 indicates to what extent the LEA policy was that professional administrators should attend interviews of short-listed candidates. The attendance increased significantly as the status of the post rose. It can be assumed from our discussions that interviews for the senior vacancies warranted the attendance of the senior administrators, e.g. staffing officer for graded post, Adviser for head of department, Assistant Education Officer for deputy head, and Chief Education Officer for head of a large school.

TABLE 9.7: *Proportion of LEAs whose policy was that professional administrators should attend interviews of short-listed candidates*

INTERVIEWS FOR	Per cent of LEAs with policy of professional administrator's attendance	
	PRIMARY	SECONDARY
Graded post	60.0	60.0
Head of department	62.6	64.5
Deputy head	80.0	78.7
Head	89.0	92.3

The professional administrator's attendance at interviews was by no means automatic, and even at interviews for headships about 10 per cent of LEAs excluded the Education Officer or his representative. Apart from headship interviews, the county council authorities exercised the policy of exclusion more than did county boroughs. While officers may have attended merely to give evidence or submit documents, we gathered it was more usual for their advice to be sought. Even so, several cases were reported where the officer's advice was either not taken or not even sought.

(d) *Managers/Governors.* In Table 9.8 is shown the proportion of LEAs whose policy was to ask managers/governors to attend the interviews of short-listed candidates. As with professional administrators, the tendency was for managers/governors to attend interviews for senior rather than junior posts, but unlike the former case, the county boroughs excluded managers/governors more than did county councils. This possibly reflected the decentralization in the geographically large council authorities where the local school was much more the centre of community interest and affairs than was the case with large urban areas.

TABLE 9.8: *Proportion of LEAs whose policy was that managers/governors should be represented at interviews of short-listed candidates*

INTERVIEWS FOR	Per cent of LEAs with policy of inviting managers/governors to attend interviews	
	PRIMARY	SECONDARY
Graded post	50.3	52.3
Head of department	60.0	66.5
Deputy head	80.0	84.0
Head	86.5	91.0

It is surprising to see in how many LEAs managers and governors did not attend interviews. How often had the Education Committee taken over the role of recommending as well as appointing? Was it (or one of its subcommittees) acting as the managing/governing body? Is the managers'/governors' authority to recommend appointments often delegated to a professional administrator or to the head? Strictly speaking, such delegation runs counter to the letter of the articles of management/government. No doubt this was a commonsense course of action where quick action was necessary but where a meeting of managers/governors was out of the question.

(e) *LEA Advisers/Inspectors.* The role of the LEA adviser in the appointment procedure varied across the authorities, and some LEAs do not involve them at all. Out findings indicated that Advisers were called to attend interviews for primary appointments in about 50 per cent of LEAs. For secondary appointments about 44 per cent of LEAs asked Advisers to attend interviews. This figure went up to 56 per cent for secondary head of department vacancies, presumably to accommodate the specialist knowledge of subject advisers.

(f) *HMI.* Officially, Inspectors appointed by DES have no connection with the arrangements for appointing staff. We did wonder if LEAs ever sought HMI advice when filling vacancies. The answer for all posts below head was an almost unanimous and unequivocal 'No'. HMI advice was sought for headships in primary schools by nine per cent of LEAs, almost all being county boroughs, while for secondary headships nearly 20 per cent of LEAs sought advice from HMIs.

Examples. Two actual examples culled from our interviews with LEAs may demonstrate the range of procedures.

LEA No. 1. (County Council)

(a) *Primary:* Posts below head—interview conducted by Staffing Subcommittee of about 20 (including 3 teachers' representatives, head, AEO). View of AEO only of limited weight. Head—same subcommittee (minus head).

(b) *Secondary:* Posts below deputy—head entirely responsible. Deputy head—Head, AEO, governors at interview (sometimes all governors, sometimes subcommittee). Head—Joint committee of 12 (6 from governors, 6 from Education Committee), AEO/CEO present, can ask questions and give opinions, but committee very strong and have sometimes ignored 'professionals' advice. (In this authority advisers have no role at all in the appointments procedure.)

LEA No. 2. (Small County Borough)

(a) *Primary:* lower status and deputy heads frequently internal promotions within authority and 'arranged over phone' between heads, and AEO; rarely interviews arranged.
Headship—2-stage interview—6 candidates seen in morning by managers, AEO and CEO and 3 selected for afternoon interview with subcommittee of Education Committee. Post usually goes to local candidate. 'It's a small borough and this relatively intimate and easy-going system works quite well'.

(b) *Secondary:* Headship—similar to primary system, but CEO takes greater interest and afternoon selection by full Education Committee.

Summary

As we have seen, variations in interviewing policy and procedure were widespread. It is possible, however, to discern from our survey certain trends about the roles taken by the various interested parties, and a summary of these may now be of some use.

Managing bodies appeared to exercise little control over appointments, although they were the official groups that recommended appointments. Governors seemed more involved, but still had little power. Teachers might regard these 'laymen' as a threat to their jobs as professional workers yet, as far as we could tell, these 'laymen' were generally on very good terms with their heads and were happy to be guided by them. While some bodies were lethargic and took little interest in the school, others prided themselves on being 'friends of the school'. If they were members of the Education Committee or knew such members, they would often bring to the LEAs attention matters which they felt affected the welfare of 'their' school.

Heads' powers in appointments depended more on their relationship with their LEA than with their managers/governors. Primary heads had less of a formal role in appointing than secondary heads. However, their professional colleagues made every effort to accommodate heads' wishes in appointments.

Education Committees varied enormously. Some leaned heavily on the professional expertise of their educational administrators and heads, being genuinely anxious to seek their advice and to learn from them. Others regarded themselves as an elected elite, were ever watchful that the professional administrators and heads should know their place as public servants and employees, and treated professional expertise with suspicion.

In the final analysis, as one LEA officer remarked, much depends on the strength of personality of the Chief Education Officer and of the heads who are appointed.

F. The Result of the Application

The vast majority of LEAs made an appointment on the day of the interview, and those who attended for interview knew the result on that day. About 4 per cent of the LEAs delayed a decision for a short while (possibly because all those called for interview could not attend on one day), and in these cases, all interviewees were told the result within a week of the interview.

We also asked LEAs if they informed applicants who had not been called for interview of the result of their application. For lower level primary appointments, 85 per cent of LEAs told all applicants the result, and for deputy head and head vacancies, 90 per cent informed all applicants of the result. In the secondary sector, about 90 per cent of

LEAs told all applicants the result, irrespective of status levels. Five LEAs said they informed applicants of the result provided they had enclosed a stamped addressed envelope with their original application.

G. The Appointment of the Head

While all appointments are important, that of the head is the most vital appointment of all, for the entire functioning of the school depends on the influence he exerts in every aspect of the school's life. Is our current system effective in appointing the best head teachers? We do do not really know, but the variety and subjectivity of present methods make it unlikely. Without any doubt whatever, many head appointments have proved first rate. However, this may have happened as much by chance as by systematic appraisal. The same system which has produced first class leaders has also made appalling blunders, and the ill-effects of these spread far and wide. Some way must be found to make the vital issue of the appointment of heads more systematic and objective. Alternatively, it may be that in future years the role of the head may undergo modifications such that his influence on a school is less of a 'make or break' one.

H. Reorganization

The reorganization of schools raises problems of allocation, re-allocation or re-advertising of promotion posts. To a great extent salaries were guaranteed under Burnham arrangements, so the critical issue is the change of status, of esteem, of responsibility. Important for later promotion applications, a teacher's record may show that his status changed from deputy head to head of department, an appointment demotion to the uniformed.

The problem was too complex for us to study in detail, as LEAs adopted different procedures and were faced with different reorganization problems. As illustrations we report how five of the LEAs we visited had dealt with the problem, or planned to deal with it.

LEA No. 1 (County Council)

General policy: Director/AEO prepares draft of proposed school structure, discuss with governors and finalize; plan issued to all teachers and given time to study; teachers state (on proforma) what post now held and what they would like to teach and status wanted within new structure. All teachers interviewed in confidence by Director, the principle being to encourage teachers to expect equivalent structure, and if equivalent post not offered, then 'next best' offered; governors make final decision. No post will be advertised till all teachers inter-

viewed and opinions vetted. Headships: If no dramatic change via
re-organization (e.g. same school, same age range etc.) Committee
consider governors' views, and latter usually want existing head. If
re-organization to be drastic (e.g. amalgamation, mixed from single
sex) post advertised nationally, with existing heads being placed on
short-list; if equivalent not given, then 'next best' offered, e.g. deputy
headship and automatically short-listed for head vacancies at any
school of similar type to previous school.

LEA No. 2 (County Council)

No plans yet for re-organization. If it happened, probably 'administrative convenience would override political or educational conviction'.
Status could not be guaranteed, but they would try to arrange things
by the 'retirement method'.

LEA No. 3 (County Council)

Usual problems did not arise because whole districts re-organized at
same time.

(a) All existing heads displaced simultaneously, and all could apply for
new headships; as there were always as many new schools (including
Middle) as before, all heads were recommended on principle of trying
to allocate to position of comparable status.

(b) LEA and head decide on school establishment, and advertise
within a district of the LEA; i.e. staff at schools being re-organized
were offered first choice (and any *not* holding posts could apply);
again, principle adopted of trying to give existing holders a post of
comparable status, though it might not be in previous school.

(c) Same procedure where just two or three schools amalgamated—
treated as the district from which applicants can come.

(d) Always—principle was, first to fill new posts with staff in affected
districts, then—if vacancies left—to advertise throughout county,
then—and only as last resort—nationally.

LEA No. 4 (County Borough)

Protecting of status not proved too difficult. Any displaced head or
deputy head sent on courses and usually apply for other headships in
smaller schools, or become housemasters in large comprehensives.

LEA No. 5 (County Council)

No problems; no policy about protecting status because 'this is
impossible.'

A few authorities appear to treat the problem purely as an administrative matter and seem insensitive to the emotional and professional
blows to individual teachers. However, if the picture presented by our
sample of LEAs is representative of other authorities, most authorities
have tried (or will try) to consult with teachers, considering the problems

in human terms as well as protecting their official obligation to the public. There is a recognition by the professional administrators, if not by the elected policy-makers on central committees, that any strong personal discontent among teachers may have serious repercussions in the schools. Hence the position of consultation and compromise adopted by many authorities must appear to be all the more commendable.

I. Career Development

Do LEAs regard it as part of their function to develop a system to identify and encourage able teachers to think of teaching as having a career structure, either generally or within a particular authority? From the somewhat vague answers to our questions on these items we gained the general impression that the notion of positive career development in the teaching profession is virtually non-existent. What little there was is summarized here.

1. *A Career with a particular LEA*

This may be encouraged in three ways: (i) by setting up a system for identifying, encouraging and counselling teachers who may be suitable for subsequent (further) promotion; (ii) by having a definite promotion system laid down by the LEA concerned; and (iii) by a system of giving preference in promotion to internal rather than external candidates.

(a) *Career development advice.* Most authorities ignored this issue, and a few relied on casual conversations between advisers and teachers, e.g. 'There is no "procedure". Advisers encourage promising teachers to apply for promotion and secondment'. (County Borough); 'Inspectors discuss personal future with each probationary teacher—and with older teachers on request.' (County Borough). Only one authority referred to a definite service specifically designed to advise teachers of the possibilities of promotion in the LEA:

'We are in the process of setting up a Careers Advisory Section, where teachers will be advised of future promotion, etc., particularly in view of a proposed system of comprehensive secondary education.' (County Borough)

(b) *Promotion schemes.* Only two of the 155 responding LEAs said they operated a formal promotion scheme. This was puzzling, as discussions with teachers and heads had suggested that such schemes were much more prevalent. An example from a County Council LEA will illustrate the practice: (i) Primary deputy headship: advertised only in divisional area; must have minimum service of five years (used to be ten) and last five must be in one of the county's primary schools. (ii) Primary headship: advertised throughout county; must have served at least five years (used to be ten) and last five in county primary school; if head applies for new headship, must have served in present headship at least four years. (iii) Secondary headship: nationally advertised, but must be graduate with at least five years' secondary experience.

(c) *Preference for internal candidates.* The practice of giving preference to promotion candidates with present or past experience with the LEA was more common in primary schools seven to ten per cent) than secondary (one to three per cent), and occurred more in county boroughs than county councils. Other LEAs encouraged their own serving teachers by operating a policy that a certain proprotion of short-listed applicants for promotion posts should always be internal candidates. Naturally this would not guarantee that the actual appointment would go to a teacher already serving with the LEA.

2. General career development

Table 9.9 shows the response to the question 'What percentage of the LEAs annual education budget is allocated to in-service training, *including* support of Teachers' Centres ?'

TABLE 9.9: *LEA expenditure on teachers' in-service training*

	PROPORTION OF ANNUAL EDUCATION BUDGET ALLOCATED TO IN-SERVICE EDUCATION				
	Less than 0.1%	0.1%– 0.39%	0.4%– 0.59%	0.6%– 0.99%	1.0% *or more*
Per cent of LEAs (N = 113)	10.6	41.6	22.1	15.1	10.6

A quarter (27 per cent) of the LEAs did not answer this question, but there is little reason to believe that if they had answered the pattern would have changed. The tendency was for county councils to allocate more than county boroughs.

We asked LEAs for details of the management/administration courses offered, as these seemed the most relevant for career development towards high status. Forty-two per cent of LEAs said they provided such courses, but we were restricted by resource limitations from studying the answers in qualitative detail. We also asked about arrangements for staff to attend such courses, and gathered that it was not the desire to attend courses that affected application levels, so much as the availability of other staff to cover teacher absences. For 23 per cent of LEAs the granting of secondment for a term or more at a course was dependent on the teacher's 'promise' to return to the LEA that seconded him.

CHAPTER TEN

The Involvement of Head Teachers

While heads may not be aware of their LEA policy on promotion procedures in all sectors of the system, they become involved in those aspects that affect their own schools. The head must fill the promotion vacancies in his own school, and become involved with the search by his own staff for promotion posts at his or other schools.

Our sample of 681 primary and 137 secondary heads (35 per cent in voluntary schools) were asked about their role in promotion procedures, in the Heads' questionnaires[1]. The depth interviews with heads yielded additional case-study examples of qualitative information.

As both the LEA and head samples were nationally representative, we are able to compare the general evidence of the Heads' questionnaires with the general findings of the LEA account given in the previous chapter. We might thus learn how far the general policies advocated by LEAs were put into practice. An incidental effect of this chapter may be to enlighten aspiring heads on their future tasks—at least as far as promotion procedures are concerned.

A. Advertising

Of 27 heads who spoke to us on this matter, 16 said they personally were involved in preparing the advertisement of vacant posts, either on a standard proforma or by telephone conversation to the 'office'. No great objection was raised where the head did not have a hand in the advertisement.

Most of the interviewed heads said their authority forwarded to applicants further details of the school and post, but they felt happier if the applicant came and saw the school personally.

The majority of heads said their LEAs allowed them between three and four weeks between advertisement and closing date, and they thought that adequate. However, certain situations can cause haste, e.g. 'If you are advertising in mid-May you have got to give a closing date in a matter of days if you want an appointment for the following

---

[1] Reproduced in Appendix B in the Supplement—see page 1.7.

September', and 'temporary teachers suddenly give a month's notice—even less for supply teachers'.

B. Application Procedures

Where the heads we spoke to received applications directly, they usually acknowledged each one and also told all applicants not called for interview when the post had been filled. Most did not feel strongly about the method of corresponding with applicants, but one commented sharply:

'I think our LEA system is bad. A general circular goes round which gives the result of the vacancy—individuals don't get cards or letters. Those not called for interview just don't know anything till they see the result in the bulletin and that can be some months after they actually applied'.

The heads were divided on the question of application forms or letters of application. A quarter wanted forms because 'letters vary so much' and 'it is so much easier to compare standardized forms'. Another quarter preferred letters of application because 'it gives the applicant scope to give his opinions', or the letter is 'most revealing'. Half favoured the combination, commenting that 'no application form can cover everything'. Some felt they learned not only from 'what is said but how they say it'. One head raised a point that must puzzle many would-be writers of letters—'teachers don't know what to put in letters'. There seems to be some disparity in what is considered relevant by some heads, committees and teachers for specific posts and schools.

Although a few wanted to retain them, most heads found testimonials useless. Not all heads were antagonistic, some effectively turning them into references. 'I follow them up with a telephone conversation to the person who has written it'.

Heads usually wanted two referees, but there were reservations about their value. Cognizance may be taken only if the reference 'comes from an important person, like the Director of Education or the head of the school'. The relevance of some referees was often challenged, 'people quote the vicar . . . but they're coming here to the school not the church'. The integrity of referees was always seen as a potential problem—'I once had an excellent written reference sent, and on ringing up the writer he admitted he was trying to get rid of the chap'.

C. Short-listing

We wished to know how heads themselves saw the role they played in shortlisting.

The status of school—county, voluntary controlled, or aided and special agreement—confers varying degrees of autonomy in the appointing powers of authorties. Consequently the role of an individual head is conditioned by global LEA policy, by the local circumstances appertaining to the school, and especially by the 'autonomy structure' built into the school's instrument and articles of management/government.

1. Short-listing of applications for deputy head

Table 10.1 shows the extent to which our sample of heads said they were involved in the short-listing of deputy headships at their school.

The total number of heads concerned in any table in this and later sections will vary from one table to another. The post concerned might not have been in existence in the head's school; or the post has never been vacant and therefore the head does not know if he might or might not be involved.

TABLE 10.1: *Heads' involvement in short-listing of applications for deputy headship*

| | | PER CENT OF HEADS WHO WERE: | | | |
SCHOOL TYPE	N	Completely responsible	Consulted	Took no part	Unclear answer
Primary heads	523	10.9	69.0	12.6	7.5
Secondary heads	137	20.4	75.9	2.2	1.5

X^2 differences between primary and secondary significant at 0.1% confidence level.

Patently secondary heads receive greater responsibility. Over the whole sample, a tenth of the heads said they had no part in the short-listing of their deputy head. Proportionately far more secondary heads short-listed entirely on their own (twice as frequently). The great majority of both primary and secondary heads were involved, even if sharing the responsibility with the Education Officer's representative, or managers/governors. Fewer heads admitted their sole power than LEAs indicated (11 per cent *v.* 23 per cent for primary and 20 per cent *v.* 34 per cent secondary), nor confessed their exclusion (13 per cent *v.* 35 per cent primary and 2 per cent *v.* 27 per cent secondary). It seems that where policy stipulated independence, both parties tended to consult each other.

More consultation between the primary head and others occurred in voluntary than in county schools, but the extremes of giving the head complete responsibility or none at all were found more in county than in voluntary schools. In the secondary sector no difference between county and voluntary sectors was evident, but grammar heads appeared to be given sole responsibility for short-listing their deputies more than comprehensive or modern school heads (46 per cent against 13 per cent and 16 per cent respectively).

2. *Short-listing of applications for other promotion costs* (Tables G10.1— G10.2 in supplement).

The heads were more closely involved with the short-listing for posts below deputy head than they were for deputy head appointments; e.g. 39 per cent were completely responsible for the short-listing of graded posts, and 25 per cent for departmental heads, and only 13 per cent for deputy head appointments. The differences in appointing deputy heads, between primary and secondary schools, and between heads in county and voluntary schools, remained characteristic for all other posts whether ungraded or involving promotion. An exception was that sole responsibility for short-listing graded posts was given less to modern school heads than to the other heads.

3. *Heads' views*

Every head whom we interviewed felt he/she ought to be involved in drawing up a short-list for any appointment that concerned his or her school. Few heads thought that they alone should select short-lists for their schools. Most believed the help of an adviser/inspector was useful, particularly if a specialist subject was involved. Secondary heads placed heads of department as the next most important selectors of a short-list. Two-thirds believed it was right for a representative of the managers/governors to have a say as 'they do know the village prejudices and local area very well'. Others felt rather strongly that managers were quite unnecessary because 'they did not know enough about the school'. About half wanted a representative from the 'office' to help because 'they can read between the lines of an application form better than anyone else'. A third sometimes asked their deputy heads to help them, but not one wanted anyone from the 'Committee' or 'Council'. Members of staff other than deputy or head of department were also not very popular 'because they change so quickly'.

Our interviews confirmed the inference from the heads' questionnaires that most heads, if not solely responsible, were at least very much involved, although perhaps with some unwanted assistance.

D. 'Confidential Information' (The Grapevine)

Many people involved in appointment procedures will be heard to refer to the 'grapevine'—the informal and unofficial seeking and receiving of confidential information about applicants. These inquiries are made of the applicant's current head or LEA office.

Heads were not asked if they *personally* used the 'grapevine' methods, but if they *believed* the method was practised, hence providing data on how far the practice is believed to exist.

1. *General contacts* (Table 10.2)

About one third of the heads in the sample believed that these contacts, whether in personal meetings, by telephone conversations or letter correspondence, happened. About a third thought they occurred rarely, and 36 per cent felt they could not answer.

TABLE 10.2: *Heads' views: collecting confidential information about applicants for promotion from sources other than those offered by applicant*

| | | PER CENT OF HEADS BELIEVING THE PRACTICE OCCURRED: | | |
SCHOOL TYPE	N	Never/ rarely	Often/ frequently/ always	No clear answer
Primary heads	681	30.9	30.3	38.8
Secondary heads	137	33.6	44.8	21.6

More primary than secondary heads were unsure about the existence of the system, but it did appear that the practice was believed to occur frequently in secondary more than primary schools. There was little difference of opinion among primary school types. In the secondary sector the modern and comprehensive heads (45 per cent and 49 per cent) were more inclined to believe the practice existed than grammar heads (36 per cent).

2. *Personal contact* (Table 10.3)

There were significant differences in the views of primary and secondary heads. Half of the secondary heads believed that it happened very rarely, compared with a third of primary heads. Fifty per cent more primary than secondary heads were unsure if the system existed. There was little difference between county and voluntary school heads, though voluntary school heads, particularly those in controlled schools, appeared a little more reluctant to give any view at all.

TABLE 10.3: *Heads' views: collecting confidential information about applicants for promotion by personal contact with sources other than those offered by applicant*

SCHOOL TYPE	N	PER CENT OF HEADS BELIEVING THE PRACTICE OCCURRED:			
		Never/ rarely	*Fairly often*	*Usually/ always*	*No clear answer*
Primary heads	681	31.4	13.8	13.2	41.6
Secondary heads	137	49.6	12.4	9.5	28.5

3. *Telephone contact* (Table 10.4)

The 'chat over the phone' is probably the grapevine method most commonly referred to in staffrooms. In fact one third of the heads believed that it was practised frequently, and another third believed it occurred rarely or never. Proportionally more primary heads said they were unsure of its existence. Among the heads who had opinions, the primary and secondary sectors did not differ. Again, heads in voluntary controlled schools offered a clear answer much less than heads of other schools.

TABLE 10.4: *Heads' views: collecting confidential information about applicants for promotion by telephone contact with sources other than those offered by applicant*

SCHOOL TYPE	N	PER CENT OF HEADS BELIEVING THE PRACTICE OCCURRED:			
		Never/ rarely	*Fairly often*	*Usually/ always*	*No clear answer*
Primary heads	681	30.8	18.4	14.4	36.4
Secondary heads	137	37.2	25.6	17.5	19.7

4. *Contact by letter* (Table 10.5)

A number of heads mentioned writing to the applicant's LEA for information. One might have expected heads to know that this was routine LEA practice, but obviously this knowledge might not be universal. Hence the figure of 37 per cent of heads believing that a source other than referees were contacted must include some heads unaware of LEA practice, and others who have not considered the LEA 'confidential' in this category.

TABLE 10.5: *Heads' views: collecting confidential information about applicants for promotion by writing to sources other than those offered by applicants*

SCHOOL TYPE	N	Never/ rarely	Fairly often	Usually/ always	No clear answer
		PER CENT OF HEADS BELIEVING THE PRACTICE OCCURRED:			
Primary heads	681	30.5	11.6	19.4	38.5
Secondary heads	137	13.9	14.6	54.7	16.8

Again 'don't know' is a feature of the response of heads of primary and voluntary controlled schools. A significantly higher proportion of primary heads believed it did not happen, and proportionately three times as many secondary heads as primary 'knew' it happened always.

The consistently high proportion of 'don't knows' among heads of primary schools and of voluntary controlled schools is intriguing. Despite our guarantee of strict confidentiality, did such heads feel too vulnerable to give their views? Do these heads have less knowledge of the appointments procedure? Were they younger, less experienced, and hence less prone to definitive statements?

5. *Which contact is used most?*

Fifty-five per cent of the secondary heads believed that very frequent use was made of the letter contact, 18 per cent believed this of telephone contacts, and 10 per cent of personal meetings. With primary heads, the corresponding figures were 19 per cent, 14 per cent and 13 per cent. There were consistent views within the secondary sector, with modern heads perhaps emphasizing the letter contact a little more. In the primary sector, infant heads regarded telephone conversations as the most often used.

6. *The ethics*

Twenty-five of our 27 interviewed heads believed the practice of these additional contacts was quite common. Four thought it wrong 'in principle'. The others (85 per cent) saw no objection to the practice, though there was little doubt that they were only thinking in terms of 'professional contacts'. These would be applicant's present head, possibly the applicant's LEA or, for internal applicants, the authority's Adviser/Inspector. Two heads felt strongly that if these contacts were made, the applicant should be told the content of what was disclosed. The majority of the heads interviewed took it as a matter of course that the applicant would expect his head to be contacted, but two felt it should be more in the open: 'If the applicant didn't quote his head as a referee, I would write for the head's opinion, but I would tell the candidate I was doing so'.

The need for accurate information on applicants was stressed by most heads. One head, with amused resignation, quoted a case to illustrate:

'We get confidential information from the Training College, which is useful though not as accurate as it could be. We had an application from a girl who had an excellent college report, and out of the four at the interview we picked her. She taught for six days and then packed it in, saying "I can't stand children". She had done three years at college!'

E. The Heads' Involvement in Interviewing

1. *Interviews for deputy headship* (Table G10.3 in supplement)

From Table 10.6 it will be seen that about 40 per cent of heads felt that their views dominated the interview proceedings, and a little more than this proportion believed their views carried as much weight as any of others on the interviewing panel. Proportionally more secondary than primary heads claimed the dominant role.

LEA policy and heads' experiences tallied closely. Five per cent of LEAs had said their policy was to exclude primary heads from attending interviews for posts of deputy head at their school, and 3.4 per cent of primary heads said they did not attend. No LEA had a policy of excluding secondary heads, and no secondary heads said they were excluded in practice.

Grammar heads felt they played the major role at the interview of deputy heads more often than did heads of comprehensive and modern schools (63 per cent, 44 per cent and 48 per cent respectively).

Forty per cent of voluntary primary and secondary school heads said they played the major role compared with 35 per cent of county heads, but four per cent of voluntary heads said their role was minor or non-existent, compared with 11 per cent of county heads.

TABLE 10.6: *Heads' involvement in interviews of applicants for deputy headship*

SCHOOL TYPE	N	Major	Equal with others on panel	Minor	Non-existent (not present)	Unclear
Primary heads	498	36.3	44.4	5.2	3.4	10.7
Secondary heads	127	50.4	40.2	5.5	0.0	3.9

PER CENT OF HEADS WHOSE ROLE AT INTERVIEW WAS:

X^2 Differences between primary and secondary significant at 0.1% confidence level.

2. *Interviews for other posts* (Table G10.4 in supplement).

Heads felt they played a more dominant role as the status of the vacancy became lower, and heads appeared to be present at interviews a little more than one might have gathered from the LEA account. Thirteen per cent of primary heads report not attending interviews for ungraded posts. This probably occurred in certain LEAs whose policy was to allocate ungraded assistants from a pool of staff rather than permit direct application to an individual school.

The heads' roles in county and voluntary schools as noted for deputy head interviews was reversed for these lower status posts. The extremes of giving the head either the major role or none at all occurred in county schools more than in voluntary schools.

3. *Heads' experiences of their interviewing role*

Most heads said that when interviewing applicants for senior posts they usually did it in company with some representatives from the 'office' (administrators and/or advisory staff) and some representatives of the managers or governors, the average number on the panel varying between four and six. For junior posts, it was the head and chairman of the managers/governors who often comprised the panel, or perhaps the head alone. Hardly any mentioned having Committee or Council members specifically on the panel with them, nor did they express a desire for their presence.

The presence of managers/governors on the interviewing panel sometimes caused disquiet, mainly because of the lack of tact or relevance of their questions. There was the other side of the picture, however, where managers' contributions were welcomed because of their local knowledge and non-professional but relevant questions. Then there was the middle-of-the-road position of several heads who thought the governors' questions were primarily to put the applicants at their ease.

A few heads complained of having had too subservient a role, but most heads' experiences were of the opposite kind:

'My Chairman gets the candidate comfortable and says "As you will be working with Mr. X, he will ask the questions". I then ask the necessary questions, and when I've finished, some of the managers may ask the odd question. After the interviews are over, the Chairman says "You have got to work with them, so which one do you want?", and usually they vote for my choice.'

4. *The interview arrangements*

To the applicant the formal interview may appear as a uniform question-and-answer affair. Yet the conduct of interviews and the way the whole proceedings are arranged vary considerably. Patently the candidate must be put at ease, usually by referring to some of his strengths as indicated in his application. This gets him talking—the essential situation. Then follow the more searching questions, perhaps on his weaknesses. The head might be expected to show by his questioning the strengths and weaknesses of each candidate for the specific post. On the other hand, the questions may be identical ('to be fair') for all candidates, and some might be given before the interview.

Heads reported that the formal interview might be morning, afternoon or evening. Although a few said the 'office' dictated the time, the general experience was that 'It has to suit the convenience of the governors'.

Many heads thought of the formal interview as part of a larger situation involving perhaps a walk round the school or a chat over tea and biscuits. Such a procedure enables one head 'to make up my mind to a certain extent about the ones who might fit in. The interview itself then takes about 20 minutes.'

Some heads ensure that members of staff help in the selection, by 'informal' meetings with the deputy head and head of department. Subsequently 'the head of department, deputy head and I discuss it, and so I don't require them at the interview proper'.

Heads repeatedly stressed a concern for putting the candidate at ease and mentioned many ways they used; 'try to keep it informàl . . . avoid interviews at the office . . . invite him to a meal . . . make sure applicants have a comfortable place to wait, with refreshments . . . provide comfortable chairs with arms . . . remember tension builds for those whose surnames begin with a letter towards the end of the alphabet . . . avoid bringing in teacups as the next candidate arrives. . . .'

The length of the formal interview. Most heads felt about 15/20 minutes was adequate for most interviewees, with possibly a little longer for deputy head appointments. Some felt lengthy interviews were unnecessary as 'First impressions are lasting impressions', and 'I often find I can sum up or get an impression of a candidate within a few minutes, either favourably or unfavourably'.

For others the first impression did not necessarily dictate the length of interviews. A quick decision that a candidate is not good enough, or is the ideal person, may not terminate the interview. In the first instance 'you have to give the chap a fair crack of the whip to see if he can redeem himself'. In the second, the interview may extend because 'he had so much to offer . . . the panel wanted to hear his views on things'. Other heads were less inclined to form hasty impressions or generalize, and felt that 'you really must give at least 20 minutes'. Flexibility to cater for interests of the applicant, the post and the panel seemed the keynote.

The outcome. The way the interview arrangements were concluded worried some heads. Instances were given of candidates, after their interview not knowing whether to stay or return home, and of not being told at the end of the day that an appointment had been made. Heads felt that all candidates should be thanked for applying and for travelling for the interview. A few heads felt that a member of the panel should 'tell the unsuccessful candidates in as nice a way as possible why they had not been selected'. Done gently and positively it would be helpful to the unsuccessful candidates to be 'given some indication where their weaknesses lay'.

5. *The qualities that applicants need*

As heads play a major role in the interviewing and appointing procedure, teachers and others might be interested to know what qualities the heads sought in the applicants being interviewed.

Twenty-three out of the 26 heads who spoke about course attendance agreed that it was a favourable influence for promotion, though an awareness existed that 'some people go deliberately to impress' rather than learn.

Twenty-two out of 23 heads believed that participating in curricular developments helped promotion, though a few cautious reservations were made about the dangers of positive prejudging of candidates from this activity.

There was less agreement about extra-curricular activities, with 14 out of 21 saying it helped. Some heads definitely looked for it, others disputed its essential nature. Several heads thought it counted less than it used to, and several were quite undecided.

Apart from the three qualifications we asked the heads about, what were the more general, less tangible qualities sought when heads interviewed candidates? The following is a selection from our discussions with heads:

'Personality—will he or she fit in? . . . professional ability and character . . . someone who is fairly direct . . . answers concisely and to the point . . . willing to join in an experimental situation and to regard experiments critically . . . sat down and thought it (their subject) out . . . intelligence, ideas in particular, enthusiasm, powers of expression . . . a becoming modesty . . . an air of shyness but quiet confidence . . . I think very poorly of them if they hesitate and shuffle . . . quick-witted . . . take trouble to dress themselves properly . . . one is looking for the human qualities . . . they'll go down well with the children . . . a warmth of personality . . . what makes them tick as people . . . their philosophy as teachers . . . seeing children not just as pupils but as people . . . they must fit into a team . . . energy, integrity . . . proficiency and teaching ability . . . a sense of humour . . . a certain toughness to stand the pace . . . the sympathetic mothering type for the five-year-olds . . . for head of department or deputy head, someone with qualities of leadership, hard-working and pleasant personality and who will fit in'. And finally 'whether he really loved his fellow humans . . .'.

6. *Unfair practice*

In our personal interview with heads they were asked if, in their role as appointers, they had seen or experienced any improprieties in procedure. Almost all heads said they had heard rumours of unfair practice, but only where they were themselves applicants. From the appointing side of the table very few could (or would?) quote direct knowledge or personal experience of impropriety. Some situations, like holding the post on an 'acting' capacity, being a senior, internal candidate or being well known by the head, all allow unique detailed knowledge of one candidate, but no head felt that this *unjustifiably* swung the balance in favour of a specific candidate.

It is possible that the heads we spoke to were not being quite frank about jobs which were 'rigged'. Most felt that, as far as their experience on the appointing side was concerned, 'these accusations are the product of very sour grapes', and 'such comments would come from failures'. Yet these same heads were fairly sure they had met unfair practice when they had themselves applied for posts, especially for headships!

F. The Head's Influence on Promotion of His Own Staff

Our interviews with heads provided a cross-section of the heads' experiences regarding the powers they exercised in the careers of their own staffs.

1. *Power to promote internally*

Most heads felt they exercised either a reasonable or powerful role where internal promotion was concerned, but a concern to share the responsibility was recorded by one head. Obviously the heads are aware of the problems in staff relationships that internal promotion can engender.

The futility of advertising some of these posts was raised by one head. Obviously this head's influence on internal staff promotion was powerful, but her LEA always insisted on the complete operation of the appointments procedure. Hence for justice to be seen to be done, an irrelevant and expensive charade had occasionally to be gone through. We found that many teachers believed that all posts of promotion had to be advertised. But the practice is not universal, and the large proportion of informal internal promotions recorded by teachers in our national questionnaire testifies to this.

2. *Power to influence promotion outside the school*

Two-thirds of the heads interviewed believed they exercised either a great deal or at least considerable influence on promotion prospects of their teachers searching for promotion beyond their own school. Most heads thought this inevitable or justified. Some discounted the head's power to influence staff promotion as overrated, but these were in the minority. All were very conscious of the responsibility and of the possibilities of abusing that power.

Some heads felt their influence was enhanced because of their national reputation, and most believed their recommendations were positive aids to the appointment of their staff. A number took advice from senior colleagues (deputy head, head of department) and felt this strengthened the impact of their reference. No head admitted to 'writing down' a teacher to keep him/her on the head's own staff.

While all heads may not agree on the precise power they exert, all are conscious of the responsibility, and most believe that the head is in the best position to know a teacher's personal and professional contribution to the school. They felt there was no better way of transmitting this information than through consultation with the teacher's current head.

Having surveyed the appointment procedures from the points of view of those who are involved on the employing side, we now turn to the experiences that the applicants—heads as well as assistant teachers—have had when applying for promotion posts.

CHAPTER ELEVEN

Appointment Procedures: Teachers' Experiences

When interviewing our subsample of 135 teachers, we asked them to give their opinions about appointment procedures, and particularly to relate any incidents or examples to illustrate their views.

Interviewing is expensive of both time and money. Both had to be optimized across the many facets of our study. As a result, the number of teachers interviewed was small although stratified by region, school type, sex and level of appointment. One-tenth of the planned 150 interviews could not be completed because of school closures and transport problems arising from industrial action. Even so, the achieved sample was suitably stratified to be representative. However, apart from the sample size, one has to be cautious because of the nature of the data. In subjective recall the extremes stand out in one's memory and the routine, the mundane and the usual experience is not even recorded let alone retained for later recall. Hence, generalization from these opinions and incidents may well give a somewhat biased impression of the true pattern. However, that certain personal experiences occurred at all, or more than rarely, is in itself germane to the study. Every effort was made to focus teachers' reports on their actual rather than imagined experiences, and on the whole we felt that teachers reported their views and experiences candidly and seriously, and with a refreshing sense of humour.

A. Advertisements

1. *Were further details of the advertised post available?*

Sixty-six per cent of secondary teachers said they had usually received further particulars of the post advertised, compared with 36 per cent of primary. The latter figure was closer to the 32 per cent of the 1172 advertisements in April 1971 for promotion posts which offered 'further particulars on application'. Among these there was little difference between secondary and primary appointments, but there was a greater willingness to offer particulars for the higher rather than lower status posts. (Tables E.6 and E.7 in supplement—see p 13).

2. *Were the further details accurate and/or sufficient?*

In theory accurate detailed information could induce the teacher to apply or drop the idea. In practice accuracy could only be properly checked once the teacher was successfully installed in the school. For this reason more than two-thirds of the teachers felt unable to comment on the accuracy of 'Further details'. Thirty-seven (27 per cent) were satisfied, but five (four per cent) had doubts as a result of some stark incongruency between the 'details' and the reality of the post.

What applicants would wish to see in 'further details' is reviewed later where teachers' suggestions are discussed (Chapter 13), but one problem raised as a result of actual experience was the 'ambiguity' of the advertisement. Information which specifies the non-specific, e.g. 'a graded post is available for a suitable candidate', places an applicant in an invidious position—especially if he is offered the post, but at a lower status (and salary) than the particulars implied.

Some had doubts about the general value of these further details which, like references, would tell the obvious and the best sides of a vacancy: '. . . nobody is going to say that the school is in the middle of a slum dwelling area . . . if I'm serious about an application, I'd go and look at the school and area myself. . . . You must expect them to paint the school in glowing colours.'

Teachers had experienced great variation in the details given, ranging from 'just a general blurb', 'just the type of post, nothing else', to 'Yes a great deal about the school, its history and the post. A carefully prepared document sent to all applicants'.

3. *The closing date for applications*

The interval between the dates of the advertisement and the return of applications should normally allow for sending for the form and details, consulting referees, obtaining testimonials, etc., and returning these to the advertiser. Only a third of the teachers thought they could remember with any certainty, but among these the average experience of the interval was two or three weeks. Our analysis of actual advertisements provided a range from 'as soon as possible' to 31 days, with an average of 14 days. Our heads said they liked to allow about three weeks before a closing date, but added that advertisements and appointments had sometimes to be arranged precipitately because the vacancy had arisen only just before the deadlines for giving notice. It was a cause of some concern and a problem not easily resolved, that when one school appointed a teacher just before the deadline for giving notice in any particular term, this inevitably meant that the school from which he was resigning was placed in a most difficult position regarding obtaining a replacement—before the same deadline! The result was that the latter school was often without a replacement for a full term.

Some of those who had experienced a long interval wanted it shortened because the long drawn-out affair left them uncertain of their position, especially when they wished to apply for several posts at the same time. Others, who had known the short interval, often interpreted this as a 'rigged' appointment, and the immediacy of the closing date a means of discouraging applications. One surprising finding was that half the advertisements for promotion posts specified no closing date of any kind. Some teachers inferred that there was a 'sitting tenant' at the school for such a post, as date of appointment, resignation and taking up the position was apparently not expected to inconvenience the school.

B. Application Procedures

1. *Acknowledgment of applications*

In this and several later sections many teachers felt unable to comment as they had made few applications, having been in one or only a very few schools. Of the 101 interviewed teachers who felt they had sufficient experience to comment, 93 said they had *usually* had applications acknowledged. Even so, many reported that there had been exceptions and, as in all walks of life, the bureaucratic machinery can break down:

'I 'phoned the Education Office about the advert. and they denied any knowledge of it, so I read it to them over the telephone, their own advert.'

2. *Notification of result*

Nearly 90 per cent of our sample said they were usually told the result of their application, even if they had not been called for interview, and this figure tallies with the 90 per cent of LEAs who said they notified all applicants of results. A few teachers said they were required to enclose a stamped-addressed envelope if they wished to be notified of the result. Where an applicant was not called for interview, he would have to wait till after the interviews had taken place, and he usually had no idea when this might be. Almost every teacher said that when called for interview he knew the result the same day. Only one teacher reported that 'one candidate was called in, the rest were left to go home and heard no more'.

3. *Method of correspondence*

Only a small proportion of interviewed teachers felt strongly about the method the employer used when corresponding about acknowledgments or results of applications. About 40 per cent said either they could not remember or were not bothered how it was done, 35 per cent said they received pre-printed letters in sealed envelopes, which was quite satisfactory to them. The acknowledgment of the application was more likely to be on a duplicated card, either open or inserted in a sealed envelope. Where teachers had attended interviews they were usually told directly, but a few said they had been telephoned later. One had been notified by telegram that he was required for interview.

The unsuccessful applicant usually received a stereotyped letter, and only one or two specifically commented that they would like to have been told who was awarded the post.

C. Success and Failure: Number of Applications

We asked the sub-sample of teachers: 'Can you estimate how many applications you submitted for a post such as you now hold, before you were successful?', and then invited any comments on their experiences.

1. *Number of applications before success*

The number of teachers concerned in each instance below is inevitably small, but the data are nevertheless of value, being based on actual personal histories within a random sample.

For 36 teachers now holding *lower status posts* (graded posts and small departmental headships): 21 teachers were successful at the first attempt, five at the second, two at the third, four at the fourth or fifth, and four applied six or seven times. Hence 22 per cent had made four or more applications for the type of post they now held.

Out of 15 teachers who were *heads of large departments or deputy heads of small schools:* four succeeded at the first application, four at the second, two at the third, two at the fourth or fifth, and three needed six or more applications before achieving their present post (the maximum recorded being 12 applications). Hence a third had applied four or more times before success.

Of particular interest is the status of *first headship*. Of 14 primary heads who were able to reply, six had succeeded in obtaining a headship for the first time on their first or second application, four needed between five and nine attempts, and four had applied ten or more times, the maximum being 20. Of 10 secondary heads who replied, three were awarded their first headship at the first or second attempt, three at their third or fourth, two needed to apply between five and nine times, and two applied ten times or more, the maximum being 31 applications.

Of course, the achievement of their present status did not imply the end of the teachers' search. For example, a senior master had applied 30 times for a headship, currently to no avail. One teacher, at a graded post Scale 2 level, had submitted up to the time we saw him 15 applications for a departmental headship.

2. *Personal comments and advice*

(a) *The element of luck* Several teachers, as we might have expected, received promotion internally—'My post was upgraded', 'the head of department died and I was asked to take over'. But even where formal application was concerned (and this was usually increasingly necessary for higher statuses) some teachers felt they had been fortunate. Some put it down to being 'a person who interviews well', others saw it as very much a matter of luck.

There were those who felt that method as well as luck were needed. Such teachers were identified by phrases such as 'I have chosen carefully. . . . It's a matter of timing and technique . . . to get more promotion I'd never have less than 20 applications in the post at one time. . . .'

Some teachers believed that luck could be 'engineered' and that a great deal of time is taken up filling in forms and writing letters and on unnecessary applications when many of those jobs were spoken for before they were advertised. Where the appointment is a 'foregone conclusion' the rejection of unwitting applicants 'can do a lot of damage to the ego of teachers'. This plaintive but penetrating comment might lead us to wonder whether advertisements that appear because of policy rather then to locate an appointee, should not be specially designated. At least teachers would know what they were up against.

(b) *Advice regarding success and failure* Different views, experiences and advice emanated from our talks with teachers. Perseverance and determination were stressed most of all:

'. . . keep on applying. . . . I put in 31 applications in one year before getting this (headship) . . . put in for anything that seems suitable . . . people who wanted promotion applied and applied and got there in the end. . . . I know of one head who applied 81 times before he got his headship . . . it was just a matter of keeping putting in applications until his luck changed . . . he got his headship at the 36th application. . . .'

though some teachers admit it does not always pay off:

'. . . a friend who is very capable has tried for headships seven times with the same LEA. I think they just use her to make the numbers up . . . a colleague of mine applied for 20 posts but without success . . . other people (have) applied and applied and got absolutely nowhere . . . a friend who has applied 36 times for headships in one year, and was shortlisted twice . . . in this school (Secondary Modern) the majority of staff have made 10 or 11 applications and all been turned down . . .'

Other suggestions included ability 'to write good letters', a change to 'a different approach' and local residence, as evidenced by 'It's a difficult area and I think they wanted someone who lived with these people'. One teacher felt that non-graduates in comprehensive schools could expect only a 'couple of small promotions', and many others 'would not think of coming into the profession without a degree'.

3. *Some personal histories*

The following three case histories put the matter into a longer perspective:

'I went from assistant to head of department after 27 applications, from head of department to deputy head after 20; for my first headship I put in 3 applications and didn't bother again till my present headship (Group 9) which I got at the first application.'

'In my assistant days, the application rate was much bigger than it is today. There was a lot of unemployment in the thirties among teachers, and I knew many graduates who couldn't get to a grammar school and who had to stay unemployed or go into an elementary school—and once there you nearly always stayed there. I was told once there were 430 applicants for a headship in 1945—they just put aside the non-graduates and those who weren't heads, and then they put aside any without a good degree, and finally got down to about 20 widely experienced, good honours graduates. Nowadays the market is much more open.'

'When I was younger, like so many married men with commitments (or even single people with commitments) it was difficult to apply around very much beyond one's own area, and I went from secondary schools to junior, as I thought there was more opportunity there for promotion. Later I went from junior to secondary where I am now, but I think that at the time when I was younger and did have a chance of promotion, I returned from a school where I was in line for the deputy headship in order to look after my parents who were ailing. In doing that I more or less damned my chances of promotion from then on.'

D. Experiences of Interviews

1. *How many interviewers ?*

Several promoted teachers had had no interviews at all, as with informal promotion, but most had attended many. Large variations in the panel size encountered by the same individual were not uncommon: 'As few as two and as many as 30 . . . between three and 50 . . . varied from one to 18 . . . anything from six to 20 . . . from four to 24. We collated the data in terms of a range.

(a) Out of 78 teachers who quoted a *minimum* number on their panels, 23 said there had been only one interviewer, 23 reported a panel of two or three, 24 quoted their panel as comprising either four, five or six members, two had panels of seven, eight or nine, and six said the minimum panel strength had been 10 or more. (This makes an average minimum panel strength of three or four members.)

(b) Out of 86 teachers who quoted a maximum number on their panels, 6 said there had been only 1 interviewer, 8 said there had been 2 or 3, 22 estimated the maximum as 4, 5 or 6, 13 quoted instances of 7, 8 or 9, and 37 remembered a maximum panel of 10 or more members. (An average maximum of 7 on the panel.)

2. *Who were the interviewers?*

Remembering the names of individuals on the panel is difficult enough during the interview, let alone recalling them after a period of time. Not that this mattered, as most teachers were rarely introduced to the individual members of their interviewing panels. As a result we were unable to compile accurate data on the composition of the panels that teachers had actually experienced. However, in trying to recall panels composition, teachers frequently quoted some experiences that our question evoked, and from these some trends could be extracted.

(a) *Interviews for lower status posts*

'The head and Chairman of managers was there'. 'School Managers and head: the managers had little idea of education and were prompted by the head.' 'There was the head, governors and advisers—six in all.' 'The head and the secondary schools inspector.'

In most cases the head was there, as were some of the managers or their chairman. Less often the deputy or head of department on his own. School inspectors, advisors, education officers and even the CEO were not unknown. Sometimes the composition of the panel could be disconcerting.

'. . . I'd lived in the district quite a time and recognized most of the faces; they were shopkeepers. . . .'

(b) *Interviews for head of department/deputy head*

For this higher level of appointment the rank of the 'office' representative tended to rise, as did the number of governors. A not uncommon recollection was of non-participating members:

'Once I had ten, of whom three were sleeping partners—or at least their eyes were closed and they asked no questions . . .' '. . . and seven governors who didn't ask a single question.' '. . . the rest of the 16 or so made up of governors who seemed to take very little interest in the proceedings. One chap had to be awakened.'

(c) *Interviews for headships*

At this level the professional staff of the 'office' were usually represented, and it was often from them that the questions teachers considered most pertinent arose. Also the numbers of councillors and governors increased, though the value of their contributions was seen very variedly: '. . . questions like, what do you think of school dinners came from the laymen . . . there were several shrewd, experienced people who know something about management. . . .'

3. *The panel's questions*

The type of question teachers were asked at interview was discussed specifically with the teachers. Those who could recall their interviews commented chiefly in terms of 'reasonable' or 'unreasonable'.

(a) *General experiences* The typical response of our teachers was that on the whole they had been asked pertinent and reasonable questions. A few teachers had mixed views, believing that the questions of large panels had more tendency to be irrelevant. Some teachers criticised the modes of questioning they had encountered, on grounds of superficiality.

(b) *Questions by laymen* Any criticisms teachers had were usually directed at the laymen on the panel. Lack of understanding or relevance were the main objections, and teachers were concerned about showing irritation or condescension in their answers. However, the laymen on the panel were by no means universally censured.

(c) *Type of questions asked* Satisfactory questioning was seen by teachers to focus on the professional issues—career, ideas, views on corporal punishment, the duties of particular posts, type of school previously attended and so forth. Equally acceptable were questions 'on the wide educational field, whether I was interested in modern developments, would I experiment to find out more?' Acceptable if they followed (we gathered) the purely professional inquiries were more personal questions 'about me as a person—my leisure activities'.

What teachers regarded as 'irrelevant' or 'unprofessional', was sometimes difficult to pinpoint. In the absence of specific knowledge of the context one might question the implication of irrelevance in examples provided by the teachers. For example, it is easy to think of a situation for which the question 'Are you going to have a family in the near future?' is extremely relevant. Teachers felt that questions about the personality of their wives and their ability to settle in a new district were irrelevant. Questions on the professional competence of a colleague or on which teachers' union the applicant belonged to were felt to border on the unethical. Whether one's parents were alive should hardly affect suitability for a post, and questions about religious activities and political affiliations were viewed as 'loaded'.

We heard examples of interviews where monologues by the candidate were expected rather than an interaction between panel and interviewee. Here the candidate was expected to talk for fifteen minutes on one to five topics, usually written on a piece of paper, which might face him as he sat down at the interview table or might have been presented some time prior to entering. The monologue method was occasionally invited in a direct way which could disconcert some teachers:

'They ask a general question like "What have you to offer?" and this is asking you to sell yourself, and if you're a bit modest, you feel embarrassed and it's difficult to answer.'

but delight others:

'I like fairly general questions: I've always been given lots of scope to talk, which is what I want to do at an interview.'

4. *The head's role at interviews*

Eighty-six teachers in our sample felt they had sufficient experience of interviews where heads were present to be able to comment on the head's role in the interview. Just under half thought the head played the sole or major role. About an eighth said it was equal with others on the panel. Another eighth said it had varied a good deal. A quarter asserted that the head had been a minor participant. This accords in the main with our earlier findings from the heads' views of their own experience as interviewers.

5. *How long were interviews?*

The formal interview is usually the only occasion when the selecting panel meet each short-listed candidate face to face. The length of time allowed each applicant to present his views and answer questions would seem an important aspect of the interview arrangements. The variations in the teachers' experiences in this respect are therefore of considerable interest.

Forty per cent of those teachers who were able to remember said their formal interviews lasted between 20 and 30 minutes. About a quarter judged it as between 10 and 20 minutes. The experiences of the remaining 35 per cent were shared equally among interviews of less than ten minutes, between 30 and 50 minutes and over 50 minutes.

Length was no guide to potential success, as different teachers had experienced success and failure after a three minute interview. Some resentment was expressed by an ultra brief (and unsuccessful?) interview 'to go 80 miles there and have an interview lasting five minutes, I felt a bit cheated'. Overlong meetings also came under criticism: 'my last interview was two-and-a-half hours. The head was bungling and inefficient—she just let the thing go on and on'. Interviews varying from three to 150 minutes clearly cannot be giving equal opportunities to all candidates. Thankfully most fell in the 10–40 minutes range.

6. *When was the interview?*

Of the 120 interviews that could be clearly recalled, a third had taken place in the morning, about 45 per cent in the afternoon and about a fifth in the evening. Often evening interviews were arranged because this was the only time when managers/governors could attend.

Several teachers reported occasions where the total procedure took up the best part of a day—looking round the school and meeting staff during the morning and having the formal interview after lunch, or perhaps a two-stage formal interview where the 'long short-list' was seen in the morning and the 'short short-list' in the afternoon; and occasionally the 'whole day' proceedings went on into the evening.

7. *Qualities that interviewers seek in interviewees*

We asked our sample of teachers if, at the various interviews they had attended, they had received any impression of what the panel were looking for, and if so, what. Many, including those who were successful, reported they had received no impression at all of what the panel was looking for. The impressions of the others are reviewed here.

(a) *Primary posts* According to assistant teachers, the qualities sought by their interviewing panels included self-assurance and pose, integrity, feeling for the children, and ability to develop their character, a wide range of experience, somebody prepared to work, to do extra work after school, someone with responsibility, organization and the ability to get on with people, someone who could speak Welsh, not rock the boat, stand up in front of a class and keep control. Two points added by heads were 'they wanted someone to give a lead to village life' and someone who had 'ideas on how to run an open plan school'.

(b) *Secondary posts* The secondary teachers considered the following had been sought: a general interest in teaching, enthusiasm for the subject, being sound in your subject, personality, humour, integrity, manners and an ability to communicate, personal qualities like initiative and adaptability, how to overcome department difficulties, and the candidate's political bias.

8. *General arrangements about interviews*

Few teachers felt strongly enough about their interview experiences to offer any comment on the general arrangements. From those who did comment, the main impression we received was that the teachers were quite satisfied with the arrangements they had experienced. Only a very few teachers were *generally* displeased with interview arrangements, with comments such as 'I think teachers are shabbily treated. . . . Generally one is given a lukewarm cup of tea and sent on your way . . . not treated as courteously as they should be'.

Certain specific aspects of procedure come under criticism.

(a) *Short notice* Some candidates had received telegrams or telephone messages to attend for interview next day which was perturbing.

(b) *Excessive waiting* This was criticised as a waste of interviewees' time (and nervous energy!) 'Why not have staggered appointments? 'Why does the interview sequence always have to be alphabetical?' inquiries Mr. W., who felt that as the interviewers have been sitting for two hours, obviously they haven't the same approach to the last as to the first.

(c) *Candidates' comfort* 'Corridor waiting, with or without draughts, was not improved by hard backed, hard seated school wooden chairs, especially if you had to get your own chair because there were more applicants than corridor chairs.'

(d) *Interview conditions* Candidates were not enamoured of being placed 'in the middle of a horseshoe of men' . . . in a very large committee-type room . . . I don't like this sitting across a desk, like facing a firing squad . . . the interviewers had their back to the window, but the sun was shining in my face . . . at the far end of the longest table I have ever seen. . . .'

(e) *Looking round the school* While many teachers felt they had been given the opportunity to look round the school, it was offered less than candidates would have wished.

(f) *Candidates asking questions* Most panels gave candidates the chance to ask questions, but opportunities varied, as did the teachers' views of the need for such questions.

(g) *Expenses* Here the irritation was the condition, occasionally met, that no expenses would be refunded to applicants who were offered but declined the post. This can rebound on LEAs, as teachers 'get very discouraged from applying to certain authorities, for the word gets round that some pay your expenses and others only pay if you toe the line'.

(h) *Courtesy to the unsuccessful*

'When interviews are over and the candidates are just waiting in the room together, the clerk puts his head round the door, calls out the name of the successful candidate to go back with him, and that is all the others hear. They just put on their coats and go without hearing another word. With some experienced clerks, they do come and talk to you and tell you they're sorry and so on. I remember at my first interview, I just sat and waited, and it was the other candidates who said "It's no use sitting there get your coat and go, it's over now".'

The speaker, who was now a head, added that experience had taught him always to go and see the unsuccessful candidates before they went, and have a quiet word before returning to his own room to talk to the successful one.

Summary

The unsensational finding that 'it was quite fair' imprints itself on a reader's mind much less vividly than isolated examples of specific, dramatically unpleasant incidents. Hence it must be stressed that the great majority of the random subsample of teachers whom we visited were in no way censorious of the general interview arrangements they had encountered. The specific criticisms were localized and isolated. Courtesy and consideration to applicants, who are sometimes under even greater tension than they might admit to, seems to be the key.

E. Unfair Practice

The 'sham' interview, the rigged appointment—does it really happen, or is this another grapevine legend ? In our interviews with teachers we asked (diplomatically, we hope, but nevertheless frankly) whether the teacher had had personal experience of unfair practice, or had suspected its occurrence, or had any comments on it. Where it was suspected, we always tried to elicit specific cases.

Of the 135 teachers we spoke to, 79 (60 per cent) believed such dubious or unfair practices existed. Some resented it, some ignored it, whilst others accepted it as a problem to be met in many other walks of life. Of those who believed that 'rigging' went on, five reported that it had concerned their own appointments—that is, four per cent of the teachers interviewed. Twenty-one (16 per cent) inferred it either from their own interview experience or from close acquaintance with the facts. Of these 21 instances, 12 were concerned with the appointment of a local or internal candidate. The large majority (53 teachers, 40 per cent of group) based their views on what they had heard from other teachers. It is of course extremely difficult to obtain direct evidence of such practice, but there was little doubt that what beliefs existed concerning unfair practices were based far more on hearsay than on close personal experience.

The following examples extracted from teachers' answers illustrate the extent to which the 'hearsay' grapevine operates. 'There are many instances in this county and I'm not alone in thinking it. It's a case of not what you know, but who you know.' Many teachers prefaced their comments with 'I've no personal experience of it' and then continued in some such manner as : 'but I do know that you can go to an interview in good faith and the interviewing panel have already made up their minds', 'but I am certain it has occurred near here', 'In this area, it is known that in the way people are selected, politics and canvassing do go on'; or sometimes 'I don't think it happens to the degree people make out. It's an excuse when they don't get the job'.

Whether unprofessional practice exists or not, that teachers believe it exists may be damaging to general morale and confidence in the justice of the system. Examples of direct experiences were few and far between. There were individuals who asserted that they had encountered unfair bias, but the evidence was often, by the nature of the case, either circumstantial or a matter of impressions:

'I've had 20 interviews in my time and I'm absolutely certain that three times it was decided prior to the interview. I was there with others just to make up the weight.'

'In one case I felt quite sure there was political bias behind it, the candidate and chairman of managers being closely connected politically.'

'Two candidates who, at one interview, had been unsuccessful like myself, told me when I met them at a later interview that the successful chap at our earlier interview had gone round to see the people and make himself known. I don't know that that is a bad thing if everybody does it.'

Some reports, however, did claim to have a direct factual basis:

'The head took me aside and said, "Look, I'll be quite honest with you. I've got a candidate for the job." Mind you, it was the acting deputy and the head knew already she'd fit in.'

'The interview was over in 10 minutes, but we'd been told by the deputy before we went in that the post was already filled by the person who'd already been teaching there on a temporary basis for two years. They had to have us along because the LEA said the post had to be advertised.'

'A lady who'd lived there all her life and was known personally to them was appointed—I didn't feel bitter at all. It was like appointing a village teacher to the village school, a very good thing.'

There are no doubt good reasons why LEAs should stipulate that particular posts or all posts should be advertised. However, it is expensive for the LEA to have mock interviews, and equally wasteful for the makeweight interviewee in terms of his time, self-esteem and frustration. A path must be steered between limiting nepotism and damaging professional trust. One more experience to conclude this section, related with great amusement though open to other reactions:

'It was for a headship post. We'd all been interviewed and, while waiting to be told the result, were told it would take a little while—why didn't we take a walk to the village? We did, and while there—the merest chance—I bought the local evening paper, and lo and behold! I saw an announcement that Mr. – – had been appointed head of the school: the very post we were being interviewed for and for which we were waiting to be told the result: I was furious and when I complained on my return to the interview place, the local inspector took me aside and in the friendliest way said, "Look you've got to understand, that's the way we do thing here in – –".'

F. Effects of Reorganization

LEAs often waive normal appointment procedures when school reorganization has taken place. Some teachers feel strongly on how LEA policies were affecting teachers' prospects. Our subsample of teachers were asked if they could comment on any effects reorganization had had or were likely to have on promotion prospects for themselves or colleagues. About two-fifths felt unable to comment as they had not yet been confronted with the problem. Of the remaining teachers half believed reorganization had multiplied or would multiply the number of posts available and thereby enhance the teacher's prospects. The other half felt exactly the opposite—amalgamation would result in reduction of posts and be detrimental to prospects. Either way a constant threat was that 'It's all very well safeguarding a person's salary, but it's not the same thing as your old job. Status can be just as important as salary'.

Examples of the problems and uncertainties experienced are reported below:

1. *Primary sector*

Undoubtedly the likely staffing strategies for the middle schools gave most concern in this sector. Who would occupy the senior posts, men or women, graduates or non-graduates, primary or secondary teachers?

'. . . the prospects for primary teachers are poor. I expect any promotion within the middle school is going to come from the secondary sector. . . .' 'with middle schools coming, will the LEA look more kindly on graduates, as they do now with secondary heads ? . . . 'For primary men it comes as rather a shattering blow to find that middle school headships are going to graduates—they (non-graduates) can only work within the middle school and have no promotion, or try for headship of first schools where they then find all the headships are going to women' . . . 'I think there'll be few (middle school) headships for women.'

Uncertainty about reorganization plans, and resultant feelings of insecurity, were cited as the cause of some premature retirements. A number of teachers felt that unhappiness about reorganization had a pervasive effect—'Everyone is rather jittery about the future'.

2. *Secondary sector*

Secondary reorganization was seen as providing more lower promotion posts and fewer at the highest level. Again the financial security was offset by the status changes—most of which were seen as downward by the occupants of high level posts.

'It works two ways. If you have bigger schools there are fewer posts at the top, but on the other hand posts underneath become much more numerous.'

'There has been a fair amount of demotion, not financial but in status, and this is more important than money.'

'These situations have already arisen, and the Teacher's Unions have slipped up badly as the pressure should have been on increased promotion instead of increased salary.'

The outstanding concern for many was the bleak future seen for non-graduate and secondary modern school teachers where amalgamation with grammar schools was planned. Here the loss was seen as likely to be financial ('They're not going to put non-graduates in charge of a maths department which has got to prepare kids for 'A' level as well as CSE') as well as in terms of status: 'The heads of departments (of the modern school) will have to stay here in the new lower school or go to the upper school where they would be very inferior members of a large department—here they're large fish in a small pond'. However, some teachers saw the possibility of improved prospects in the non-academic fields: 'For me personally, I suppose the prospects will improve purely because there won't be any competition from grammar school—my subject is remedial work', 'People whose skills are not primarily academic can fulfil pastoral roles in the school or house masterships, quite a senior post in the school that four or five years ago they would not have had a chance of obtaining.'

Were the expressed fears justified? A few teachers were in a position to report the effects of reorganization of their own school. Teachers sometimes recognized that, with the best will in the world, it had not been possible to find equivalent posts to satisfy every teacher 'although an attempt has been made to do this'. Some teachers felt that occasionally the opportunity was taken to attempt some weeding out, 'I think everyone who has been on the permanent staff has been offered some kind of job although it has been made clear that if they would like to find a job elsewhere it would suit everybody better'. Once the situation settled down some teachers had found that 'more people have got better jobs than would have happened in either of the two separate identities'; 'Most people who are full-time have been accommodated into posts of equal or increased status rather than the other way round';

'There were more and bigger allowances. . . .' The experiences of a few teachers confirmed anxieties about opportunities for non-graduates. 'The grammar had taken the head of department posts, which was true as far as concerned academic subjects and I think quite rightly so. We tried to balance it up by looking favourably on ex-secondary modern staff who had pastoral responsibilities.'

CHAPTER TWELVE

Appointment Procedures: Teachers' Questionnaire Opinions

In the questionnaire to teachers and heads we asked for their opinions on appointment procedures. After consultation with teachers and their representatives, a list of 17 items considered to be sources of dissatisfaction was drawn up, and these, plus an item 'nothing unsatisfactory', were listed and each teacher was invited to record the five items he thought most unsatisfactory.

The general survey

Table 12.1 gives the percentages of teachers who considered a particular item was in the top five sources of dissatisfaction with appointment procedures.

TABLE 21.1: *Dissatisfaction with appointment procedures: all 'normal career' teachers (primary and secondary)*

RANK	UNSATISFACTORY ITEM	PER CENT OF TEACHERS (N = 4770)
1.	Qualifications of interviewers	57.5
2.	Interview questions	37.2
3.	Testimonials	30.5
4.	Opportunity to look round schools	25.5
5.	Opportunity to meet staff	24.6
6.	Notification of result	20.7
7.	Advertisements	19.5
8.	Application forms	19.4
9.	Acknowledgements	18.7
10.	Quoting referees	17.9
11.	Further details received	14.4
12.	Number of interviewers	14.2
13.	Notice allowed interviewees	11.7
14.	Letters of application	10.9
15.	Opportunity to ask questions	9.5
16.	Time allowed for interview	6.7
17.	Interview expenses	3.5

The qualifications of the interviewing panel disturbed the majority of teachers more than any other item and, if we may anticipate a little, the presence of 'laymen' was the particular source of dissatisfaction. This related to the next most unsatisfactory item, viz. the questions asked by interviewers, for it was the laymen who, according to our teachers' experiences, were the most guilty of asking irrelevant questions.

Groups of teachers

The general pattern of opinion was similar for most teacher groups. The reader is reminded that differences both in the rank and the relative vote are important when comparing the teacher groups.

1. Primary and secondary teachers (Table 12.2)

Primary and secondary teachers had the same top ten items of dissatisfaction. Both were unhappy with the qualifications and questioning of interviewers. Secondary teachers were significantly more dissatisfied than primary teachers about the use of testimonials and about the opportunities given to meet staff at the prospective school. Primary teachers were significantly more unhappy about the opportunities offered to look around the school itself.

TABLE 12.2: *Dissatisfaction with appointment procedures: (primary and secondary teachers)*

	PRIMARY			SECONDARY	
	(N = 2442)			(N = 2328)	
		Per cent of			Per cent of
Rank	Unsatisfactory item	teachers	Rank	Unsatisfactory item	teachers
1.	Qualifications of interviewers	58.0	1.	Qualifications of interviewers	57.0
2.	Interview questions	37.8	2.	Testimonials	37.2
3.	Opportunity to look round school	28.7	3.	Interview questions	36.6
4.	Testimonials	24.1	4.	Opportunity to meet staff	27.5
5.	Opportunity to meet staff	21.7	5.	Opportunity to look round school	22.3
6.	Advertisements	20.7	6.	Notification of result	22.0
7.	Notification of result	19.5	7.	Acknowledgements	21.1
8.	Quoting referees	18.7	8.	Application forms	21.1
9.	Application forms	17.7	9.	Advertisements	18.3
10.	Acknowledgements	16.4	10.	Quoting referees	17.1

Secondary-school type (Table G12.1 in supplement—see p. 14) Grammar
teachers were happiest with the appointment procedures, with 21.0 per
cent recording 'no unsatisfactory item'. Only 14.0 per cent of their
colleagues in other types of school were as content. Teachers in all
three types of secondary school objected most to the qualifications of
interviewers, and most strongly in secondary moderns (63.4 per cent),
(comprehensive 56.4 per cent and grammar 46.0 per cent). The higher
dissatisfaction in the modern school can be seen in other differences—
interview questions: modern 40.1 per cent, comprehensive 36.2 per
cent, grammar 30.0 per cent; opportunity to look round school:
modern 24.9 per cent, comprehensive 23.2 per cent, grammar 18.3 per
cent; quoting of referees: modern 19.7 per cent, comprehensive 15.0
per cent, grammar 14.7 per cent.

2. *Sex* (Table G12.2 in supplement)

a) *Primary teachers* (Table 12.3)   For both men and women the most-
selected unsatisfactory item was qualifications of interviewers, though
primary men felt more strongly about this than primary women. Nine
of the ten items were common, the strangers being number of interviewers (men) and acknowledgements (women). Men were significantly more dissatisfied than women with the use of testimonials,
application forms and questions asked at interviews. Women were
equally less satisfied with the opportunities offered to look round the
prospective school and with advertisements (placed by men 11th, with
13.7 per cent).

b) *Sex—secondary teachers* (Table 12.4)   Eight of the top ten items were
shared. Secondary men were significantly more dissatisfied than women
about the use of testimonials, the qualifications of interviewers, and
application forms (this latter item being placed 11th in the women's
rankings with 15.7 per cent). Women were unhappier than men about
the opportunity offered to look over the prospective school.

3. *Secondary teachers—qualifications* (Table G12.3 in supplement)

Graduates and non-graduates rated qualification of interviewers as
number one irritant, with non-graduates feeling more strongly (60.1 per
cent compared with graduates 53.5 per cent). The other two significant
differences were that non-graduates were less satisfied with the opportunity to look round the prospective school (5th with 24.2 per cent) than
were graduates (8th with 19.1 per cent), and relatively less disturbed
about the use of testimonials (3rd with 32 per cent compared with 2nd
with 44 per cent).

4. *Age* (Tables G12.4—G12.6 in supplement)

Older teachers saw the appointment procedures in a different light from their younger colleagues.

TABLE 12.3: *Dissatisfactions with appointment procedures: men and women* (*primary*)

	MEN (N = 649)			WOMEN (N = 1790)	
Rank	Unsatisfactory item	Per cent of teachers	Rank	Unsatisfactory item	Per cent of teachers
1.	Qualifications of interviewers	65.5	1.	Qualifications of interviewers	55.4
2.	Interview questions	41.9	2.	Interview questions	36.4
3.	Testimonials	36.4	3.	Opportunity to look round school	30.8
4.	Application forms	23.9	4.	Advertisements	23.3
5.	Opportunity to look round school	22.8	5.	Opportunity to meet staff	22.5
6.	Quoting referees	21.0	6.	Testimonials	19.7
7.	Notification of result	21.0	7.	Notification of result	19.0
8.	Opportunity to meet staff	19.9	8.	Quoting referees	17.9
9.	Number of interviewers	19.4	9.	Acknowledgements	16.6
10.	Acknowledgements	15.9	10.	Application forms	15.5

(a) *Age groups—primary teachers* While qualification of interviewers was the prime dissatisfaction at all age levels, its importance rose from below half the teachers under 30 years to two-thirds of the 30–plus teachers. Similarly the older teachers were less tolerant of the questioning, dissatisfaction rising from third to second in rating and 12 per cent to 15 per cent in vote across the 30 year boundary. Dislike of testimonials rose steadily in both ranking and percentage with age to 49 years, then levelled. There was a steady decline with age in the percentage who wanted more opportunity to meet staff.

Younger rather than older teachers were dissatisfied with advertisements of posts, opportunities to look round the prospective school and to meet the staff, the acknowledgement of their application and the notification of the result of their applications.

(b) *Age groups—secondary teachers* The top rank order—interviewers' qualifications and questions, and testimonials—was the same (1, 3, 2) for all but the oldest group (1, 2, 3). In terms of percentages the older groups (30 and over) were 15 per cent less concerned with the interviewers' qualifications and 10 per cent less concerned with their questions and the testimonials than the under-30s. Application forms

TABLE 12.4: *Dissatisfactions with appointment procedures: men and women (secondary)*

	MEN (N = 1400)			WOMEN (N = 927)	
Rank	Unsatisfactory item	Per cent of teachers	Rank	Unsatisfactory item	Per cent of teachers
1.	Qualifications of interviewers	60.0	1.	Qualifications of interviewers	52.4
2.	Testimonials	43.7	2.	Interview questions	37.6
3.	Interview questions	36.6	3.	Opportunity to meet staff	28.7
4.	Opportunity to meet staff	26.7	4.	Testimonials	27.5
5.	Application forms	24.7	5.	Opportunity to look round school	25.7
6.	Notification of result	22.0	6.	Notification of result	22.0
7.	Acknowledgements	20.9	7.	Acknowledgements	20.2
8.	Opportunity to look round school	20.0	8.	Advertisements	20.4
9.	Quoting referees	18.9	9.	Further details received	18.3
10.	Advertisements	16.9	10.	Notice allowed interviewees	17.5

were a greater irritant to the over-30s teacher (four ranks and five to 10 per cent votes) than the youngest teachers. Relatively more younger than older teachers were dissatisfied with advertisements, opportunity to look round the prospective school, the acknowledgement of applications and the notification of the result.

5. *Present post* (Tables G12.7 and G12.8 in supplement)

Higher status implies experience of and success in applying for promotion posts. One might expect different opinions, yet the same items were revealed as unsatisfactory but the strength of feeling differed with status.

(*a*) *Present post—primary teachers* Over three-quarters of deputy heads and heads voted that the qualifications of interviewers were unsatis-

factory. Overall the picture is a more acute but not dissimilar version of
that found in the age stratification. Perhaps the added emphasis comes
from the sex difference, as there were relatively more men than women
among primary promoted teachers. The higher status holders were more
dissatisfied than the lower about the qualifications of the interviewers,
the questions they asked, and the use of testimonials. Ungraded
teachers were more dissatisfied than holders of graded posts about
advertisements, while deputy heads and heads were almost unconcerned
about this item.

(b) *Present post—secondary teachers* 'Qualifications of the interviewers'
was the least satisfactory for all levels, the percentage votes being
ungraded 47 per cent, graded 59 per cent, head of department 63 per
cent, deputy 63 per cent, and heads 68 per cent. These percentages
were not as extreme (12–14 per cent lower) as in the primary sector.
Are the interview panels for secondary promotions better qualified ? Do
they have a higher proportion of 'professional' representation ? The
questions, too, though ranked second or third, tend to cause less
irritation (by nine to 18 per cent of the vote). With better qualified
interviewers the questions might be more pertinent. Even so, between
half and two-thirds of promoted teachers were still dissatisfied with the
interview panel, and between 33 per cent and 44 per cent of them felt
the questions were irrelevant.

Few significant differences among secondary status groups were
found. Higher rather than lower status holders were dissatisfied with the
qualifications of interviewers and with application forms. Lower rather
than higher status holders were dissatisfied with advertisements and the
acknowledgements of applications. The questions asked by interviewers
dissatisfied heads of department and deputy heads more than they did
either lower status and ungraded teachers or head teachers.

CHAPTER THIRTEEN

Appointment Procedures: Teachers' Suggestions

The previous chapter surveyed the sources of teachers' dissatisfactions with appointment procedures, as revealed across the whole sample completing the teachers' questionnaires. Some insight into the *reasons* for their opinions was obtained from the sub-sample of teachers whom we interviewed. In this chapter we report their suggestions for improving each stage of the application procedure, from advertisement to interview and appointment.

A. Advertisements (Appendix E in supplement—see p. 13)

Greatest dissatisfaction with advertisements was expressed by younger teachers, those on lower promotion levels, women, and more by primary than secondary teachers. In our interviews, teachers were asked for their views on the interval between the advertisement and the closing date by which applications had to be posted, and what they wanted to know about the posts before deciding to apply.

1. *Closing date for applications*

About a quarter of the interviewed teachers had no strong views on this issue. Hardly any wanted less than a week. Positive preferences were more or less evenly distributed at about one fifth of teachers for two weeks and three weeks, while about a third wanted at least a month.

The chief concern for those wanting the longer periods was the need for time to organize referees and testimonials. This might well be needed for a first application, but then subsequent applications would have the testimonials, referees, etc. available so 'there's no need to drag out the closing date'. One suggestion was to standardize the interval at 28 days, but whatever the system, there is the practical problem of finding a replacement for a teacher who resigns only a few days before the accepted date for notice in any particular term.

2. *The contents of 'further particulars'*

Advertisement in a local bulletin or the educational press usually provides only limited information, and only a third of the advertisements we studied offered to provide any further details of the post. One hundred of the interviewed teachers could recall the matter of 'further details' with some assurance, and about two-fifths said they had not received such additional information.

A few teachers felt that the further particulars usually sent were not of much help as 'a glowing picture of the school is always presented', and anyway 'you'll never know what a school's like till you're working in it'. Nevertheless, some indicated that if they had known 'such and such' about the school or post they would never have wasted their time with an application. This did not refer to 'rigged' appointments, but to facts about the pupils or school or post, e.g. 'when I got the particulars I saw that I hadn't realized the children were going to be so handicapped, so I didn't apply'.

What kind of information did teachers want? A large number had strong views. The most frequently mentioned item was *school size*. Sixty-three (47 per cent) of the 135 teachers wanted this, and it was the most-wanted item regardless of the teacher's status, sex or type of school. Fifty-one (38 per cent) believed some kind of *job specification* was important. As one teacher put it—'I've been lumbered with things when I've got there . . . they ought to be honest about such things like extra duties'. For many teachers, the job specification should state a great deal about teaching commitment, e.g. 'the subjects to be covered, the grade and ability of the children to be taught . . . the possibility of sixth-form teaching'. Heads seemed less concerned about job specification than were other teachers, among whom those in secondary were more concerned than colleagues in primary school.

The school's immediate *environment* was mentioned by just under a third of the teachers, particularly the catchment areas 'so that I would know whether the background of the pupils was rural, industrial or deprived'. Men appeared to want information on the school area more than women did.

Specified by just under a quarter of the teachers, *teaching methods* was the fourth most-mentioned factor, and all types of teacher seemed equally concerned. 'I want an indication of the teaching methods— traditional or team teaching . . . is it mixed or family grouping? . . . knowledge about the freedom I would have in running my own department, in the syllabus I chose and the teaching methods I would be free to adopt'.

Number of staff was quoted by about a tenth of the teachers and, combined with school size, it would give some idea of pupil-teacher ratio. For primary teachers the stress was on class size, for secondary the size of the department.

Other items lower down the overall priority list were demanded more by one teacher group than another, e.g. the facilities of the school and department was an item more important to secondary than to primary teachers; the *age range of pupils* to be taught was mentioned more often by primary teachers; the *schools buildings* was noted as third on the heads' list but ninth for other teachers, and was mentioned more often by primary than secondary teachers. Any *reorganization plan* was considered more important by heads and by men.

Secondary teachers sometimes mentioned their *subject specialism* as an item about which they would like more information:

'I'd want to know whether my own subject, divinity, was treated seriously, was a Cinderella subject, if it was an examination subject'.

'With PE I want to know what teams are run, what pursuits followed, amount of time on the timetable; you get in the school and find you're doing it all by yourself'.

The *housing situation* was not mentioned often, though some teachers wanted to know 'what efforts are made by the LEA to help with housing?' Other items which occurred sporadically, as important to individual teachers, included the *school organization* ('was it streamed or mixed ability . . . was there a house system?'); *discipline* ('how they deal with trouble-makers'); the *school's philosophy* ('the school's basic aims'); *special curricular features* at the school; the *extra-curricular activities* at the school.

Some teachers asked for estimates of intangibles like staff morale or staff relationships, items which an employer or head would scarcely be ready to characterize as 'poor', even if they were so. Some teachers asked for the impossible, as exemplified by the teacher who wanted 'to know something about the head, because I've had experience of working with a person who was bad-tempered, upset people, made life miserable'. Such explicit opinion would require the 'further particulars' of that school to be printed on asbestos, especially if it were true.

The teachers were obviously most concerned with obtaining details of the job; only a few mentioned the other side of the coin, the details of the person required. Yet considerable effort would be saved if better job specification and *applicant specification* were available, e.g. 'whether they wanted a young person or a more experienced teacher . . . (is it) a post for which a graduate is needed . . . when I got to the interview I found it was for a senior mistress and they wouldn't look at anyone who hadn't had experience with third and fourth year juniors'.

B. Application Procedures

Certain aspects of the 'mechanics' of applying were regarded as less satisfactory than others.

1. *Application forms and letters of application*

We asked the teachers we visited whether they preferred letter or forms or a combination of the two. Letters were preferred by 21 per cent of the sub-sample and forms by 31 per cent. Thirty eight per cent preferred to complete both (sometimes with the letter being included as part of the form), and the remaining one tenth expressed no feelings either way.

The analysis of the questionnaires had indicated the teachers' dissatisfaction with forms. One might have expected therefore that in their interviews teachers would have preferred letters of application. The apparent contradiction might arise because teachers may think forms necessary and preferable, but believe the *content* should be improved by omitting 'war experience . . . national insurance number . . . when I finished or started school'. Often preference arose by elimination rather than selection, as in preferring a form because of not knowing what was expected in a letter, or favouring a letter because forms are poorly designed. A teacher with 16 years of experience behind him summed it up:

'This really needs organizing. To have a national form used by all authorities would be absolutely the thing—or else do away with the form altogether and just have a letter: it's got to be one or the other, and perhaps there's more to be said for the letter if the authority gives guidance as to what should be included'.

2. *Testimonials*

From the questionnaire replies, testimonials were one of the most unsatisfactory items. The comments of our interviewed sub-sample of teachers showed a divergence. Of the 135, 50 wanted testimonials abandoned completely, yet 44 preferred two testimonials. Women preferred testimonials more than men, and primary more than secondary teachers—and this reflected the questionnaire findings. However, the split between wanting them abandoned and preferring the sending of two was maintained within all these groups.

Most teachers who wished to see the end of the use of testimonials were fairly concise and terse about their view—'they're a farce . . . useless . . . get rid of them'. The main objection was their alleged unreliability, stemming from not knowing if the author's stated view was true or not. In some instances the integrity of the head was challenged as he might be 'very willing to give a very good testimonial to get rid of a teacher'.

Some teachers who wanted to retain the use of testimonials thought a teacher had a right to them, e.g. 'If you have spent years in a certain school you should be able to go from that school with your good qualities pointed out'. A few saw testimonials as overcoming the difficulty sometimes experienced when 'there are a very few people I can approach for a reference'. A practical problem arose for those teachers whose heads refused 'on principle' to give testimonials even when other people demanded them.

The following was the view of one head who attempted to take a 'balanced position:

I think they are very valuable provided you know the person that has written them and the quality of the school they have taught in. It is silly to ask for three testimonials from someone who has been in the same job for a long time. It is equally ridiculous to ask it of someone that has just started teaching. If you have a teacher who has been in several posts rather rapidly it might be reasonable to ask for a lot of testimonials to see why they have been changing'.

3. References

The analysis of the teachers' questionnaires had found that the quoting of referees was not a particularly unsatisfactory aspect of the application procedure. One hundred and eighteen of the 135 interviewed teachers had views on this topic. Most—nearly 60 per cent— thought two referees the ideal number to be asked to quote. About 15 per cent wanted one referee, and the same proportion wanted three or more referees. Only a minority of about 12 per cent thought references should not be requested at all.

Most teachers had reservations though, mentioning the difficulty in obtaining suitable referees, especially at the beginning of one's career. Some teachers pointed out that the quoted references might not necessarily be the most pertinent people for the employer. A definite problem was that few employers specified the kind of referee wanted. The teachers themselves were divided. Some believed that references should be more concerned with character than professional ability, others stressed that only the candidate's professional competence should be considered. Many suggested that two referees should be quoted, one who knew the candidate at school and one who was independent of the school. If the teachers knew definitely the kind of reference required, perhaps the problem of who to quote as a referee might resolve itself. An equally valid character reference might be sought from either a non-educationist *or* from someone acquainted with the candidate in his professional work, but only the latter could comment on the teacher's professional competence.

Many teachers thought the present head ought to be one of the referees, if not the only one, who should be quoted, and some regarded the quoting of the head as an assumed obligation ('If you don't quote the head, one would think there was something strange'; 'They're probably going to ask your head whether you quote him or not'). However, as with testimonials, the validity of the head's report was questioned by some teachers, on the grounds that he might supply a good reference in order to get rid of a teacher, or a bad one in order to retain him.

C. Short-listing

Who, in the teachers' view, ought to draw up the short list of candidates to be called for interview? We did not ask this in the questionnaires, but did so in our personal interviews. As some teachers might not have been familiar with the short-listing process and the possible options open for a selecting panel, we listed the five most usual groups, viz. the head of the prospective school, the managers/governors, the head of department, the LEA officers and the LEA advisers. We asked each teacher if he thought each of the groups should be involved in the short-listing process, and if there were any other individuals or groups who should be involved. Teachers differentiated between short-listing for headships and short-listing for other posts, and this is reflected in our analysis.

1. *Short-listing for posts other than headships*

The teachers were almost unanimous (95 per cent) in saying the *head* ought to be involved in short-listing candidates for posts at his school. About half (51 per cent) thought the *LEA Inspector/Adviser* ought to help; 63 (47 per cent) mentioned the *head of department* but this, as might be expected, was noted for secondary rather than primary teachers; 61 teachers (45 per cent) thought an *LEA official*, e.g. the CEO or his representative, should be involved; and 55 (41 per cent) wanted the *managers or governors*. The deputy head was mentioned by 23 teachers (17 per cent) but other groups by only small numbers, e.g. other staff (11), Education Committee members (3), parents (2), union official (1).

2. *Short-listing for headships*

Apart from eliminating head and head of department, the teachers felt as they did with non-head posts, i.e. the *LEA Inspector/Adviser*, an *LEA official* and the *managers/governors* were all mentioned by half or just under half the teachers.

There was considerable diversion of opinion on how these various interests should be combined as short-listing panels. Apart from the constant presence of the head, all the named individuals were permutated, e.g. 'head, adviser and definitely no managers or governors . . . head, managers or governors and definitely no adviser . . . head, LEA official and head of department but no one else'.

Primary teachers were divided about all possible selectors except the head. In particular while some felt the managers were not qualified to select a short-list, others believed they ought to have a say. The adviser/ inspector was wanted by some teachers, but others doubted their value. Most *secondary* teachers insisted that the head should be the principal person involved, and that he should consult one or more members of staff. Opinion was divided, as with primary teachers, concerning the value and role of the inspectorate, the LEA officers and the governors.

D. Confidentials and 'The Grapevine'

From our preliminary discussion we became aware that some of the spokesmen for the teachers' associations, no doubt reflecting the views of some of their members, felt strongly about confidential assessments. In our interviews we explored this delicate area rather more thoroughly than would have been politic in the questionnaire, which covered the openly recognized testimonial and reference only. Each teacher was asked a fairly impartial question:

'It is often suggested that apart from the confidential information from a referee, further information about an applicant is also sought and received confidentially from other sources, without the knowledge of the applicant. What are your views or experiences of this ?'

The teacher then answered freely. If he indicated knowledge of the practice we then asked why he thought it was used. Finally, if the teacher had not included the point in his comments thus far, we asked if he would personally object to such confidential information about himself being used without his knowledge, as part of the application procedure.

This last question is perhaps the most important, at least as far as the individual teachers' attitudes are concerned. Only eight (six per cent) of the 135 teachers gave a 'don't know' answer. Fifty-seven per cent answered unequivocally that they would have no objection whatever, with another 12 per cent giving qualified acceptance, e.g. no objection but would like to be told it was being done. Twenty per cent said they would object whatever the circumstances. Another five per cent said they would object unless told the contents of the information which could then no longer be confidential. Thus a fair summary would be that the great majority (69 per cent) did not object to the principle of seeking confidential information (*additional* to what the candidate offered), a quarter did object, and six per cent did not care. This distribution was roughly the same for men and women, for heads and non-heads, for primary and secondary teachers.

These findings are rather unexpected. The articles and letters in the educational press would have suggested that most practising teachers objected strongly to the 'grapevine' practise. Our observations were different. Moreover, the lack of objection to confidentials and 'the grapevine' was not just negative—many teachers thought such seeking of confidential information a necessary obligation on the part of the LEA or head to protect their schools, their staffs and their pupils. The teachers' attitude to the interviewer when answering this question (as with other sensitive issues such as 'unfair interviews', 'social contacts', 'the head's role') appeared no different from their attitude when replying to the more factual and less sensitive areas of questioning. So there is no reason to suspect that teachers were less honest in this isolated issue.

The lack of full credibility of testimonials and references was the reason given for the need to seek additional information in confidence. This doubt was expressed by many teachers. It is significant that, even though few teachers seemed aware of it, LEAs exchanged 'confidentials' (usually only on short-listed candidates) presumably because they were deemed necessary. The initial source of those confidentials was usually the present head of the candidate's school, i.e. the same principal source of the 'grapevine', the testimonial and one reference. The teachers, with some reservations, raised little objection to the head as the source of this additional confidential information. It would appear that, in principle, teachers are not in conflict with present policy and practices regarding confidentials and the grapevine, and even regard it as the best system available in present circumstances.

The time sequence is one important aspect that should not be overlooked. Whereas the LEA confidentials are usually requested and sent only after short-listing, the grapevine could come into operation prior to or as an essential concomitant of the short-listing process. Acceptance of the grapevine process by some teachers may reflect a hope that it can boost the prospects of teachers whose paper qualifications or contacts are relatively inferior. Everything, of course, depends on the integrity of present heads.

E. The Interview

The analysis of the teachers' questionnaire showed that the interview itself incurred great displeasure. Our discussions with the sub-sample of teachers gave them a chance to suggest how to improve the system.

1. *Number of interviewers*

A third of the teachers seen offered no comment on the number preferred on the panel, being keener to talk about the panel's qualifications. The choice of the other two-thirds varied between two and six, as a desirable panel size, the upper range of from four to six appearing to be the most satisfactory.

Those who preferred very small panels did so because they found 'being asked questions by a lot of people is overwhelming', or they were not sure to whom they should direct their answers. A problem of too small a panel was also mentioned—'if the one person interviewing happens to be against a particular remark you make, or a particular line you have taken, that is more or less conclusive'. No one mentioned the advantages of saying the 'right' thing in front of one interviewer. Between four and six on the panel was popular because 'all avenues can then be explored', and the various panel members are 'all looking at it from different angles'.

2. *Who should interview teachers?*

The teachers' questionnaire showed that the qualifications of interviewing panels was the most unsatisfactory aspect of the whole appointments procedure. How did our sub-sample of teachers think an interviewing panel ought to be constituted?

Of the 122 teachers (90 per cent) who volunteered opinions, 121 wanted the *head* of the prospective school to be at the interview, but beyond that many teachers merely stipulated that the panel should comprise people who 'know about teaching' or 'who have professional qualifications'. However, certain groups or individuals were specifically named, as follows: 57 (42 per cent) thought that the *managers or governors* should attend interviews, 42 (31 per cent) said a *representative of the LEA* should be present, 35 (26 per cent) wanted an *adviser*, and

28 (21 per cent) a *head of department*, the latter being requested mostly by secondary teachers. The deputy head was mentioned by about a tenth of the teachers. A few teachers mentioned staff representatives, parents and councillors.

Apart from the universal agreement on the head's presence, there was much division of opinion as to who should accompany him. Teachers' reasoning for the exclusions and inclusions in their ideal interviewing panel emerged in the comments some teachers added. Exclusion of the non-professional was justified by:

'Although the governor may have the school's best interests at heart, I don't think he's qualified to appoint staff—he doesn't know the problems involved.'

'I think they should have people with experience in interviewing people and knowledge of schools and teaching. Here we have farmers and all kinds of people on the panels.'

'Political nominees of education committees find themselves on Governing Boards or Managing Boards. I don't know of other professions where appointment has to depend upon the well-intentioned but nevertheless politically-biased opinions of different people. . . . I think it wrong that these amateurs with the best will in the world, should have the right to make appointments. . . . You don't appoint a doctor to a hospital upon the word of a bus driver, a road sweeper, etc., but you do in teaching.'

'So many from the Office are merely administrators and know nothing at all about actual teaching.'

The exclusion of 'non-professionals' was questioned by teachers who considered the interview an attempt to summarize a person's personality and character. They wondered if purely educational background and experience were sufficient to endow a panel member with 'interviewing calibre'.

'It is a danger to underestimate laymen—they can ask questions which are pertinent. I wouldn't want them short-listing, but I would want them at the interview . . . I believe there is a case for one man on the panel who comes in without teaching experience but who is a good judge of character!

The value of 'somebody with a knowledge of local affairs' on the panel was recognized by some teachers, to answer, if not ask, pertinent questions.

One teacher added that, whoever was on the panel, they should have some knowledge of interviewing techniques.

Some teachers wanted to eliminate the interview as a formal occasion, preferring a personal discussion with the head and head of department. Finally, one teacher was not happy about there being an interview at all, and suggested that personality testing, as used in industry, should be substituted for the interview.

3. *The head's role at interviews*

The teachers we saw believed that the head ought to play a major role at the interview. Of the 76 non-heads who commented on this, only one thought he should take a minor part, and 65 (68 per cent) thought his role ought to be the principal one. Ten thought the head's role at interviews should be equal to that of the other panel members.

4. *The questions that should be asked*

Over a third of all surveyed teachers regarded the kind of questions asked at interviews as unsatisfactory. The chief concern of the interviewed teachers was that the questions should be confined to educational matters of the kind:

'Your past experience; your interests and aims; your ideas on education and what you think about teaching methods; the role you think you should play in your subject, and your role in pastoral care; extra-curricular work you have engaged in, and courses you have attended; the kind of work you would like to do, and the kind of syllabus you would like to evolve.'

Many teachers were clear about the two areas in which questions should *not* be asked. Rejected first were personal questions, questions on the teacher's politics or religion and 'personal beliefs'. Next were the questions where the answers are already known, e.g. facts recorded on the application form.

Some teachers felt the interview questions should be directed at finding out about the candidate's personality, '. . . whether he will be the right sort of person, character and personality-wise, for the particular post; whether he will fit in to an existing situation with colleagues'. Others felt the very opposite '. . . We must get rid of the attitude of checking on characteristics and personality'. Some teachers felt that interview time was wasted establishing facts that could have been more systematically obtained beforehand, e.g. 'It's no good asking at an interview what a person thinks about streaming or non-streaming—

these specific questions should have been asked and answered in the initial application form'. Some teachers stressed that it was not the questions that mattered as much as the manner in which they were put.

Finally, the most important question, according to one teacher, should be 'Are there any questions you would like to ask us?' The interview, he thought, was a two-way process, and other teachers also commented on the need to know from the interviewers, and particularly from the head, the way the school was organized and what was expected of the candidate.

5. *Time and length of interview*

(a) *Time of day*   About half the teachers were not concerned when the interview took place, but of the remainder hardly any favoured an evening interview. The choice was evenly split between morning and afternoon, with some secondary teachers favouring the less formal arrangement that spanned both morning and afternoon.

Those who specifically disliked an evening interview listed the lack of opportunity to see the school at work, tiredness at the end of a working day, and personal inconvenience. Of those who favoured mornings, some mentioned feeling fresher, others a desire to 'get it over and done with'. Afternoons were favoured by those who had to travel and by those who wanted to see the school during the morning. The overall impression was that few teachers felt strongly on the matter.

(b) *Length of interview*   Although a few of the teachers we spoke to wanted interviews to last over 45 minutes, the great majority favoured between 10 minutes and a half-hour. Primary women appeared to favour the 10–20 minute interview, whilst other teachers preferred between 20 and 30 minutes. This general pattern of preference applied, whether the post concerned was junior or senior.

6. *General arrangements*

Whilst nearly two-thirds of our sub-sample would be happy with the suggestions covered earlier, one third re-emphasized two opportunities, to look round the school and, less strongly, to ask questions at the interview. The first concern reflected the similar dissatisfaction of a fifth of the total teacher sample on the questionnaire. The greater opportunity to ask questions at interview did not, however, appear as a cause of complaint from the questionnaire analysis. On the other hand, the general survey suggested dissatisfaction (24.6 per cent) with the limited opportunity to meet the staff of the prospective school, yet only eight (six per cent) of the 135 sub-sample of interviewed teachers raised the matter.

As an inventory of arrangements preferred by teachers, the following list might be of interest.

1 Applicants should be allowed to look round the prospective school.
2 There should be an opportunity to meet the staff of the school.
3 Applicants should be treated with courtesy and offered refreshment, if possible.
4 Reasonably comfortable accommodation should be available while applicants wait to be interviewed.
5 Long waiting periods for applicants should be avoided, preferably by having set times for each applicant's interview.
6 The order in which applicants are called for interview from a communal waiting room should not necessarily be alphabetical.
7 Interviewers should be introduced to the candidate.
8 The interview should be as relaxed as possible.
9 Applicants should be allowed to ask questions at the interview.
10 If there are many applicants to be interviewed, the interviewing panel should have a rest period and refreshment during the total session, to ensure freshness of attitude and parity of treatment to candidates seen later in the session (this rest period and refreshment should not be taken during an interview).
11 Candidates should be informed of the decision of the panels regarding the appointment.
12 Candidates' expenses should be paid regardless of acceptance or refusal of an offered post.

F. Reliability of the Appointment Procedures

Whatever specific satisfactions or dissatisfactions there may be, do the appointment procedures work? There are no criteria universally established to answer such a question. Stipulated requirements are hardly criteria by which the system can be evaluated, e.g. the successful candidate must be a graduate, male, have taught in comprehensive schools, etc. We are forced to accept that within teaching there are no currently acceptable criteria for teacher effectiveness *that are defined in measurable terms*. Promotion to different levels may (or may not) call for different attributes. What these qualities are, or how selectors can measure them, is rarely stated in terms more precise than personality, competence, character, energy, enthusiasm, etc. It is assumed that those who select know what they are looking for in candidates, and that they will be able to identify and recognize whatever it is that is being sought. Yet there is considerable evidence now to question this assumption (Wiseman and Start 1965, Koskenniemi 1965, Start 1966, 1967, 1972, Start and Laundy 1973).

Whether or not the appointment procedures are efficient must await effective criteria, but it is important to know if the teacher believed that posts of promotion had been filled successfully. Was he aware of many square pegs in round holes? How did he think the system of promoting could be improved?

1. *Was the system reliable?*

Of the 135 teachers interviewed, 31 (23 per cent) felt they had not had enough experience to judge, or were non-committal. Fifty-two (38.5 per cent) thought the system was reliable, and 52 thought it unreliable. This pattern was roughly the same when considering appointments for both headships and posts below headship, and the dichotomy of view was found within the various teacher groups—men and women, primary and secondary, heads and non-heads.

The division of opinion among the teachers was frequently illustrated in the teachers' comments, based, as many were, on their personal experiences.

(a) *Headships* Nor unexpectedly, some of those who were now heads were fairly content with the headship appointments they had known, e.g. 'In 75 per cent of the cases, they've got the right man', or 'There haven't been many errors', but others were less sure.

Many non-heads were content with the headship appointments they had come across, a typical comment being 'On the whole, I've not seen many in the wrong job'. Those who spoke unfavourably of the system usually did so fairly caustically— '. . . one or two heads I've worked with on teaching practice (had) no more idea of managing staff than pussy-cats . . . he was so insignificant . . . he could be the last one you would pick out . . . I know a case where the priest had the casting vote and it wasn't a man's ability to be head of the school that was wanted, but a man's ability to do exactly as the priest wanted regarding religious education. . . . To appoint, as head of a comprehensive, someone whose previous experience has been limited to a grammar school, is looking for disaster'.

(b) *Posts below headship* It was interesting to hear the heads' comments on appointments made to their own school. Some were content—'In my personal experience, which probably means four or five hundred interviews, I would look back happily and say we only made a mistake twice. . . . Generally one doesn't make the mistake with senior posts'. Other heads were less enthusiastic, particularly for some appointments made by 'committee'. Some admitted their personal errors in appoint-ing—'Time and again in my experience of interviews I find I have picked the wrong one. . . . At the interview they say they are willing to do this or that, but once they're collecting the money they don't want to do anything for the school any more. . . . I had a girl for interview who was efficient and friendly and I thought she was my answer to a prayer, but she was different when she came. I was completely wrong about her. . . . We know we make mistakes. You let people slip in who are not really capable of doing the job. . . . (Selection procedures are) emphatically not reliable'.

Among the non-heads, about half the teachers thought that promotions to posts below headship had been satisfactory and that 'people in wrong appointments are just isolated cases'. The other half felt quite differently. One teacher succinctly remarked 'We have a hell of a lot of square pegs in round holes'. Some teachers echoed heads' opinions of teachers 'who have perfected an interview manner and can appear to be very good'. One quoted a personal experience where an inexperienced colleague was appointed 'because she threatened to leave if she didn't get the post'. Another recalled 'three people who were so outrageously impossible and unsuitable' and the relief of the staff when these individuals left.

A fairly common complaint was that paper qualifications were relied on too much, occasionally overriding discipline, teaching, leadership or personality.

Some teachers saw the position from the appointed teacher's side, when insufficient or incorrect detail about a post or school causes a mismatch—'Some advertisements don't state what is wanted and you're not told enough about the job—and so a person can get appointed to the school and then finds that the job doesn't suit them. . . . It might be that you've got yourself in the wrong school—I couldn't teach in a progressive school, it just wouldn't work'.

With approximately one third approving the system and one third criticising it, and the non-commital third including in their comments, remarks such as 'I'd say fifty-fifty', it does seem that on this issue teachers are fairly and decisively divided.

2. How to improve the appointment procedures

Very few teachers, even among those who thought the present system unreliable, could suggest any radically different system that would be an improvement. Typical answers were 'It's not a good system, but it's as reliable as it can be. . . . I can't propose an alternative which hasn't greater drawbacks'.

Of the 135 teachers interviewed, 70 (52 per cent) could offer no change, major or minor, that would noticeably improve the system. Tentative changes were frequently countered by arguments posited by other teachers to explain why such a change would not be desirable.

The great majority wanted to retain the interview as part of the procedure for appointing. Only one teacher wanted it abandoned and substituted by computerised tests of personality and other characteristics. Some, however, thought the interview could be supplemented by this kind of information. Others were wary of such quantitative devices and preferred observation to measurement. They suggested informal talks with various members of staff or even various members of the appointing panel, perhaps over a residential weekend. Such prolonged interviewing was not welcomed by those who preferred to 'get the thing over and done with', although there was a general acceptance of the need for greater informality in interviewing.

Improvement in interviewing techniques was suggested by some, and inevitably this was linked to appointments by professionals, not laymen. There emerged a fundamental conflict of views about the purpose of the interview. For some teachers, all the applicants appearing at interview were equally capable of doing the job in question; hence the purpose of the interview was to discriminate among their characters and personalities. For others, it was this very attempt to make such discriminations that produced the mistakes in appointment. For them the interview panel determined and compared candidates' attitudes on professional educational problems and issues.

Several teachers suggested that the unreliability of appointments could be reduced by ensuring that only the best possible candidates were short-listed in the first place. But this begs the question. Reliance on assessments of competence in the school and classroom was threatening for those teachers who were uneasy about the infallibility of those formulating these assessments, notably heads and inspectors. Some teachers suggested that the interview panel should see the candidate teaching in his 'natural setting'—it would help them judge him and also let him perform in an atmosphere he was accustomed to rather than in the foreign setting of an interview room. Opposition to this suggestion came from those teachers who said they disliked being observed and would never be able to perform naturally in such a situation. A few teachers, perhaps cynically, believed that unreliability was more likely to be avoided by choosing from among 'the devils you know' and not having appointments open to all candidates.

The interviewed teachers were divided about the effectiveness of the appointments procedure, but they could offer little of positive reforming nature that commanded more than token support. This reflected the opinions gathered by questionnaire from the whole teacher sample. Though many items relating to appointment procedures were regarded with differing degrees of disfavour by teachers, very few items were strongly disliked by a majority of teachers, and about a fifth of the whole sample were completely satisfied.

CHAPTER FOURTEEN

Policy, Practice and Opinion

This chapter is concerned with the extent to which policy, practice and opinion among those concerned differ with regard to the procedures for appointing to promotion posts.

A. Advertising

1. *Open advertising*

Whilst there is considerable disagreement among teachers on this issue, most LEAs had the policy of opening appointments to allcomers, especially in secondary schools. Yet the teacher questionnaire showed nearly half (46.8 per cent) of all promotion appointments were made internally in the primary school, and over half (66.3 per cent) in the secondary schools (see Chapter 6, Table 6.1).

2. *Head's involvement*

Two-thirds of the heads we spoke to said they were fully responsible for or closely involved in the compiling of the advertisement, but this appeared to be true much more of secondary heads. The analysis of advertisements indicated that it was common practice for applicants to be asked to return applications to the Education Office in the case of primary schools, and to the head for secondary appointments. This difference could have implications regarding the head's role in short-listing.

3. *Further particulars*

Just over half our interviewed teachers received further details about posts, when only a third of the advertisements mentioned the availability of such details. The practice seemed more common when advertising senior than lower level promotion posts. Neither the surveyed nor the interviewed teachers seemed unduly disturbed about the sending of further particulars or their contents.

4. *Closing date*

The average interval before applications were to be received was found to be about two weeks. The teachers interviewed would have preferred longer, three weeks to a month.

B. Application Procedure

1. *Acknowledgements*

The LEAs indicated a general policy of acknowledging applications, though county councils tended to do this less than county boroughs. Heads also said they acknowledged applications when they received them directly. Nearly 10 per cent of the surveyed teachers who were dissatisfied with application procedures regarded acknowledgements as an unsatisfactory item, yet only eight (six per cent) of the 135 teachers we interviewed said their applications had usually not been acknowledged. Most of the teachers interviewed were satisfied with the LEA correspondence with teachers.

2. *Application forms and letters of application*

Almost all LEAs asked applicants to complete application forms, and about a third generally requested a letter, whether as substitute or additional information. About 19 per cent of all the dissatisfied teachers felt that the application form was an unsatisfactory item in the procedure, but they were not so disturbed concerning letters. The teachers interviewed offered reasons for dissatisfaction with forms, and our analysis of application forms appeared to justify some of their criticisms. Nevertheless, there was no general desire among teachers to replace forms with letters.

3. *Testimonials*

Testimonials were high on the survey teachers' list of unsatisfactory aspects of the application procedure, and the teachers interviewed were divided about their value. The odd feature of this matter, however, was that while a large number of teachers were not happy about testimonials, only about a third of the LEAs said they asked for them, and only a fifth asked for more than one. Heads indicated that they too did not ask for testimonials, nor did they have much faith in their value. Teachers' anxieties about testimonials, therefore, seemed superfluous or at least exaggerated.

4. *References*

The LEAs' report that it was usual policy to ask for references was confirmed by the experiences of the teachers interviewed, and only 18 per cent of all the dissatisfied sample thought the practice unsatisfactory. The chief complaint of the interviewed teachers was that little indication was given of the kind of reference required. The teachers disagreed among themselves on whether referees should be professional or laymen, and about whether the reference should comment on character as well as ability. Heads were generally not happy with references from persons unacquainted with education.

5. *Notification of the outcome*

Over 90 per cent of LEAs said their policy was to notify all applicants of the result of applications. Heads directly involved in the advertisement agreed this was their policy also. The teachers we spoke to confirmed that *not* being notified of the result was the exception rather than the rule. As several of the teachers we interviewed complained about the delay in notification, it might be this delay rather than non-notification that placed the item sixth of the unsatisfactory aspects of the application procedure identified by the questionnaire.

C. Short-listing

1. *Posts below headship*

(a) *Deputy headship* From the LEA questionnaire heads were said to be given sole responsibility for short-listing their deputy headship by about a quarter of LEAs for primary vacancies and about a third in secondary schools. On the other hand, heads on their questionnaire claimed sole responsibility for 11 per cent of primary deputy positions and 20 per cent for secondary—both about 13 per cent less than the LEAs' figures. At the other extremes, heads reported themselves less excluded than the LEA policy statements might lead us to believe, e.g. in the primary field LEAs suggested 35 per cent and heads report 13 per cent, in the secondary the LEA figure was a little over 25 per cent whereas only two per cent of heads experienced it. In both sectors there was a consistent 22 per cent move to more consultation.

(b) *Graded post/head of department* There was little discrepancy between LEAs and heads on the proportion with sole responsibility for shortlisting posts below deputy head, the figures for exclusion revealing the same 20 per cent leavening of practice over policy. But while about a quarter of the LEAs said primary heads took no part in short-listing posts below deputy, only five per cent of primary heads agreed. And while 10 per cent of the LEAs said secondary heads played no part, not a single secondary head admitted complete exclusion.

These differences suggest that there is much more consultation than is 'policy'. Neither sole responsibility nor exclusion occurred as frequently as 'policy' would suggest. On the other hand, these discrepancies may have arisen from the different bases for LEAs and heads. Certainly the policy of counties was to grant their heads more authority than county boroughs. Heads of voluntary schools were given greater freedom than heads of county schools, and LEAs differed considerably in the balance of voluntary/county schools maintained by them.

Whatever the role of heads in short-listing posts below headship, the teachers interviewed were almost unanimous in wanting the head involved, either alone or with senior members of staff.

Although some teachers expressed extreme hostility to the idea of laymen taking any part at this stage of the appointment procedure, about a third felt that managers or governors ought to be consulted. Similar contrasts in view were expressed regarding the 'professionals'— either administrators or advisers.

2. Headships

The variations in the policy for short-listing of applicants for headship vacancies ranged from placing almost the whole responsibility with the professional administrators (e.g. CEO, AEO, county inspectorate) to denying the professionals anything more than a clerical role. Then full responsibility for short-listing was either with members of the Education Committee or with such members in conjunction with school governors.

The teachers we interviewed were divided concerning the roles of managers and professional administrators. It was noticeable that whereas managers or governors were sometimes referred to as lay people who ought to be consulted because of their interests in the locality, very few teachers mentioned the need to consult the lay persons on the central or divisional education committees.

D. Confidential Reports

Generally, LEA policy was to collect confidential assessments of teachers who were short-listed for interview. It was acknowledged also that much confidential information was exchanged informally between the heads of present and prospective schools. The heads confirmed, in their questionnaire, that such exchange of information was made, and those interviewed felt this to be a necessary step both to protect pupils and staff of the prospective school and to be fair to their own staff seeking appointments elsewhere.

The majority of teachers interviewed had no personal objection to the 'grapevine' system, though they were concerned about the source and content of the information passed. They believed that such confidential information should come only from professional people like the head or the LEA advisers. According to LEAs and heads, this *is* the practice. Most teachers felt their personal experience justified faith in the integrity and fairness of most heads. At the same time, it is known that teachers' associations sometimes receive complaints from members concerning the nature of confidential reports supplied by LEA advisers. It is sometimes unclear whether the LEA adviser is in a position to give confidential information based on first hand knowledge or whether his report is a summary, possibly inadequate, of information collected from others, in which case teachers feel that this should be clearly stated.

E. Interviews

1. *Number of interviewers*

About a tenth of the total teacher sample regarded the number of people on the interviewing panel as a source of dissatisfaction. Our interviews with teachers showed that panels could be too large *or* too small. Our talks with both LEA officers and teachers indicated that the size of interviewing panels could vary from one to over 20, even for a fairly junior post. While the most popular ideal number for our teachers was four, five or six, some wanted larger and others smaller panels.

2. *Qualifications of interviewers*

(a) *Posts below headship* The great majority of LEAs said it was their policy that heads should be present at interviews for promotion posts, and the heads' replies in their questionnaires and interviews confirmed this as their own experience. Where the post concerned a deputy headship, between 80 and 90 per cent of LEAs said their policy was that a professional administrator (CEO or representative) should be present, as well as representatives of the managers. About half wanted advisers also present. For posts below deputy head, the professional administrator attended interviews in only 50 to 60 per cent of LEAs, and about the same proportion of managers and governors attended. Advisers were still present, according to about half the LEAs. The talks with teachers tended to confirm this variation in policy, but they could not be sure, as frequently the panel were not introduced to candidates.

The teachers' questionnaires showed that the type of person on the interviewing panel disturbed teachers greatly. From our talks with the subsample, it seemed that they disliked the presence of laymen, particularly because they asked apparently irrelevant questions. The teachers wanted the head of department and/or deputy head to be involved more at interviewing. They did not wish to exclude the managers or governors, but the advisers and professional administrators were not especially popular. Patently, teachers wanted the head, in conjunction with others on the school staff, to play the major role in interviewing and appointing. According to the teachers' experiences at interviews the head had often taken this major role, but there were many teachers who related that the head's role had frequently been a minor one.

A few education committees do insist on being almost entirely responsible for interview decisions, as for short-listing decisions. However, according to our talks with LEA officers, the influence played by managers and governors is, in general, minimal when the decision on appointment is actually made. The lay members usually lean very heavily on the advice of the head or professional administrators. The heads who spoke to us confirmed this opinion. So it would appear that the presence of managers and governors at interviews is not likely to exert a decisive influence on promotion.

From their questionnaire replies, very few heads felt that their views at interviews carried little weight. At interviews for lower promotion posts 67 per cent of secondary and 50 per cent of primary heads thought their views carried more weight than those of other panel members. For deputy headships these figures were lowered to 50 per cent and 36 per cent respectively. If, as the LEA officers believed, the managers' or governors' views did count for little, it must have been the opinions of the professional administrators or advisers that were being weighed closely with the views of heads. As the level of the post rose to a point that could affect school policy or establish a personal link with the 'office' (e.g. the deputy) the views of those at the office weighed more in the balance (14–17 per cent more.).

(b) *Headships* For interviews for headships, about 90 per cent of LEAs said that managers or governors were present. The same proportion reported that LEA officers usually attended (CEO or representative). Only 45 per cent had a policy of asking advisers to attend. Of course, attendance at the interview does not imply that an important role is being taken in decision-making. Even the kind of questions asked or the people asking do not indicate where the power to appoint actually lies. The LEA officers we spoke to indicated a vast range of circumstances, from the LEAs who gave the CEO almost total responsibility, to the LEAs who encouraged managers and governors to seek advice but take the responsibility, thence to LEAs whose education committees did not seek and did not want advice from the 'professionals'.

In their questionnaires and interviews some LEA officers remarked on the positive value of the presence of managers or governors: 'Managers and governors can be a useful commonsense balance of heads' views. . . . The attitude and interest of the managers or governors far outweigh qualifications. . . . I do not think that teaching posts should be a gift from the head'.

Several LEA officers reported that their authority was attempting to alter the structure of managing or governing bodies, possibly to include parents and members of school staff, and to increase their powers 'particularly as far as appointments are concerned'.

3. *Other points regarding interviews*

The total teacher sample were not disturbed about the *time given to applicants* at interviews. Most of the interviewed teachers wanted an interview of 20–30 minutes, and the majority reported that this was indeed their general experience, though very short and very long interviews were not unknown. The questionnaires revealed that teachers were not satisfied about opportunities offered to *look around the school*, but most of the teachers spoken to, said they had been given the opportunity. Lack of *opportunity to meet staff* at the school was another unsatisfactory circumstance according to the questionnaire, but very few teachers mentioned this item in our talks with them. The teacher questionnaire indicated that teachers were not generally critical concerning opportunities offered candidates *to ask questions* at the interview, and the teachers spoken to confirmed that they had usually been asked if they had any questions. Most thought this a very desirable practice.

CHAPTER FIFTEEN

Other Important Issues

The Power of the Head Over Teachers' Promotion Prospects

We have already noted some LEA and heads' views of the head's role within the system. Other teachers were generally not in a position to know the exact extent of the head's power or role, but what did they believe his power to be and what did they think it ought to be? We asked whether the teacher thought, from his general experience, the head's role was restricted, powerful or reasonably balanced, when appointing teachers to his staff, when promoting teachers within his school, and when his staff sought promotion elsewhere. The teacher was then asked for his views of the role the head ought to play.

1. *The head's power to appoint staff*

Ninety-one of the non-heads we interviewed felt their experience or knowledge enabled them to comment on the head's power to appoint staff to his school. Thirty-four (37 per cent) thought it was reasonably balanced, with the LEA administrative officers, or managers or governors being equally powerful. Forty (44 per cent) believed he wielded a powerful role, and nearly a fifth (19 per cent) thought his powers were restricted.

The majority who estimated that the head played a powerful role in appointing, justified this and were content. There were a few teachers who believed the head's power should be more restricted . . . 'we've still got the Divine Rights of Heads with us very much, I'm afraid'. Several of the teachers who saw the head's role as a restricted one, believed he ought to be given greater power: 'All hands should have a greater say in appointing staff'; 'He ought to have more say (in appointing a deputy) as it's very important for a head and deputy to get along, otherwise it's very difficult for the school'.

2. *The head's power to promote staff within the school*

Fewer teachers felt able to estimate the head's role in promoting his own staff. Of the 73 non-heads who commented, the majority (45, or 61.7 per cent) thought he played a major role, with 26 (35.6 per cent) considering his part reasonably balanced, and only two (2.7 per cent) saying it was restricted. From our earlier findings we know that many teachers in the total sample received their promotions internally within the school. It is very likely therefore that the views of the interviewed teachers were based reliably on experience and that heads were not restricted when it came to recommending their own staff for promotion.

But did the teachers approve or disapprove of the head's power in this respect? There were several who were unsure, or who, while approving in general, were concerned about some of the problems internal recommendation brought: 'There has been a certain amount of ill-feeling among other members of staff when we have had internal appointments'. Whether or not exclusion of the head from the process would reduce tensions must be debateable, however.

A few felt that too much reliance was placed on the head's personal recommendation. They believed that the power to recommend internally was correct in principle but that it should be delegated to others, chiefly heads of department. One teacher disliked the head's power over promotion because he might choose *not* to recommend internal applicants within the school: 'They'd sooner bring in someone from outside'. The great majority of teachers, however, either raised no objection to the head's having a large influence over internal promotion, or positively approved of it. His power was regarded as perfectly justified and appropriate, because 'Let's face it. He's the man on hand, he knows whether the chap deserves promotion, he should be allowed to give it.'

3. The head's power when staff seek promotion elsewhere

The head's power was seen as marginally (seven per cent) more balanced when his staff sought promotion outside rather than inside the school. Of 74 non-heads who offered a definite opinion, 40 (54 per cent) believed his role was powerful, 31 (42 per cent) reasonably balanced, and three (four per cent) rather restricted.

Most teachers saw the testimonial, the reference and the 'grapevine' as the methods by which a head might exert influence, but those who believed that the head's role was 'reasonably balanced' felt that the present head's opinions would be placed in perspective by the prospective head or appointing panel, e.g. 'They don't just take the work of the head as being the final word . . . the interviewing head may feel that your present head may want to get rid of you'.

Most teachers thought the head did play a major role when their staff sought promotion: 'Their head's letter is going to have far more value to the interviewing panel than anything else'. Some believed this was perfectly justified by the head's knowledge: 'If you work with somebody for a long time you know their qualities. You're the right person to say to the next school, "Yes, this is a good person for the job" or "No, dead loss, no good".'

The possibility of the head's abusing his powers was recognized by a number of teachers. Some thought he might allow personal relationships to become involved: 'He can make or break you; if you get on with him he can push you ahead, but if you don't, well. . . . I certainly know of cases where promotion prospects have been inhibited because the teachers have not got on with the headmaster for various reasons'.

But for most of those concerned about possible abuse of the head's power, the teachers' doubts revolved more around the head's reluctance to lose good staff: 'The head will tend to try and hold on to staff that he wants to keep, and therefore not give such a good reference'; 'As he didn't want to lose him, the reference he gave him was only fractionally as helpful as it should have been'. Positive support for weak teachers was seen as an abuse more by heads than other teachers—not unexpectedly for it is the head who has to live with the outcome.

Despite the doubts expressed by some teachers, the general view of teachers who commented implied complete confidence that heads would not abuse their powers during a teacher's search for promotion.

'If anyone phoned the head about what I had done and what I was like, I'd be prepared to take my chances. He would not be unfair.'

'I know the headmistress fairly well, and her concern would be for the member of staff to get on. Consequently she would not push too hard to stop them going or push too hard to make them go.'

'The heads I have known have been very fair. Obviously they are disappointed to see some members of staff go, but they are there to give help.'

'I found my heads were all satisfactory. They have always acted as referee and I have no reason to think they have not acted properly.

'I have never heard of a head stopping or using his influence unfairly when his staff are leaving.'

'Our head is very reluctant to lose staff; but he can see that everybody wants promotion, especially the men, and he doesn't stand in their way; he helps.'

Summary

The great majority of the teachers we interviewed believed that the head exercised considerable influence on their personal promotion, whether within the school or outside. They were content that he should have these powers, and many felt they should be increased. A quarter of the total teacher sample believed good relations with the head was a factor favouring promotion. But this is not necessarily Machiavellian as it would be a natural concomitant for a teacher to have good relations with his head if he were also competent with children, colleagues, parents and administrators.

Teachers' generally expressed trust in the head's sense of fairness and non-abuse of power. The few doubts expressed were in most cases related to hearsay about the experiences of others.

Open Advertisements: Internal and External Appointments

Few topics engendered greater feeling on the part of our interviewed teachers than that of the 'closed-open advertisement'. For these, teachers went through the whole process of applying and, sometimes, being interviewed, only to find that the result had always been a foregone conclusion, at least in their opinion. The teachers were not antagonistic to 'closed appointments' as such. It was the futility and waste of pretending they were open that was so annoying. Apart from the practical vexation, did teachers believe a case could be made for all vacancies to be completely open, i.e. nationally advertised? Were teachers in favour of some form of restriction—to the local authority's own employees, or even perhaps to the staff of the school where the vacancy occurred?

1. *Opinions of LEA officers*

We have already reported the extent to which internal promotion within schools or within an LEA was policy and practice. Most LEAs omitted any comment on the pros and cons of internal and external appointments. The comments here therefore cannot be seen as representative in any way, and serve as examples only to illustrate points of view.

(a) *In favour of internal appointments*

A number of LEA questionnaires indicated that a policy of internal appointments was encouraged. Some stated that 'All posts are advertised internally initially, and if sufficient numbers of applicants of the right calibre are not produced, then nationally'. Restriction could be effected by requiring experience within the LEA, as exemplified by 'there are service qualifications for applicants for headship: Groups

0–3, 5 years; Group 4, 8 years; Group 5 and over, 10 years.' One or two LEAs who were much in favour provided rationales for the procedure, e.g. 'Internal promotion helps to retain a corps of experienced teachers'. One LEA, while weighing the pros and cons ('The reward of long and valuable service is clearly very important, but complete exclusion of external candidates in all cases seems inadvisable'), practised the 'pros' in the primary sector where all appointments below headship were restricted to the LEA's own teachers, and headships were advertised locally in the first instance.

(b) *In favour of open advertisements*

The practical problems of small LEAs were put by one officer . . . 'Internal promotion means the choice is too small'. Wider educational implications were evoked by others . . . 'Promotion should be open in order to revitalize the service . . . the "in-breeding" which occurs when, in the service of a comparatively small LEA, promotion is confined solely to internal candidates . . . there is too little "cross-fertilization" of minds among teachers'.

(c) *Mixed feelings*

Many LEA officers were aware of the advantages and disadvantages of either open or closed systems. The benefits of a national pool of teachers from which to draw, and the cross-fertilization that new blood would bring, were balanced by the desire not to undermine the morale of local teachers, to retain an able, experienced and knowledgeable teaching force and to develop a mutual loyalty. The problem, as always, was where to draw the line. Individual LEAs placed and justified the line at widely different places between the completely open and completely closed system.

2. *Teachers' opinions*

Forty-four per cent of the 135 interviewed teachers were in favour of completely open advertisements. Sixteen per cent wanted advertising restricted initially to local advertisements. Thirty per cent wanted no advertising at all, preferring a policy of 'within school' appointments. Two-thirds of the latter group said that if no-one at the school could be found who was suitable, the post should then be advertised nationally, not just locally.

(a) *Present school staff favoured*

While comments were initially qualified by 'individual circumstances', the main feeling of both heads and teachers was expressed by one headteacher '. . . first priority to the school, second to the authority, and lastly outside'. All agreed that in the presence of a competent internal candidate 'the charade of going outside is unnecessary'. Loyalty was highly valued by some heads and teachers to such a degree that one got the impression that it should, in their opinion, intrude across competence differences that were other than stark. Among those who favoured internal appointments for competent teachers, many believed that the second stage should be national not local advertising as 'I do not think there is anything to be gained by having someone from within a fairly near radius'. A third reason advanced for internal appointments was that with only outside applications, 'this can be very disruptive in a large school and produce a large turnover'. Certainly if external appointments were the rule and promotion opportunities many, then a stable staff with all its advantages (and disadvantages) would be unlikely.

(b) *Local advertising favoured*

Those who favoured internal appointments and local advertising only argued the case for the thorough knowledge of a serving teacher a school of LEA *should* have, and a value to be placed on long service and loyalty. Another point of view was that in a large authority the pool of talent was a good as could be obtained, with very few exceptions. There was an element among teachers favouring a 'local shop' of seeking the best of both worlds, e.g. '. . . it is right that they should give me that slight touch of preference over someone else from outside. At the same time I would like to feel myself free to go outside if I wanted to'.

Some who favoured local advertising were critical of promotion within a school as 'fresh blood is needed' or because such close competition 'can be a cut-throat business'. Whatever the limitation, there was strong and unanimous feeling against advertising 'foregone conclusions'. '. . . . It's unreasonable to go through a sham of advertising the post and holding interviews, etc., when the outcome is already known.'

(c) *Open advertisements favoured*

Educational benefits and 'fairness' were the two reasons for wanting open advertisement of all promotion vacancies. A typical comment by a head was that 'the head and LEA have a duty to appoint the best staff they can get'. Some assistant teachers supported this approach, asserting that where LEAs give priority to their own employees they 'tend to get very closed-in communities. . . . the teachers never move and get into a rut . . . you never get any fresh ideas and you get very insular.'

Teachers valuing the 'fairness' of open advertisements considered that 'everybody has an equal opportunity whether inside the school, the area or outside the area . . . a teacher should be appointed solely on worth and suitability for the job. Where she comes from doesn't matter a scrap.'

Some teachers who desired 'genuinely open advertisements' were concerned that local teachers had been penalized by LEAs whose policy seemed to be to favour outsiders. How this would help is not clear, as they could have applied for the vacancy in their own school from the national advertisement in the first place. Discrimination among applicants rather than exclusion of application was obviously the true concern here '. . . I know my own authority has sometimes given great preference to outsiders. I would want to make sure it is genuine open advertisements, so that local people and particularly people in the school are given as much opportunity as anybody else'.

A few heads had been appointed from within the school. No broadly based information was available on the outcome of such appointments (in fact no study has produced *hard data* on the 'success' and problems of internal appointments at the different levels). Hence the views of our sample can only be regarded as anecdotal. One of our heads explained her change of heart about such internal appointments:

'I think it is a mistake to make promotion within the school. There was a time when I thought that this would be fair—I thought, well if you have worked in a school and you have been there years and years, and the head retires and you know just how it ought to go, then a person who is getting on in years and who is a loyal member of that staff should be given the chance of promotion. I experienced this once and it made me change my mind. It is an extremely difficult position to take up from assistant head to a head, and in this particular case—everyone had been friendly with the person who got the headship. Then he changed and we changed, and he was no longer the chap we knew across the table at dinner time and the one that you had a little moan to sometimes; he became a different person. It wasn't long before every member of staff had sought another post. I think he should have left to get his promotion, and left the school intact.'

(d) *Balancing the promotions*

Several teachers, like some LEA officers, felt there should be a balance between internal and external appointing. The common fulcrum saw senior posts being advertised nationally and the junior vacancies being offered to staff within the school 'to reward loyalty'. Alternatively these lower promotion posts should be available only within the area of the LEA because 'if they go too far and wide, it would cause a lot of dissatisfaction and too much movement or desire for movement, which is not good'. Both teachers and officers saw the needs of individual schools cutting across any general practice—'diversity within reason', as one teacher put it.

Finally, a plea for some kind of uniformity was made by one teacher, in the name of greater fairness. Both open and closed opportunities had good points, but for him it should be either one or the other. It gave teachers in 'closed' authorities two bites of the cherry. However, open advertisements with a practice of closed appointments would only increase the number of 'non' vacancies.

Summary

A large number of teachers felt that long service within a school or an authority should be rewarded 'for loyalty'. Whether long-service, in itself, is a suitable criterion for promotion is a matter of opinion. Some suggested that rewarding long service engendered a better school or corporate spirit; others that it merely encouraged insularity of outlook. Actually, long service in an area or school need not be an indication of loyalty, it might equally be dislike of personal and domestic inconvenience. The opposite extreme, that of *deliberately* selecting outsiders, would undoubtedly lower internal morale and stimulate excessive staff turnover.

Some teachers soundly reasoned that preference should be given to the present staff of a school who know the pupils and the problems. Just as reasonable is the logic of other teachers that many problems would be more likely to be reduced if a fresh outlook were imported into the school. In addition, as several teachers pointed out, internal promotion, far from generating a corporate spirit, can lead to internal recriminations and bitterness.

Open advertisement of all promotion posts suggests a little naiveté, for appointing panels may still, possibly justifiably, choose the local teacher from among the applicants. How will the unsuccessful outsiders know the appointment was genuinely open?

Obviously, a compromise between principle and practicality must be found. Teachers accept the *principle* that the best person should get the job, and this in theory means completely open advertisement. But then the *practical step* of finding out first if a member of staff, or a locally-serving teacher could fit the bill would save the unnecessary expense, time and inconvenience, and frustration that all parties endure when posts are openly advertised merely for the sake of form.

Promotion for the Classroom Teacher

The history of the Burnham settlements reveals that responsibilities additional to classroom teaching should be the chief justification for a teacher's promotion. More recently, LEAs have used the limited discretion granted them to promote and hence retain well reputed teachers without formally specifying additional duties. However, such promotions were the exceptions and not the rule. Promotion has been linked to duties additional to or even in place of normal teaching responsibilities. The particular promotion status was tied to the school and not attached personally to the teacher. In principle, if the promoted teacher moved school he lost his promoted status, but in practice he usually assumed similar or greater responsibilities and thereby maintained or enhanced his promotion level. Hence promotion is linked with increasing absence from the classroom, and the search for the 'additional responsibilities' has produced a more mobile teaching staff. In some schools this has led to excessive staff turnover and a consequent undermining of stability and continuity of the teaching within these schools.

According to our evidence, promoted staff had to satisfy appointing panels of their professional competence in the classroom as well as of their capabilities for future additional responsibilities. But where the promoted teacher has increasingly to assume non-classroom responsibilities, classroom competence may well diminish in importance, and the ability to administer, organize and get on well with colleagues might become more important considerations. While the 1971 Burnham settlement officially removed additional responsibility as a condition for promotion to all posts below deputy head or its equivalent, journal advertisements show that the responsibility is still assumed.[1]

Although teaching competence should be the most fundamental teacher quality affecting the education of pupils, it has received no formal recognition as such as a path to promotion. If it had, then like years of service and graduate allowance, more promotion would have been geared to it, rather than to features of the school. Unlike time and degrees, however, the assessment of teacher competence creates many practical problems, and fearsome professional ones. It has been suggested that the very idea of recognizing degrees of competence will cause dissension in the school. Yet college lecturers are not deterred from

[1] The principle that promotion posts should imply extra duties has in practice operated in conjunction with the other principle underlying the Burnham settlements, i.e. that the number and type of promotion posts available to a school should depend on the school's unit total. These principles, however, are not inter-dependent.

invoking such criteria when grading teaching practice, nor heads when providing 'confidentials' or references—though it must be admitted that such forms of judgment have never yet been shown to be objective. Nevertheless, it seems extraordinary, and worth investigating further, that while similarly elusive qualities like capacity for leadership, administration and management are quoted as reasons for promotion, teaching competence itself is not often invoked.

We asked all the teachers we interviewed if they believed that the present basis for promotion affected adversely those teachers who wished to remain in the classroom, thereby discouraging them from remaining classroom teachers. Of the 135 teachers, 29 did not commit themselves either way, saying they did not understand what the question referred to, despite explanation. Eighty-seven teachers (64.4 per cent) saw the present promotion system discriminating against the classroom teacher, and 19 (14.1 per cent) thought it did not. A representative selection from teachers' views is given below.

1. *No adverse effect on classroom teacher*

Some teachers thought that classroom teachers had no cause for complaint, because the present system linking promotion to additional responsibility was the correct way to approach promotion prospects: 'I think promotion should only be given for responsibility over and above teaching. . . . Teachers who want more money should take on more responsibility'. Some believed the teacher who wished to stay in the classroom did not deserve promotion because he was too insular '. . . the person who just stays inside the classroom shows a limited vision'. An acceptance of the system rather than agreement with it was voiced: 'If you want to stay in the classroom, which I do, then you obviously expect your promotion to be limited. . . . If they don't want to leave the classroom they shouldn't go in for promotion'.

Several teachers did not agree that the promoted teacher did become distant from the classroom. This view was most emphatic about small schools and the lower levels of promotion—'In small schools most of those who hold promoted posts, including heads, are classroom teachers anyhow, so the problem doesn't arise . . . certainly up to head of department, the teacher who takes on responsibility is still a classroom teacher. . . . This might be true of deputy head or senior mistress who spend half their time on administration, but most heads of department do considerable amounts of teaching'.

2. *An adverse effect on classroom teacher*

Nearly two-thirds of those interviewed thought the present system of promotion was unfair to the teacher who did not seek administrative responsibility. As one head put it, 'Classroom teachers do not get recognition until in fact they leave the classroom'. Another head thought that if you distinguished 'the classroom teacher who does not want responsibility because he wants to teach, then such teachers do have a grievance'.

Promoted and unpromoted assistant teachers believed that the system gave too little recognition to the good classroom teacher, who should 'earn as much as someone who does take on administrative responsibility'. Throughout, the comments were full of references to the 'good' teacher or teaching that merited status and financial recognition—'if a teacher is *good* in the classroom but does not wish to take up administration . . . if you are prepared to stay in the classroom, and want to, and do a *good* job . . . not just service, but *competence*. . . .' Regrettably, no-one defined good or competent, and the literature would suggest that there would be little agreement on relevant criteria which could be defined in such a way as to be quantified or even establish reliability between subjective assessors. How can the classroom teacher be rewarded for his teaching competence if there is no agreement on its precise definition or measurement?

Despite the assurances quoted earlier that promoted teachers still taught in classrooms, many teachers believed there was an increasing distance from the classroom that came with promotion—'The further you want to go, then the further away from the classroom you get. . . . It is a known fact that as you get promotion you do move out of the classroom, teaching does become less . . . (as) a head of department you still can't do as much teaching as the other members of your department, because you have got to administer it'.

The system was seen by some teachers as harmful to the profession and to the pupils—'There are absolutely first-class teachers who can be completely lost to the profession once they decide they have to get promotion. . . . We lose far too many good teachers to other fields outside the classroom itself . . . the system attracts able men out of a job that they are able at. . . . The best teachers tend to get promoted and then end up sitting in an office'.

One ungraded teacher expressed some rancour towards the promotion of a younger colleague whom he defined as 'a career teacher rather than a class teacher'. This suggests that the classroom and the career have separated, and that a group of young teachers exist who for promotion have to plan on moving between classrooms and schools and from teaching to administration to further their career.

Reorganization and the advent of large comprehensive schools have

not eased the classroom teacher's problem as some teachers had hoped—
'In my own experience, particularly in this reorganization, a great many
of the better teachers are drawn off the teaching side into the pastoral
side. . . . Reorganization is making the situation worse; you are pulling
people out of the classroom for all kinds of administrative jobs. . . . The
arrangements of posts in comprehensive schools leads to people doing
less and less classroom teaching and assuming more responsibility;
therefore the teaching load on the people remaining is increased'.

Finally, some teachers were quick to point out that the system not
only discouraged the dedicated teachers from staying in the classroom,
but positively encouraged those who *disliked* teaching—'I think a lot of
people go for promotion because they want to get out of the classroom'.

3. *Improving the classroom teacher's prospects*

While the majority of the interviewed teachers had some sympathy
with the notion that the promotion system neglected the very persons
who were most directly concerned with pupils' education, they could
offer little to mitigate the situation—'I can't suggest any way of giving
classroom teachers recognition, although they are far more valuable'.

A few thought that the normal annual financial increments would have
to suffice as the classroom teacher's incentive. Possibly an increment for
long service as such could be instituted. Such suggestions would benefit
all classroom teachers, whereas the teachers' chief concern was that it
was the specially skilled classroom teacher who was being neglected.

One teacher thought that the new Senior Teacher Scale above Scale
5 would go some way to meet the problem, but this is hardly applicable
to many teachers, as such posts can be awarded only in large secondary
schools. One head solved the problem for a classroom teacher by
'pushing' her off on a few audio-visual courses and then said she had
been taking unofficial responsibility for this feature in the school: 'If
you think hard enough you can probably think of something'.

A secondary head's suggestion was to recognize that the selected
classroom teacher's 'extra responsibility will be in his subject'. Such a
solution does not help the head or school which, under the present
system, is not allowed many posts to distribute. A number of teachers
believed there was a need for a change of approach, whereby competence
became a criterion for promotion. This did not necessarily mean eliminating responsibility as a criterion, but rather creating two routes to
promotion.

Inevitably, the teachers who suggested rewarding competence saw the
problems that would ensue regarding the assessment of a 'good' teacher.

'To give merit allowances to classroom teachers is an interesting thought, but who do you leave it up to and how do you decide who is worth another £100 ?'

'I have not thought how this could be done unless one moves in the direction of grading teaching ability, which is very difficult and slightly distasteful.'

'Well, I can't ever see it coming to anything, but I suppose the only way you could do anything about that would be to have a proper assessment system of work done in the classroom and therefore in effect be paying by results, but this seems to me that it would be so unpopular it would never get off the ground.'[1]

Other teachers were not deterred by these doubts:

'I think it would have to be done on the heads' recommendation: he should have a (competence) grade for which a man might apply, a grade that would be comparable with, say, a head of department but which would not give administrative responsibility.'

'I think that a good teacher who has had examination successes and that sort of thing—there is a case for promotion for them, in some sort of way, in recognition of this, to save them from being lost.'

'You would presumably need some continuous assessment; anybody who wanted to be promoted and remain in the classroom would have to be inspected regularly.'

'Teachers can, through proving themselves more expert at their jobs, receive extra allowances as time goes on, as happens in the public school where I taught. The headmaster and governors have the discretion to allow people to go on rising up a salary scale, almost indefinitely.'

A few teachers took the view that there would be no problem if there were no differentials, 'by having no disparity in salary between administrators and others. . . . I would like to see a kind of anti-hierarchy. I am more in favour of a general drawing-together of the wage scale'.

In addition to the opinions summarized above, mention should perhaps be made of two criticisms concerning appointment and promotion practices which did not loom large in our sample but which are known to have been made by a number of teachers. These criticisms

---

[1] Incidentally apart from success with examination pupils, this was the only definite suggestion that children's progress should be considered in assessing teacher competence.

allege that some LEAs and individual heads fail to make full use of the opportunities that the Burnham reports provide. Since 1971 the number of teachers in a school who can be promoted to the higher scales is determined by the 'points score range' for the school, which is based on the school's 'unit total'. LEAs are required to use the minimum of the points score range, but what they do beyond that is left to their discretion, and the first criticism is that some LEAs fail to take account of the particular needs of individual schools, allocating instead an intermediate 'score' to all schools or to all schools of a certain type. The second criticism is that some heads do not make full use of the score allocated to them by the LEA. An undue number of points may be kept in reserve in case they are wanted for a new recruit to the staff.

We cannot estimate the importance or justice of these criticisms on the basis of our survey, but they are included as it is known that considerable importance is given to them by some groups of teachers.

Summary

Many teachers believed that the promotion system does little to encourage teachers to stay in the classroom. As a result, competent teachers are lost from the classroom, and the children and education in general must suffer. Moreover, there is some discontent at having to leave the classroom for promotion, and resentment by those who stay in the classroom and feel their talents go unrecognized and unrewarded. Some heads and LEAs have tried to recognize such talented teachers by engineering 'posts of responsibility', but they have been limited by the numbers and range of posts allowed under Burnham settlements.

The majority of the teachers spoken to were sympathetic to the idea that teaching competence should be tangibly rewarded as a skill in its own right. The problem comes in trying to assess teaching competence and establishing which teachers deserve the accolade of 'superior' or 'master teacher'. Most teachers hesitated about implementing such an idea, while a few were fully prepared to take their chances. There are real difficulties in providing these assessments. Yet the present system of promoting to responsibility is informally based on such assessments, and while many teachers may find fault with this system, they nevertheless accept it.

Teachers being promoted at present are deemed 'superior' in some way. Should 'superiority' in teaching skill be less acceptable? Do not teachers and their employers believe that some teachers are better at teaching than others, or better at teaching in certain situations than others? They appear to believe that some teachers are better administrators than others. Is the idea so alien to any supposed code of professional conduct? Perhaps teachers are less sensitive to the idea than many believe. It might be worthwhile finding out. There are few schools where certain teachers are not particularly highly regarded. The comments of our interviewed teachers revealed, this in the frequent references to the 'best teachers', so unofficially the assessment is recognized.

Many teachers pointed out that most of the 'best teachers' are promoted from and lost to the classroom. One could argue that they exercise a wider influence, for as deputies or heads (or lecturers or inspectors) they are influencing the teaching of many more pupils than if they had remained in the classroom. If our sample are in any way representative, few teachers accept this argument.

It is vital that the issue of teacher assessments be thoroughly explored and not set aside as 'too difficult' or 'impossible to implement' even before such an inquiry is undertaken. It is essential that the teachers' associations be fully consulted. The aim would be to study the problems in depth, to examine the feasibility of different assessment methods, their acceptability, and if possible to propose and implement agreed solutions, such that teaching talent was given its full due and therefore was not, for the lack of this, lost to the education system.

SECTION IV
TEACHING AS A CAREER

CHAPTER SIXTEEN

Satisfaction and Dissatisfactions with Teaching Career

I. Questionnaire and Interviews[1]

The teachers' questionnaire listed 38 items related to aspects of teaching, and teachers were asked to select the five they thought the most satisfactory and the five considered the most unsatisfactory. Most of the analyses concerned the 'normal career' teacher, and in the present chapter this is the teacher sample referred to unless specified otherwise. The general tables, which pool primary and secondary 'votes', show the items selected by over a fifth of the sample. The remaining tables present the 'top ten' items selected by each teacher group. In looking at the percentage 'vote' it should be borne in mind that if votes were shared equally among the items (i.e. randomly) each would have a shade more than 13 per cent—that is, a five in 38 chance.

A. Satisfactions

1. General survey

Table 16.1 shows the items selected by over a fifth of all 'normal career' teachers, and the reader can see which aspects of teaching appeal to the sample as a whole.

TABLE 16.1: *Teachers' satisfaction with teaching: all teachers (normal career)*

Rank	Satisfactory item	Per cent of Sample (N = 5794)
1.	Holidays	58.1
2.	Opportunity to practice own ideas	48.2
3.	Economic security	40.4
4.	Staff-pupil relationships	38.7
5.	Working hours	37.0
6.	Staffroom relationships	34.6
7.	Time to pursue personal interests	20.3

[1] We are indebted to Dr. Jean Ross for an initial draft of this chapter.

2. School type

(a) *Primary and secondary* (Table 16.2)   Though ordered differently, the first six items were the same for both primary and secondary teachers. However, the former were more likely to give working hours as a cause of satisfaction, and regard as more satisfactory the relationships established with parents and the amount of consultation between head and staff. For secondary teachers the benefits of holidays were highly prized, and economic security was more highly valued than it was by primary teachers, and there was more satisfaction with staffroom relationships and staff-pupil relationships. In addition, the secondary rather than primary teachers were pleased with the time teaching gave them to pursue academic interests, and with the pastoral care shown to pupils.

TABLE 16.2: *Teachers' satisfactions with teaching: primary and secondary*

	PRIMARY (N = 3021)			SECONDARY (N = 2773)	
Rank	Satisfactory item	Per cent of teachers	Rank	Satisfactory item	Per cent of teachers
1.	Holidays	55.2	1.	Holidays	61.2
2.	Opportunity to practise own ideas	50.0	2.	Opportunity to practise own ideas	46.3
3.	Working hours	41.7	3.	Economic security	45.3
4.	Staff-pupil relationships	36.3	4.	Staff-pupil relationships	41.2
5.	Economic security	35.8	5.	Staffroom relationships	37.5
6.	Staffroom relationships	32.0	6.	Working hours	31.8
7.	Relationships with parents	22.3	7.	Time to pursue personal interests	21.5
8.	Head-staff consultation	21.3	8.	Pastoral care for pupils	15.6
9.	Time to pursue personal interests	19.3	9.	Time to pursue academic interests	14.7
10.	Opportunity to pursue qualifications	17.8	10.	Opportunity to pursue qualifications	14.3

(b) *Infant and junior* (Table G16.1 in supplement—see p. 14).   Overall, infant teachers spread their votes over a wider range of items than did their women colleagues in junior and junior/infant schools. Compared with teachers in infant schools, teachers in junior and junior/infant schools valued much more highly holidays (54 per cent and 66 per cent), the opportunity to practise their own ideas (50 per cent and 56 per cent) and staff-pupil relationships (33 per cent and 44 per cent).

(c) *Secondary types* (Table G16.2 in supplement—see page 17)   Holidays rated first among the satisfactions of teachers in any secondary school (61–63 per cent of votes). Grammar school teachers found the staff-pupil relationship more satisfying (50 per cent) than their colleagues in comprehensive (42 per cent) or secondary modern (36 per cent) schools, and also the staffroom relationships (grammar 46 per cent, comprehenisve 40 per cent, secondary modern 34 per cent). Working hours pleased the secondary modern teachers most (secondary modern 40 per cent, comprehensive 29 per cent, grammar 26 per cent), as did the time to pursue personal interests (secondary modern 24 per cent, comprehensive 22 per cent, grammar 16 per cent). Pastoral activities pleased the comprehensive teachers (18 per cent) more than the secondary modern (15 per cent) or grammar (12 per cent). Opportunities to pursue academic interests appealed to the grammar teachers (18 per cent) more than to the comprehensive (15 per cent) or the secondary modern (not in top ten—less than 13 per cent).

3. Sex (Tables G16.3–G16.5 in supplement)

(a) *Sex—primary teachers*   Men were more pleased than women with the time their work gave them to pursue personal interests (27 per cent and 17 per cent), and the opportunity the career offered to practise their own ideas (55 per cent and 48 per cent). Women rather than men were satisfied with working hours (46 per cent and 29 per cent) and head-staff consultation (23 per cent and 17 per cent).

(b) *Sex—secondary teachers*   Among the secondary teachers, proportionately more men than women were satisfied with the time for personal interests (28 per cent and 13 per cent), economic security (49 per cent, 41 per cent), and holidays (64 per cent and 58 per cent). Women, like primary teachers, were more satisfied than men with working hours (35 per cent, 30 per cent), but in addition they were more contented with staffroom relationships (40 per cent, 36 per cent).

The findings for sex and school sector suggest that the extremes may well be the primary woman and the secondary man.

4. Qualifications (Table G16.6 in supplement)

Holidays were paramount for all secondary teachers (non-graduate 48 per cent, graduate 50 per cent and good honours graduate 57 per cent). Non-graduates valued the working hours (30 per cent) more than

did their colleagues (graduate 25 per cent, good honours 22 per cent).
Pupil-staff relationships were more satisfying for honours graduates
(43 per cent) than for other graduates (36 per cent) or non-graduate
teachers (30 per cent), as were staffroom relationships (good honours
graduates 40 per cent, graduates 33 per cent, non-graduates 28 per cent).
Economic security was valued more by honours graduates (41 per cent
than by other graduates (38 per cent) or non-graduates (34 per cent).

5. *Age* (Tables G16.7—G16.9 in supplement)

Most of the differences among the age groups appeared to arise in the
primary sector.

(a) *Age groups—primary teachers* The significant differences found were
that the younger teachers seemed to be more satisfied than older
colleagues with holidays, working hours and the opportunity to practise
their own ideas, while the older teachers were more pleased than
younger teachers regarding head-staff consultations and relationships
with parents.

(b) *Age groups—secondary teachers* The chief differences among secondary age groups were: younger rather than older teachers were satisfied
with holidays, and older rather than younger were satisfied with the
pastoral care given pupils and with economic security.

6. *Present post*

In Tables 16.3 and 16.4 the lists of ranked items are shown for
primary and secondary post-holders respectively. In each case, three
groups were compared—heads, other promoted teachers, and ungraded
teachers (now Scale 1).

Satisfaction with holidays and working hours was greatest among the
unpromoted teachers and least among the heads of both primary and
secondary sectors. Probably with promotion comes encroachment of
responsibility into both 'free' time and holidays. Among *primary*
teachers, the promoted teachers felt more satisfied than the unpromoted
about relationships with parents and the time allowed to pursue further
qualifications. *Secondary* teachers differed in that the promoted rather
than the unpromoted were pleased with economic security, head-staff
consultations (only 7.6 per cent of unpromoted selected this item),
staff-pupil relationships and pastoral care given pupils. Heads in
particular were more satisfied than others with the opportunities offered
to teachers to practise their own ideas, and the time allowed to pursue
academic interests.

TABLE 16.3: *Teachers' satisfactions with teaching: present status (primary)*

	UNPROMOTED (N = 1582)	Per cent of Teachers		PROMOTED ASSISTANTS (N = 826)	Per cent of Teachers		HEADS (N = 461)	Per cent of Teachers
Rank	Satisfactory Item		Rank	Satisfactory Item		Rank	Satisfactory Item	
1.	Holidays	58.6	1.	Holidays	56.9	1.	Opportunity to practise own ideas	52.7
2.	Opportunity to practise own ideas	49.7	2.	Opportunity to practise own ideas	50.8	2.	Holidays	43.8
3.	Working hours	47.5	3.	Economic security	37.8	3.	Economic security	35.8
4.	Staff-pupil relationships	37.6	4.	Working hours	37.5	4.	Staff-pupil relationships	34.3
5.	Economic security	35.4	5.	Staff-pupil relationships	36.8	5.	Relationships with parents	32.5
6.	Staffroom relationships	31.7	6.	Staffroom relationships	35.7	6.	Staffroom relationships	28.2
7.	Head-staff consultations	19.7	7.	Head-staff consultations	26.3	7.	Working hours	27.8
8.	Time to pursue personal interests	19.4	8.	Relationships with parents	25.3	8.	Opportunity to pursue qualifications	23.0
9.	Relationships with parents	18.7	9.	Time to pursue personal interests	20.5	9.	Head-staff consultations	21.3
10.	Opportunity to pursue qualifications	16.9	10.	Opportunity to pursue qualifications	17.4	10.	Time to pursue personal interests	18.4

TABLE 16.4: *Teachers' satisfactions: present status (secondary)*

	UNPROMOTED (N = 802) (Present Scale 1)		PROMOTED ASSISTANTS (N = 1788) (Present Scales 2–5/Deputy head)		HEADS (N = 83)	
Rank	Satisfactory Item	Per cent of Teachers	Satisfactory Item	Per cent of Teachers	Satisfactory Item	Per cent of Teachers
1.	Holidays	66.6	Holidays	60.7	Economic security	63.9
2.	Opportunity to practise own ideas	46.3	Economic security	48.9	Opportunity to practise own ideas	60.2
3.	Working hours	38.9	Opportunity to practise own ideas	46.7	Holidays	56.6
4.	Economic security	38.3	Staff-pupil relationships	43.7	Staff-pupil relationships	51.8
5.	Staffroom relationships	38.3	Staffroom relationships	38.2	Pastoral care for pupils	39.8
6.	Staff-pupil relationships	38.2	Working hours	29.5	Staffroom relationships	37.3
7.	Time to pursue personal interests	22.2	Time to pursue personal interests	21.7	Working hours	26.5
8.	Opportunity to pursue qualifications	15.6	Pastoral care for pupils	16.7	Head-staff consultations	25.3
9.	Time to pursue academic interests	13.7	Time to pursue academic interests	15.2	Time to pursue academic interests	25.3
10.	Pastoral care for pupils	11.3	Head-staff consultations	14.3	Time to pursue personal interests	19.3

7. *Career type* (Tables G16.10—G16.15 in supplement)

It was thought that satisfaction might vary among teachers according to whether they were 'normal career' teachers, re-entrants or late entrants. While there was considerable agreement, late entrants were more satisfied with the opportunity to practise their own ideas (50 per cent) than were re-entrants (43 per cent), though similar to 'normals' (48 per cent) in this. Working hours were less appealing (31 per cent) for late entrants than re-entrants (42 per cent) or normals (37 per cent). An interesting group, late entrant secondary women, did not rank holidays as the most satisfactory item—in fact it was 10th with 6.5 per cent. Apart from this, the popularity of other aspects followed the usual pattern.

B. *Dissatisfactions*

1. *General survey*

There were only five items among the 38 'possibles' that were selected by over a fifth of all the 'normal career' teachers (N = 5794) as unsatisfactory. Two items stood out above all others—class size (49.2 per cent) and the professions's status in society (49.0 per cent). The other three were school/classroom accommodation (27.5 per cent), promotion prospects (23.0 per cent) and extent of non-professional work (21.0 per cent).

2. *Primary and secondary* (Table 16.5)

Far more primary than secondary teachers were dissatisfied with the size of classes, with the general accommodation in the school and classroom, and with the supervision of students by their tutors. Secondary teachers were significantly less happy about the influences of external examinations, pupil discipline, and school equipment.

3. *School types* (Tables G16.16 and 17 in supplement)

(a) *Primary* (women only)   The two groups were very similar. Eight out of ten infant teachers and seven out of ten junior or junior/infant teachers listed class size as unsatisfactory. Next was the status of teaching, with half of each group of teachers. Next was the school/classroom accommodation listed by four out of ten teachers.

(b) *Secondary*   Status, presumably the lack of it, was of concern to half of each group of secondary teachers. Class size irritated more than a third of comprehensive and secondary modern teachers, but only a quarter of their grammar school colleagues. Physical conditions upset

25 per cent of grammar teachers, 21 per cent of secondary modern teachers and 18 per cent of comprehensive teachers. Textbooks and equipment problems for comprehensives (18 per cent and 19 per cent) and grammar teachers (21 per cent and 20 per cent) did not appear

TABLE 16.5: *Teachers' dissatisfaction with teaching: primary and secondary*

	PRIMARY (N = 3021)			SECONDARY (N = 2773)	
Rank	Unsatisfactory Item	Per cent of teachers	Rank	Unsatisfactory Item	Per cent of teachers
1.	Class size	62.6	1.	Status of profession in society	50.7
2.	Status of profession in society	47.4	2.	Class size	34.7
3.	School/classroom accommodation	34.5	3.	Influence of external examinations	24.7
4.	Student supervision by tutors	22.8	4.	Promotion prospects	23.5
5.	Promotion prospects	22.5	5.	Extent of non-professional work	22.1
6.	Inter-school consultation	21.7	6.	School/classroom accommodation	19.9
7.	Extent of non-professional work	20.1	7.	Inter-school consultation	17.6
8.	Staffroom accommodation	17.9	8.	Pupil discipline	17.4
9.	Interruptions to lessons	15.6	9.	Textbooks	16.5
10.	Textbooks	14.1	10.	Equipment	15.5

among the top ten dissatisfactions of secondary modern teachers (less than 13 per cent) who felt interruptions to lessons more crucial (18 per cent), whilst this 'did not rate' for comprehensive and grammar teachers. Discipline, a problem for 20 per cent of teachers in secondary modern and comprehensive schools, did not draw complaint from one in seven grammar teachers.

4. *Sex* (Tables G16.18–G16.20 in supplement)

(a) *Sex—primary teachers* Relatively more men than women were dissatisfied with the profession's status (54.3 per cent against 45.1 per cent) and with promotion prospects (24.2 per cent against 21.9 per cent). Women rather than men were unhappy about the size of classes (65.2 per cent, 55.3 per cent).

(b) *Sex—secondary teachers*   As with primary teachers, men were more discontented than women with the profession's status in society (men 55.7 per cent, women 43.7 per cent) and with promotion prospects (men 27.0 per cent, women 18.7 per cent). The only other difference of note was that 18.0 per cent of women thought lesson interruptions an unsatisfactory aspect compared with 11.3 per cent of men.

5. *Qualifications* (Table G16.21 in supplement)

The differences in dissatisfactions found among graduates and non-graduates in secondary schools follow, but in interpreting them one must remember that certain groups will be under greater pressure than others from specific items. For example, it is much more likely that a graduate will be preparing children for GCE 'O' and 'A' levels and hence be more aware of the required syllabus than his non-graduate colleague (even allowing for CSE involvement).

Influence of external examinations: Good honours graduates, 25.2 per cent; 'ordinary' graduate, 20.2 per cent; non-graduate, 18.4 per cent.

Extent of non-professional work: Good honours graduate, 22.8 per cent; 'ordinary' graduate, 22.3 per cent; non-graduate, 15.7 per cent.

Promotion prospects: Non-graduate, 21.5 per cent; good honours graduate, 17.2 per cent; 'ordinary' graduate, 16.7 per cent.

6. *Age* (Tables G16.22—G16.24 in supplement)

(a) *Age groups: primary teachers*   Among the primary teachers, dissatisfaction was felt more by older teachers than younger concerning promotion prospects, the profession's status and interruptions to lessons. The oldest group were not as dissatisfied with the extent of non-professional work as other groups were.

(b) *Age groups: secondary teachers*   The older rather than younger teachers were dissatisfied with the profession's status, class size and pupil discipline, only the oldest groups registering strong dissatisfaction with interruption to lessons. The influence of external examinations was selected as an unsatisfactory item by younger teachers more than by older.

7. *Present post*

(a) *Present post: primary teachers* (Table 16.6)   Dissatisfactions with class size was remarkably different across the groups. Least irritated were the unpromoted teachers (29 per cent) and most concerned were the promoted assistants (71 per cent). Both would still be in the primary

TABLE 16.6: *Teachers' dissatisfaction with teaching: present status (primary)*

	UNPROMOTED (N = 1582) (Present Scale 1)		PROMOTED ASSISTANTS (N = 826) (Present Scales 2–5/Deputy Head)		HEADS (N = 461)	
Rank	Unsatisfactory Item	Per cent of Teachers	Unsatisfactory Item	Per cent of Teachers	Unsatisfactory Item	Per cent of Teachers
1.	Status of profession in society	40.2	Class size	70.5	Status of profession in society	62.5
2.	School/classroom accommodation	33.2	Status of profession in society	55.1	Class size	51.2
3.	Class size	29.0	School/classroom accommodation	35.7	School/classroom accommodation	38.0
4.	Promotion prospects	23.6	Student supervision by tutors	25.4	Extent of non-professional work	29.1
5.	Inter-school consultation	20.9	Inter-school consultation	23.8	Student supervision by tutors	28.2
6.	Student supervision by tutors	20.7	Promotion prospects	23.6	Staffroom accommodation	22.6
7.	Extent of non-professional work	18.3	Extent of non-professional work	19.4	Inter-school consultation	20.8
8.	Staffroom accommodation	18.1	Interruption to lessons	17.2	Interruptions to lessons	18.9
9.	Textbooks	14.9	Staffroom accommodation	16.0	Promotion prospects	18.2
10.	Interruptions to lessons	14.3	Guidance by advisers	15.5	Guidance by advisers	15.6

classroom, but the latter would have duties additional to teaching to perform. Class size is of dramatically less concern to the purely classroom teacher than to those who supervise her! Dissatisfaction with the status of the profession increased with promotional level, being 50 per cent higher in primary heads than among their unpromoted colleagues. Other significant differences were that proportionately more promoted than ungraded teachers were dissatisfied with supervision of students by their tutors, and heads were more disturbed than others regarding the extent of non-professional work.

(b) *Present post: secondary teachers* (Table 16.7) Class size irritated a third of classroom teachers but nearly half of heads—distance from the classroom accentuating the issue perhaps. However, the striking difference is the growing concern (with rank) for the lack of status of secondary teaching—doubling from the unpromoted teacher 41 per cent) to his/her head (82 per cent). Why ? Promoted secondary teachers also expressed significantly greater dissatisfaction about the extent of non-professional work and staffroom accommodation (only 11.7 per cent of the unpromoted listed this as unsatisfactory). Both heads and ungraded teachers appeared to be more dissatisfied with textbooks than were teachers holding promotion posts below headship.

8. *Career type* (Tables G16.25—G16.30 in supplement)

Overall, it was only dissatisfaction with the status of the profession that distinguished re-entrants (56 per cent) from late entrants (45 per cent). Over two thirds of re-entrants and late entrants in the primary sector listed class size, with late entrant men lowest (60 per cent) and late entrant women highest (73 per cent). In the secondary sector the low prestige irritated 62 per cent of re-entrants and only 49 per cent of late entrants (late entrant women seemed to have little to complain about, the most frequent item, status, only drawing a 39 per cent vote).

C. *Why teach?* (*The interviewed teachers*)

Of the 117 teachers who gave a reason for choosing a teaching career, the largest group (32 teachers—27.4 per cent) liked children. The second largest group (18—15.4 per cent) said there were no positive reasons—it was a case of 'drifting in'. The limited openings elsewhere persuaded 14 teachers (12 per cent). Other reasons offered by smaller groups covered a miscellaneous range, e.g. family/friends' connection with the profession, long holidays, security, previous youth work, better financial reward, and the straightforward 'always wanted to be a teacher'. Two teachers thought it was a job 'worth doing'.

TABLE 16.7: *Teachers' dissatisfaction with teaching: present status (secondary)*

	UNPROMOTED (N = 802) (Present Scale 1)		PROMOTED ASSISTANTS (N = 1788) (Present Scales 2–5/Deputy Head)		HEADS (N = 83)	
Rank	Unsatisfactory Item	Per cent of Teachers	Unsatisfactory Item	Per cent of Teachers	Unsatisfactory Item	Per cent of Teachers
1.	Status of profession in society	40.5	Status of profession in society	55.3	Status of profession in society	81.9
2.	Class size	32.8	Class size	35.6	Class size	47.0
3.	Influence of external examinations	25.3	Influence of external examinations	25.0	Extent of non-professional work	26.1
4.	Promotion prospects	25.1	Extent of non-professional work	23.7	School/classroom accommodation	28.9
5.	Textbooks	21.1	Promotion prospects	23.5	Influence of external examinations	25.3
6.	School/classroom accommodation	19.3	School/classroom accommodation	20.4	Textbooks	21.7
7.	Extent of non-professional work	18.8	Inter-school consultation	18.0	Pupil discipline	21.7
8.	Head-staff consultation	18.2	Pupil discipline	17.6	Staffroom accommodation	20.5
9.	Equipment	17.8	Interruptions to lessons	15.0	Interruptions to lessons	19.3
10.	Pupil discipline	17.7	Staffroom accommodation	14.9	Promotion prospects	16.9
11.			Textbooks	14.5		

While 36 (26.7 per cent) were non-committal, 96 (71.1 per cent) of the 135 interviewed teachers thought their decision to teach had been justified in terms of their general satisfaction. In answer to the question that possibly revealed more than anything else their feelings about the career, viz. 'If starting again, would you choose teaching as a career?', their replies were as follows: 20 (15 per cent) were undecided, 11 (eight per cent) gave an unqualified 'No', and 104 (77 per cent) said 'Yes'. Of the latter, 75 (55.5 per cent) did so without reservation and 29 (21.5 per cent) added a rider such as 'I'd like to get experience in another job first', 'But I'd choose another subject', 'But I'm still not happy about the poor pay'.

II. Following in Parents' Footsteps (Tables G16.31–G16.34 in supplement)

Other researches by Nisbet (1956) and Start (1967, 1973) have attempted to discover how teachers feel about their chosen profession, by asking if they would recommend it for their own children. In the teacher questionnaire we asked (Q.34) whether the teacher would *encourage* his own children (or any hypothetical children) to take up teaching as a career. Eighty-seven per cent of teachers answered either yes or no, and 13 per cent qualified their replies—'Yes, if . . . No, unless . . .' The question listed sons and daughters separately, and the analysis of the data was confined to those teachers who had followed a 'normal career'.

1. *The general position*

The views of the sample as a whole can be gauged from the figures in Table 16.8, under the column for all teachers. There was an unmistakable preference among the sample that daughters rather than sons should take up teaching.

Over three-quarters of the sample said they would not encourage their sons to choose teaching as a career, although one must not conclude from this that teachers would actively discourage their sons from the career. The position was almost reversed where daughters were concerned. Over two-thirds of the sample would encourage their daughters to follow a career in teaching.

2. *Primary and secondary teachers*

There was little difference between the two school types in the teachers' views (Table 16.8). Both primary and secondary teachers revealed the same attitudes as for the whole sample—much greater

TABLE 16.8: *Encouragement to children to choose a teaching career: all teachers and school type*

CHILDREN	ALL TEACHERS (Prim. & Sec.)			PRIMARY			SECONDARY		
		Per cent who would			Per cent who would			Per cent who would	
	N	Encourage	Not encourage	N	Encourage	Not encourage	N	Encourage	Not encourage
Son	5042	23.7	76.3	2632	23.4	76.6	2410	24.0	76.0
Daughter	5065	67.8	32.2	2644	70.7	29.3	2421	64.6	35.4

χ^2 All differences between son and daughter significant at 0.1 per cent confidence level stress on encouraging daughters (two-thirds) rather than sons (one-quarter). There was a tendency for primary teachers to encourage daughters more (71 per cent) than secondary teachers (65 per cent).

3. Sex (Table 16.9)

While both women and men appeared to favour a career in teaching for their daughters (68 per cent and 67 per cent respectively), only 20 per cent of women wanted it for their sons, compared with 29 per cent of men. Evidently women are even less enthusiastic about teaching as a career for a man than the man himself.

TABLE 16.9: *Encouragement to children to choose a teaching career: men and women (primary plus secondary)*

| | MEN | | | WOMEN | | |
| | | *Per cent who would* | | | *Per cent who would* | |
CHILDREN	N	En-courage	Not en-courage	N	En-courage	Not en-courage
Son	2145	28.7	71.3	2897	20.0	80.0
Daughter	2149	67.3	32.7	2916	68.1	31.9

χ^2 Difference between men and women for *Son* significant at 0.1 per cent confidence level.

Roughly the same pattern was seen among primary men and women as in the whole sample, and secondary men felt as did primary men. Secondary women were the least happy about a teaching career—for both men and women. Only 17 per cent said they would encourage their sons, and 62 per cent their daughters.

4. Age groups

We compared four groups—under 30 years, 30–39 years, 40–49 years and over 49 years.

(a) *Primary* All four age groups would encourage a daughter towards a teaching career but not a son.

Whereas between 72 per cent and 74 per cent of the three oldest groups would *not* encourage their sons, this attitude was more firmly held (83 per cent) by the under-30 group, of whom only 17 per cent said they would encourage a son towards a teaching career. This disfavour towards a teaching career for a son was felt even more by the young women than the young men.

The enthusiasm for a daughter to undertake a teaching career waned slightly with the oldest groups. Seventy-one per cent of the under-30 group favoured the career for daughters and 77 per cent of the 30–39 group. This encouragement dropped to 69 per cent of the 40–49 group and to 64 per cent of those who had been teaching longest.

Four out of five young primary teachers viewed a career in teaching for men with a disfavour which became slightly less (seven out of 10) once the initial years of teaching were over. Teaching is seen as a satisfactory career for women by three-quarters of primary teachers, though once middle-age is reached only two out of three teachers remain enthusiastic.

(b) *Secondary*   Again three-quarters of each age group were not enthusiastic about a teaching career for a son. This time both the youngest and the oldest were least keen.

Nearly 70 per cent of the 30–39 years secondary teachers said they would encourage their daughters towards a teaching career, but the figure dropped to 65 per cent for the 40–49 group and to 56 per cent for the over-49 group. In this, secondary and primary teachers thought alike—the oldest teachers generally thought less of teaching as a career for their daughters.

5. *Present post*

Status made little difference to the teacher's viewpoint.

(a) *Primary*   The proportion of teachers who said they would encourage a son to teach was low for all status groups—21 per cent for ungraded teachers, 26 per cent for promoted assistants, and 28 per cent for heads. Ungraded women teachers were even less enthusiastic than ungraded men teachers. For all status groups the proportion encouraging a daughter to teach was relatively high—between 68 per cent and 72 per cent.

(b) *Secondary*   The encouragement to sons was again low, 20 per cent among the ungraded teachers, 25 per cent for promoted assistants and 31 per cent among the head teachers. Once more, the ungraded women were even less encouraging than the ungraded men. The wish for a daughter to take up teaching was comparatively strong—between 62 per cent and 71 per cent.

6. *Summary*

Teachers would not encourage their sons to make a career in teaching, but would their daughters. This was one of the few findings throughout this report where teachers were fairly unanimous. Older teachers seemed less sure that it was even a satisfactory career for women, and women teachers believed even more strongly than men that it was not a satisfactory career for their sons. The extreme position would be held by an ungraded, young, female secondary teacher. If these attitudes influence the career decisions of their offspring, there will be few sons of teachers among the next generation of teachers.

III. Teacher Turnover and Wastage: Leavers and Dissatisfaction

Teachers may leave school to take another position inside or outside the school system. To leave teaching almost certainly implies dissatisfaction. Leaving one school for another usually implies the latter has more to satisfy the teacher. Hence teacher movement can be an informative source of data on satisfaction.

We asked heads to list the teachers on their staff who had left their school between Easter 1970 and Easter 1971, and to state where they had gone (if this was known). This incidentally provided a one-year snapshot of staff turnover.

1. *Number of teachers leaving*

Seven hundred and ninety-nine heads answered the relevant question, and reported that 1598 teachers left the schools during the preceding year—exactly two teachers per school. Our original records showed that the average number of full-time staff for all types of school pooled together was 11.2. In other words, one in every five to six teachers had left the schools that year.

The rates of turnover may be of greater interest if made to refer to the different school types, and these data are shown in Table 16.10.

It would seem that in our sampled primary schools, a fifth of the staff left during the year, and in the secondary schools slightly fewer—about a sixth. The leaving rate was somewhat higher in grammar schools (one teacher in 5.7) than in modern (one in 6.3) or in comprehensive schools (one in 6.8 teachers), perhaps leaving for promotion posts in newly formed or expanding comprehensives.

Fifty-seven per cent of the teachers who left their schools merely crossed over to other schools, 55 per cent to the maintained sector. A relatively small proportion (3.5 per cent) moved into other educational work. This means that nearly 40 per cent left the educational scene completely—whether for retirement, domestic or other reasons. After retirement, the largest cause, emigration took one in 20 of those leaving a school. Some of these might subsequently return. How did this turnover vary with school type?

Obviously the fact that infant teachers were almost all women accounted for the higher level of domestic destinations of infant leavers. The low level of administrative/advisory work among junior leavers' destinations and its complete absence as a destination for the other

TABLE 16.10: *Turnover of full-time staff in 1970–71*

SCHOOL TYPE	Average full-time complement of staff in 1971	Average number of full-time staff who left in 1970-71	Percentage leavers of camplement
Infant	7.3	1.3	17.8
Junior–Infant	6.5	1.2	18.5
Junior	10.3	2.3	22.3
All Primary	7.5	1.5	20.0
Modern	21.5	3.4	15.8
Comprehensive	43.4	6.4	14.7
Grammar	32.5	5.7	17.5
All Secondary	29.6	4.6	15.5

teacher types was a little surprising. The 1.8 per cent going on to lecturing work would hopefully train future generations of teachers in the realities of infant and junior method.

2. *Destination of teachers who left* (Table 16.11)

TABLE 16.11: *Destination of teachers who left schools in* 1970–71

DESTINATION	PER CENT OF TEACHERS WHO LEFT IN 1970–71 (N = 1598)
Another maintained school	54.7
Domestic commitment	16.2
Retirement	11.0
Emigration	5.7
Non-educational field	4.6
Independent/Direct Grant School	2.4
Unknown	1.9
College/University Lecturer	1.6
Further Education Lecturer	1.3
Administration/Inspectorate	0.6

TABLE 16.12: *Destination of teachers who left schools in 1970–71: primary school type*

INFANT LEAVERS (N = 171)		JUNIOR–INFANT LEAVERS (N = 464)		JUNIOR LEAVERS (N = 340)	
Destination	Per cent	Destination	Per cent	Destination	Per cent
Another maintained school	47.4	Another maintained school	55.8	Another maintained school	60.9
Domestic	26.3	Domestic	16.3	Domestic	17.3
Retirement	11.1	Retirement	15.5	Retirement	8.8
Emigration	5.2	Emigration	5.8	Emigration	4.4
Non-educational work	4.1	Non-educational work	2.4	Non-educational work	2.6
Unknown	2.3	Direct Grant/ Indep. school	2.4	Direct Grant/ Indep. school	1.8
College/University Lecturer	1.8	College/University Lecturer	0.9	College/University Lecturer	1.8
Direct Grant/ Indep. school	1.8	Unknown	0.9	Unknown	1.8
				Administrative/ Adviser	0.6

TABLE 16.13: *Destination of teachers who left schools in 1970–71: secondary school type*

MODERN LEAVERS (N = 249)		COMPREHENSIVE LEAVERS (N = 244)		GRAMMAR LEAVERS (N = 130)	
Destination	Per cent	Destination	Per cent	Destination	Per cent
Another maintained school	52.6	Another maintained school	56.6	Another maintained school	44.6
Domestic	13.3	Domestic	12.3	Domestic	12.3
Non-educational work	8.5	Retirement	9.0	Retirement	10.0
Retirement	7.6	Emigration	7.8	Non-educational work	9.2
Emigration	5.2	Non-educational work	5.8	Direct Grant/ Indep. school	6.2
Further Education Lecturer	4.0	Direct Grant/ Indep. school	3.3	Emigration	6.2
College/University Lecturer	4.0	Further Education Lecturer	2.0	Further Education Lecturer	4.6
Unknown	2.8	Unknown	1.6	Unknown	3.9
Direct Grant/ Indep. school	1.2	Administrative/ Adviser	1.2	Administrative/ Adviser	1.5
Administrative/ Adviser	0.8	College/University Lecturer	0.4	College/University Lecturer	1.5

Among the secondary leavers, there appeared a relatively large number who took up non-educational work. The administrative/advisory filed claimed few of the leavers, but emigration increased (1/19 secondary modern, 1/16 grammar and 1/13 comprehensive). Secondary modern schools provided proportionately more college/university lecturers than comprehensive and grammar schools. There was a steady loss of grammar teachers to the direct grant and independent schools, perhaps in search of the academic tradition they might have felt to be threatened by the move to non-selective comprehensive schools in this period.

3. *Future plans and present dissatisfactions*

What dissatisfactions with teaching did those who had expressed a desire to leave teaching voice in the teachers' questionnaires? We examined four groups of teachers: (1) those who wished to do other educational work, as in lecturing at college or the advisory service or youth employment; (2) those who wished to take up work not connected with education or who wanted to emigrate; (3) those who wanted to retire (normally or prematurely); and, as a reference point for comparison, (4) those who wished to continue teaching in schools. The analyses looked at primary and secondary teachers separately, and were confined to 'normal career' teachers only.

(a) *Primary teachers* (Table G16.35 in supplement) There were remarkable similarities in the dissatisfactions of those leaving and those staying—in fact across all four groups. There were marginal differences, sometimes in the 'wrong direction', such as departing teachers being less fed-up with promotion chances than those who remained. In most areas of dissatisfaction the remaining teachers expressed stronger views than those who were leaving.

(b) *Secondary teachers* (Table G16.36 in supplement) Within two or three per cent and two or three ranks the dissatisfactions of teachers leaving and remaining in the profession were similar. One of the exceptions was pupil discipline, which had 26.4 per cent of the dissatisfaction vote of the group leaving for other work or emigrating, compared with 17 per cent for those remaining and those entering other educational work, and 20 per cent for retirements. The other was lack of staff consultation mentioned by 21 per cent of those leaving for other work, 15 per cent of those entering another educational post, 10 per cent of retirements and 14 per cent of those remaining in the classroom. Lack of promotion prospects was of more concern for those remaining in education (24 per cent teaching, 27 per cent other educational work) than those leaving (16 per cent other work, 17 per cent retirements).

SECTION V
THE FUTURE

CHAPTER SEVENTEEN

Future Plans: Aspirations and Expectations

In the teacher questionnaire we asked teachers about their career aspirations. How realistic these were may be seen by comparison with the promotion structure we found.

The Data Collected

Teachers were asked what position they would *like* to hold in 10 years' time, from among 26 possible choices, both in and out of schools; and then which of the 26 posts he *expected* to hold in 10 years' time. In retrospect some of the 26 choices were combined. For example, we grouped related non-school posts which were chosen infrequently; Lecturer in Further Education, in College of Education and in University were all categorized as 'lecturer'. Similarly, to emphasize the future at a time when the career structure was changing, posts which in the questionnaire were identified under the old promotion structure were combined to present a picture in terms of the new. As a result the 26 choices have been combined to make 11 'posts' for primary teachers and 14 for secondary teachers.

When looking at the whole sample, the 26 posts were reduced to seven. Six of these covered non-school intentions, and only one covered all teaching in schools. The combined groups are: *Teaching in schools*, including all posts from unpromoted assistant to head of large school; *Lecturer*, including work in further education, college or university; *Administration*, including educational administration in LEA departments and work in the inspectorate (HMI or LEA); *Related educational work*, including child guidance, educational psychology, educational research, youth employment service and 'other educational work'; *Non-educational/emigrate*, comprising employment outside education and plans to emigrate (this last category may have included plans to teach overseas permanently). The other two categories were retirement and 'don't know'.

The analysis that follows is confined entirely to the sample of 'normal career' teachers, except where indicated otherwise.

All Teachers

The figures in Table 17.1 provide a summary of the hopes and expectations of the sample as a whole regarding their jobs ten years hence.

TABLE 17.1: *Teachers' aspirations and expectations—all teachers (primary plus secondary) given as a percentage of 5970 teachers*

	ASPIRATION		EXPECTATION	
ACTIVITY	Rank	Per cent	Rank	Per cent
Teaching in schools	1	58.8	1	67.0
Retirement	2	10.1	2	13.3
Lecturer	3	9.3	4	4.5
Don't know	4	7.8	3	7.9
Related educational work	4	5.4	6	1.9
Administration	6	4.9	7	1.4
Non-educational/emigrate	7	3.7	5	4.0

About one in every 13 teachers (eight per cent) expressed no definitive aspiration or expectation for the future, but 92 per cent seemed to know what they wanted and expected.

Nearly 59 per cent wished to remain as teachers in school, but an additional eight per cent expected to be there though they would have liked to be elsewhere. This could well have been lecturing, where the expectation was less than half the aspiration, or administration and related educational work where the same ratio was one-third. Three-point-two per cent more teachers expected to have retired than wished to, and these perhaps would be those who in 10 years time would be eligible for early retirement at 60 and would prefer that to not getting suitable promotion in the schools or into other educational fields.

About one-fifth wished to retain some connection with educational work but only one-thirteenth expected to do so. Only about four per cent wanted and expected to leave the educational scene in this country, and these would include women who wished to devote themselves full-time to a family.

Whatever satisfactions or dissatisfactions may have been expressed about teaching as a career, and whatever encouragement or discouragement to offspring may be given to take up a teaching career, four out of five teachers wanted either to stay as teachers in schools (three-fifths) or to be employed in work connected with education (one-fifth). The three-fifths who wished to remain in the classroom (and the two-thirds who expected to) might be inadequate to meet the demand for teachers. But other educational fields often—and teachers may well say rightly—demand teaching experience as a qualification, hence must 'poach' from the schools (school inspectors, college lecturers, educational researchers, child guidance personnel). The desire of teachers to stay in teaching (or near to it), taken with their expressions of strong dissatisfaction with some aspects of the occupation, suggests that the grievances of the profession are at least to some extent balanced by the satisfactions.

Primary and Secondary Teachers

From Table 17.2 the reader may see the spread of aspirations and expectations within the primary and secondary samples. These can be compared with each other and with the percentage of teachers in the survey who actually held each of the aspired levels.

1. *Primary teachers*

Among primary teachers more than 62 per cent intended remaining in teaching, though 40 per cent aspired to head (25.7 per cent) or deputy (14.3 per cent) positions. Nearly seven per cent wanted no responsibility, wishing to remain on Scale 1 (a further seven per cent *expected* not to be promoted from the bottom scale in the next 10 years). One in seven primary teachers would have liked to leave the classroom for other educational work. Expectation showed the awareness of reality, with fewer expecting to land one of the top jobs—heads (20.5 per cent) and deputies (13.0 per cent). Those expecting to be in the classroom were at 34.6 per cent. some 12.3 per cent more than had wished to be there. Of those aspiring to other educational work nearly two-thirds did not expect to get it, and four per cent more expected to retire than wished to.

Just as the aspirations of primary teachers were higher than their expectations, so were the expectations higher, though not dramatically, than the reality of what seemed likely to be available. Twenty-five point seven per cent would have liked headships, 20.5 per cent expected them and 16 per cent would probably get them. At the level of deputy 14.3 per cent had hopes, 13 per cent expected and 10 per cent should be satisfied. For Scales 2/3 the figures were 16, 21 and 18.

2. *Secondary teachers*

Fifty-five per cent of secondary teachers wished to remain in the schools, but 66 per cent expected to be there. Twelve per cent hoped for

TABLE 17.2: *The aspirations and expectations of primary and secondary teachers*

	PRIMARY					SECONDARY				
	Aspirations		Expectations		Reality	Aspirations		Expectations		Reality
DESCRIPTION	Rank	Per cent	Rank	Per cent	Per cent	Rank	Per cent	Rank	Per cent	Per cent
Head (G7 & over)	—	—	—	—	—	6	8.1	7	5.1	—
Head (below G7)	—	—	—	—	—	11	3.7	12	1.8	—
Head (G3 and over)	1	19.8	2	16.8	—	—	—	—	—	—
Head (below G3)	8	5.9	7	3.7	—	—	—	—	—	—
ALL HEADS		25.7		20.5	16		11.8		6.9	5
Deputy (G7 & over)	—	—	—	—	—	5	8.5	6	7.2	—
Deputy (below G7)	—	—	—	—	—	12	2.3	13	1.6	—
DEPUTY HEADS	3	14.3	5	13.0	10		10.8		8.8	6
Teacher (Scale 5)	—	—	—	—	—	3	11.9	2	11.7	6
Teacher (Scale 3/4)	—	—	—	—	—	1	18.7	1	32.5	36
Teacher (Scale 2/3)	2	15.5	1	20.8	18	—	—	—	—	—
Teacher (Scale 2)	—	—	—	—	—	14	0.8	9	3.8	—
Teacher (Scale 1)	6	6.8	4	13.8	—	13	0.9	10	2.3	19
ALL TEACHERS		62.3		68.1			54.9		66.0	
Related Educ. Work	7	6.1	10	1.8		9	4.7	11	1.9	
Lecturer	9	4.2	9	1.9		2	14.8	5	7.2	
Administration	10	4.0	11	1.4		8	5.8	14	1.5	
OTHER EDUCATION		14.3		5.1			25.3		10.6	
Retire	4	11.2	3	15.1		4	8.9	3	11.3	
Don't know	5	9.2	6	8.5		7	6.2	4	7.3	
Non-education/emigrate	11	3.0	8	3.2		10	4.6	8	4.8	

headships but only seven per cent expected them. Eleven per cent wanted and nine per cent expected deputy headships, though the hopes and expectations at Scale 5 level were the same (12 per cent). The 'disappointed' heads, deputy heads and lecturers presumably expect to fill up the higher teaching scales, particularly scales 3/4 where 14 per cent *more* expected to be at that rank than hoped to be (19 per cent). Less than half the teachers hoping to be in other educational activities expected to be there (25 per cent and 11 per cent). Among this group lecturing seemed a popular activity, with one in seven of all secondary teachers aspiring to it. More retirements were expected than wished for. However, only two per cent of secondary teachers expected to be on the basic unpromoted scale in 10 years time.

Reality is going to come as a surprise to many teachers. The levels of head and deputy do not seem alarmingly 'oversubscribed'—head: aspire 11.8 per cent, expect 6.9 per cent, available five per cent; deputy: aspire 10.8 per cent, expect 8.8 per cent, available six per cent. But for Scale 5 there are twice as many teachers expecting to fill the available posts. For Scales 3 and 4 the ratio is .90, while at Scale 2 it is .20. Hence there are many secondary teachers going to fill much lower levels in the teaching hierarchy than they expect and certainly than they wish.

3. Comparison of primary and secondary teachers

Any comparison is bedevilled by the greater range of opportunities open to secondary teachers and the fewer headships and deputy headships in the secondary field. Hence we see that more primary than secondary teachers aspire to and expect head and deputy positions. However, between deputy and the basic Scale 1 position (i.e. Scales 2–5, posts involving some responsibility) there were rather more than twice as many secondary as primary teachers hoping for posts. On the other hand, although few, there were seven times the proportion of primary teachers wanting (seven per cent) and expecting (14 per cent) to remain on the basic Scale 1 with posts involving no responsibility in 10 years time.

Far more secondary teachers hoped to enter lecturing (15 per cent secondary, four per cent primary), and in the same ratio they expected to get there (seven per cent and two per cent). Aspirations and expectations for administration and other related educational work were the same for the two sectors. The subject specialism of secondary teachers could well have greater marketability in further education colleges and perhaps even in subject departments of colleges and university faculties of education. Fewer secondary teachers wished or expected to retire, though more intended to leave English education.

In terms of their awareness of reality, the aspirations and expectations of secondary teachers seem less in tune with promotion opportunities in their system, particularly with regard to the numbers of assistant teachers at the highest (Scale 5) and lowest (Scale 2) promoted positions.

School Type

1. *Primary*

In comparing teachers in infant schools with teachers in other primary schools, the particular analysis was limited to women teachers. The detailed data appear in Table 17.3.

About the same proportion of infant and other primary teachers wished to remain in teaching (62 per cent and 60 per cent) and expected to (66 per cent and 65 per cent). On the other hand, 23 per cent of infant teachers aspired to headships but only 13 per cent of their colleagues in junior and junior/infant schools did. Of these 17 per cent of infant teachers expected to make the grade, and eight per cent of other women primary teachers. These differences could well reflect the competition anticipated from male colleagues in the junior sector. As if to compensate, more junior and junior/infant teachers wished to have Scale 2/3 posts (23 per cent and 14 per cent) and expected them too (27 per cent and 18 per cent). The greater expectancy at this and Scale 1 level allows for 9.7 per cent and 9.9 per cent disappointed hopes for deputy and head positions among infant and other junior teachers.

2. *Secondary*

Whereas about two-thirds of each group expected to be in teaching, less than half of grammar school teachers wished it, and the figures for comprehensive and secondary modern teachers were 53 per cent and 58 per cent respectively. Among those remaining, 11 per cent of secondary modern wished for headships, compared with 12 per cent and 10 per cent of their comprehensive and grammar colleagues. However, only 5.3 per cent of secondary modern and grammar teachers expected headships, and this was very realistic, if a slight underestimate (six per cent). The comprehensive teachers had an unreal expectancy of 7.7 per cent which was two and a half times the currently available proportion. Teachers in all categories of school were astray in their expectancies of deputy head positions—grammar schools most of all. Comprehensive teachers were closer and secondary modern teachers closest. Higher levels of promotion as assistant saw comprehensive and

TABLE 17.3: *Teachers' aspirations and expectations: school type*

STATUS	PRIMARY—WOMEN ONLY								SECONDARY—MEN AND WOMEN														
	INFANT (648)				JUN. & JUN/INF. (1543)				SEC. MODERN (836)					COMPREHENSIVE (985)					GRAMMAR (466)				
	Aspiration		Expectation		Aspiration		Expectation		Aspiration		Expectation		Reality N=836	Aspiration		Expectation		Reality N=985	Aspiration		Expectation		Reality N=466
	Rank	Per cent	Rank	Per cent	Rank	Per cent	Rank	Per cent	Rank	Per cent	Rank	Per cent	Per cent	Rank	Per cent	Rank	Per cent	Per cent	Rank	Per cent	Rank	Per cent	Per cent
Head (G7 & over)	—	—	—	—	—	—	—	—	6	6.6	9	3.9	4	4	11.0	6	7.3	3	5	8.8	7	4.7	6
Head (Below G7)	2	14.7	4	12.8	—	—	—	—	11	4.3	13	1.4		12	1.1	14	0.4		11	1.5	13	0.6	
Head (G3 & over)	8	8.0	7	4.5	6	8.0	6	5.1	—	—	—	—		—	—	—	—		—	—	—	—	
Head (below G3)	—	—	—	—	8	5.2	8	2.8	—	—	—	—		—	—	—	—		—	—	—	—	
Deputy Head (G7 & over)	1	16.8	5	12.5	2	16.3	4	11.7	3	10.0	3	8.4	8	5	8.6	4	8.2	5	6	7.5	5	7.3	4
Deputy Head (below G7)	—	—	—	—	—	—	—	—	—	—	—	—		11	1.4	13	0.8		12	0.4	14	0.6	
Deputy Head (below G3)	—	—	—	—	—	—	—	—	12	3.2	12	1.9		—	—	—	—		—	—	—	—	
Teacher Scale 5	—	—	—	—	—	—	—	—	5	8.0	6	5.4	—	3	13.6	2	15.2	10	3	13.6	2	15.7	9
Teacher Scale 3/4	3	13.9	2	18.1	1	21.3	1	26.8	1	23.9	1	39.4	33	2	15.7	1	29.4	41	1	16.8	1	34.2	40
Teacher Scale 2/3	—	—	—	—	—	—	—	—	—	—	—	—		—	—	—	—		—	—	—	—	
Teacher Scale 2	—	—	—	—	—	—	—	—	13	1.1	7	4.7	21	14	0.8	9	3.0	15	13	0.2	9	1.9	16
Teacher Scale 1	7	8.2	3	18.0	5	9.5	2	18.2	14	0.8	10	2.4		13	0.9	10	2.2		13	0.2	12	1.1	
ALL TEACHERS		61.6		65.9		60.3		64.6		57.9		67.5			53.1		66.5			49.0		66.1	
Related Educational Work	6	8.6	9	2.2	7	6.9	9	2.5	9	4.4	11	2.0		10	4.8	12	1.4		10	4.3	10	1.7	
Lecturer	11	2.0	10	0.9	10	3.2	10	1.2	2	12.6	5	6.0		1	17.1	5	8.0		2	16.5	6	6.0	
Administration	9	2.3	11	0.5	11	2.4	11	0.9	8	5.1	14	1.1		7	6.4	11	1.5		9	5.1	11	1.5	
OTHER EDUCATIONAL	5	12.9	6	3.6	4	12.5	5	4.6	7	22.1	4	9.1		8	28.3	7	10.9		7	26.9	4	9.2	
Don't know	10	10.7	6	8.6	5	10.7	3	10.4	7	5.9	4	6.7		6	5.8	3	6.9		4	6.7	3	9.0	
Retirement	4	12.5	1	18.8	3	12.8	3	16.7	4	9.7	2	12.3		4	7.9	3	10.0		3	9.9	3	11.4	
Non-educational/emigrate	9	2.3	8	3.1	9	3.7	7	3.7	9	4.4	8	4.4		9	4.9	8	5.7		8	5.8	8	4.3	

grammar teachers expecting twice as many Scale 5 posts as the secondary modern teachers—fair enough perhaps, as Scale 5 is not as common in secondary modern as in other secondary schools. The surge in expected over sought stay in teaching (10 per cent secondary modern, 13 per cent comprehensive, 17 per cent grammar) appeared at the expense of disappointment regarding posts in other educational activities, particularly lecturing (seven per cent secondary modern, nine per cent comprehensive, 11 per cent grammar) and administration (four per cent secondary modern, five per cent comprehensive, four per cent grammar).

Sex (Tables G17.5 and 6 in supplement—see p. 14)

As the primary and secondary sectors differ a great deal, they will be examined separately regarding the aspirations and expectations of men and women.

1. *Sex: primary teachers* (Table 17.4)

(a) *Men* Two-thirds of the men wished to be in teaching 10 years hence, and three-quarters expected to. Half of these aspired to and expected headships. Sixty-two per cent hoped for deputy or head status and 66 per cent expected it. Administration and lecturing were hoped for by 17 per cent, and seven per cent expected it. While 49 per cent expected headship, 37 per cent would probably get it. Where they were wildly out was that there would be many more (25 per cent) holding Scale 2/3 posts than wanted to (five per cent) or expected to (nine per cent).

(b) *Women* Sixty-one per cent of women wanted and 65 per cent expected to be in schools in 10 years time. Of these, only 16 per cent wanted headships and 11 per cent expected them. This is a strikingly low promotion orientation. Deputy headships had equal figures, 16 per cent sought, 12 per cent expected. The bulk of the teaching force (43 per cent of the 65 per cent) expected to be in Scale 1-3 posts. More expected to be at these levels than wished to be (28.5 per cent) presumably anticipating lack of success at deputy, head and other educational posts, 17 per cent not expecting what they hoped for in these areas. There was a retirement expectation of over one in six.

(c) *Men and women compared* Crucial to the career structure is the very much lower aspiration of women. Forty-eight per cent of men and 10 per cent of women wanted headships of large primary schools. Since this was wish and not expectation, this does seem to suggest that lower aspiration for responsibility *is* a major feature in the ratio of men to women in headships and other senior posts. The paucity of applications from women, mentioned earlier, seems based on the 5:1 lower inclination of women. Men focussed their attention on headships, women spread their interests and expectations among the promotion levels.

TABLE 17.4: *Primary teachers' aspirations and expectations: men and women*

	MEN (N = 753)				WOMEN (N = 2202)			
STATUS	Aspirations Rank	Per cent	Expectations Rank	Per cent	Aspirations Rank	Per cent	Expectations Rank	Per cent
Head (G3 and over)	1	48.0	1	44.4	5	10.0	6	7.4
Head (below G3)	6	5.9	5	4.9	8	5.8	8	3.3
All Heads		53.9		49.3		15.8		10.7
Deputy Head	4	8.2	2	16.7	2	16.4	4	11.9
Teacher Scale 2/3	7	4.8	3	9.0	1	19.3	1	24.7
Teacher Scale 1	11	0.3	10	1.6	6	9.2	2	17.9
ALL TEACHERS		67.2		76.6		60.7		65.2
Related Educational Work	9	2.1	11	0.5	7	7.3	9	2.3
Administration	2	8.6	8	3.0	11	2.4	11	0.9
Lecturer	3	8.2	7	4.2	10	3.0	10	1.1
Retirement	5	7.6	4	9.0	3	12.6	3	17.9
Don't know	8	4.5	6	4.3	4	10.8	5	9.9
Non-educational/ emigrate	10	1.8	9	2.4	9	3.2	7	3.5

2. Sex: secondary teachers (Table 17.5)

(a) *Men* Fifty-eight per cent of teachers wanted to remain in schools (73 per cent expected to, presumably being unable to get other education jobs). Seventeen per cent hoped for headships (10 per cent expected). 11 per cent aspired to deputy with 10 per cent expecting them. Virtually no-one wanted (0.2 per cent) or expected (2.6 per cent) to be on Scales 1 and 2 in 10 years time. Other educational work was liked (28.6 per cent wanted, 12.5 per cent expected such posts). Ten per cent of men expected headships but only about half that number would get them, and the same was true for deputy head and Scale 5 posts. Balancing these were low expectations for Scales 3/4 (expectancy 33 per cent, reality 41 per cent) and Scale 2 (expectancy 1.7, reality 18).

(b) *Women* Fifty-one per cent of women wished to remain in teaching and 56 per cent expected they would. Of these, 14.4 per cent wanted head or deputy posts though only 9.2 per cent expected them (a very realistic figure) 34.4 per cent wanted a promotion to below deputy (i.e. Scales 2–5) and 47.2 per cent expected it, presumably from lack of success at higher position levels and other educational occupations. The greatest discrepancy with reality was for Scale 2 where 6.8 per cent expected it and yet 19 per cent would be likely to stay at this level. The low wish for headships was noteworthy.

TABLE 17.5: *Aspirations and expectations of men and women in secondary schools*

STATUS	MEN (N = 1597)				WOMEN (N = 1121)			
	Aspirations Rank	*Per cent*	*Expectations Rank*	*Per cent*	*Aspirations Rank*	*Per cent*	*Expectations Rank*	*Per cent*
Head (G7 and over)	4	12.5	4	8.0	13	1.8	13	0.9
Head (below G7)	8	4.8	9	2.2	10	2.2	11	1.1
Deputy Head (G7 and over)	5	8.1	5	7.9	5	9.0	5	6.2
,, (below G7)	12	2.9	12	1.9	14	1.4	12	1.0
Teacher Scale 5	2	15.1	2	17.0	6	7.1	9	4.1
,, Scale 3/4	3	14.2	1	33.1	1	25.2	1	32.0
,, Scale 2	14	0	12	1.7	11	2.1	4	6.8
,, Scale 1	13	0.2	14	0.9	12	2.0	8	4.3
ALL TEACHERS		57.8		72.7		50.8		56.4
Lecturer	1	17.5	3	9.0	3	11.0	7	4.7
Administration	6	7.8	11	2.1	9	3.4	14	0.6
Related Educational Work	11	3.3	13	1.4	7	6.5	10	2.6
Retirement	7	5.5	6	6.3	2	13.4	2	18.4
Don't know	9	4.1	7	4.6	4	9.2	3	11.1
Non-educational/ emigrate	10	4.0	8	3.9	8	5.7	5	6.2

(c) *Men and women compared*　The large headships were wanted seven times as much by men as women. For small schools the ratio was rather more than two to one. Women wanted deputy headships in large schools marginally more than men, but half as much in smaller schools. This attitude was probably the basis for the disproportionate applications from and appointments of men in the secondary headship field mentioned earlier. Fewer women than men wished and expected to remain in the schools, twice as many men hoping for administrative posts and half as many in related educational work. Men tended to overestimate their chances of upper promotion posts, whereas women were more realistic. Both tended to underestimate the proportion in the lower promotion levels. Three times the proportion of women as men expected to retire.

Qualifications (secondary teachers)

In general the respective aspirations, expectations and realities of the non-graduate, ordinary graduate and honours graduate follow the pattern of secondary modern, comprehensive and grammar; the details are given in Table 17.6. Fifty-seven per cent of non-graduates wished to remain in teaching, whilst at 53 per cent the teachers in comprehensives and grammar schools were only marginally behind. The now common finding of more expecting than wishing to remain in schools was continued—by 12 per cent among non-graduates and ordinary graduates and by nine per cent among honours graduates. One notable feature was the relative ambition for the top positions—the heads of large schools (G7 and above). Whereas three per cent of non-graduates wanted them, 11 per cent and 16 per cent of ordinary and honours graduates respectively were interested. As regards expectation, the pattern of ambition remained one per cent non-graduates, seven per cent ordinary graduates and 12 per cent honours graduates. Yet all were unrealistic. Secondary modern teachers underestimated the reality of their headship opportunities whilst graduates overestimated. Ordinary graduates were again over-optimistic at the level of deputy whilst their non-graduate and honours graduate colleagues were more realistic. Non-graduates and ordinary graduates expected too much at Scale 5, but it is the graduates who grossly underestimated their numbers at Scales 2, 3 and 4. In this extravagance they were joined by the non-graduates at Scale 2. About one in 20 secondary teachers expected to leave teaching, and this was common to all groups. More graduates were uncertain about their futures; and whilst about a quarter of all three groups would have liked an educational post outside school, nine per cent of non-graduates and 13 per cent of graduates expected it. Lecturing was the favoured educational route out of teaching.

Age Groups (Tables G17.9 to G17.10 in supplement)

This is one of the most interesting and relevant of the comparisons that can be made for we may see how the teachers' hopes and expectations rise or are blunted as they gain more experience.

1. *Age groups—primary*

Aspirations for headship rise to a peak of 42 per cent in the 40- to 49-year-old group, coming from 16 per cent in the youngest and falling to 17 per cent in the oldest group. The degree of similarity of aspiration and expectation followed a similar curve. Of young teachers aspiring to headships, 47 per cent expected to get them. For the 30- to 39-year-olds

TABLE 17.6: *Secondary teachers' aspirations and expectations by qualifications*

	NON-GRADUATES (1488)					ORDINARY GRADUATES (539)					HONS. GRADUATES (733)				
	Aspirations R	Per cent	Expectations R	Per cent	Reality	Aspirations R	Per cent	Expectations R	Per cent	Reality	Aspirations R	Per cent	Expectations R	Per cent	Reality
Head (G7 & over)	11	3.3	13	1.4	⎫6	4	10.8	7	6.5	⎫3	2	16.0	4	11.8	⎫7
Head (below G7)	8	5.3	10	2.6	⎭	11	2.8	12	1.3	⎭	11	1.1	13	0.5	⎭
Deputy Head (G7 & over)	3	10.1	4	6.9	⎫8	7	6.7	6	7.1	⎫5	7	6.8	7	8.0	⎫8
(below G7)	11	3.3	11	2.2	⎭	12	1.5	12	1.5	⎭	12	0.8	14	0.4	⎭
Teacher Scale 5	5	8.9	3	8.4	—	2	16.3	2	16.9	10	3	15.0	2	14.6	8
Teacher Scale 3/4	1	23.3	1	38.8	33	3	14.2	1	27.0	41	4	12.2	1	23.7	13
Teacher Scale 2	13	1.2	7	5.2	21	14	0.4	9	2.6	15	13	0.4	10	1.9	35
Teacher Scale 1	13	1.2	9	3.1		13	0.7	11	1.9		13	0.4	12	1.1	11
ALL TEACHERS		56.6		68.6			53.4		64.8		1	52.7		62.0	
Lecturer	2	12.3	6	5.9		1	17.6	4	9.3			17.7	6	8.2	
Related Educational work	10	4.5	12	1.5		9	5.4	10	2.0		8	4.5	9	2.6	
Administration	6	7.1	13	1.4		8	5.9	13	1.3		9	3.5	11	1.8	
OTHER EDUCATIONAL POSTS		23.9		8.8			28.9		12.6			25.7		12.6	
Don't know	7	5.4	5	6.2		5	7.1	5	7.8		6	7.1	5	8.9	
Retirement	4	9.1	2	11.4		6	6.9	3	9.8		5	10.0	3	12.3	
Non-academic/emigrate	9	5.0	8	5.0		10	3.7	8	5.0		8	4.5	8	4.2	

the percentage was 91 per cent, 96 per cent for the 40- to 49-year-olds, and it dropped to 74 per cent for the oldest group (49+).

The percentage of those wishing to remain in the classroom rose from 69 per cent of the youngest teachers, peaked at 72 per cent for the 30- to 39-year-olds, and held at 71 per cent for the next decade before tumbling to 26 per cent for the oldest group. Of the latter a third would have reached 65 in the next ten years, and a further third could retire earlier (at 60) if they wished. The expectation of remaining in the class-room followed the same curve but a decade later—74 per cent for the youngest, 80 per cent 30–39 years, 84 per cent 40–49 years, and 22 per cent for the oldest. The difference between expectancy and wish followed a similar trajectory—4.9 per cent, 7.9 per cent, 12.5 per cent and 3.6 per cent. Forty-four per cent of the oldest group wished to retire in the next 10 years, but 65 per cent of them expected to, suggest-ing that at least 21 per cent had this option. If we assume a quarter of those aspiring to retirement (44 per cent) were below 55, then it becomes possible that one in three primary teachers over the age of 49 would choose to retire early, for what would probably be a heterogen-eous set of reasons. It appeared that nearly a quarter of the oldest group of teachers did not know what they wanted in the next 10 years, and this was perplexing. Probably uncertainty rather than lack of aspiration was the cause, as whether or not to retire seemed a major issue, with a move towards 'I expect I shall have retired after all' bolstering the retirement expectancy percentage. Of the youngest group, more expected to leave than wished to, but the percentages were very small (four per cent and six per cent). One conundrum was how teachers below the age of 49 could aspire to or expect retirement, yet between three and six per cent of teachers in this age group did both.

The desire for deputy head and Scale 2/3 posts fell with age, pre-sumably complementing the aspirations for headships. The expecta-tion for deputy headships trailed hope by decreasing amounts (3.6 per cent for the youngest, 1.6 per cent for the next decade) until among the 40–49 year age group 2.4 per cent more teachers expected deputy headships than would have wished for them. Presumably these had been hoping for headships.

More teachers expected grade 2/3 posts than wanted them in 10 years time, particularly amongst the youngest teachers where expecta-tion exceeded aspiration by 18 per cent (5.3 per cent for the 30s and 4.3 per cent for the 40s). The first figure is probably inflated because the youngest teachers' wishes for head and deputy head posts (35 per cent) were not expected to be realized (22 per cent). At all levels twice as many teachers expected no promotion as wanted it.

TABLE 17.7: Primary teachers' aspirations and expectations—by age groups

Status	<30 Years (N = 1149)					30–39 Years (N = 624)					40–49 Years (N = 646)					Over 49 Years (N = 538)			
	Aspirations R	Per cent	Expectations R	Per cent	Actual N = 596	Aspirations R	Per cent	Expectations R	Per cent	Actual N = 624	Aspirations R	Per cent	Expectations R	Per cent	Actual N = 410	Aspirations R	Per cent	Expectations R	Per cent
Head (G3 & over)	3	10.0	6	5.7	12 ⎫	1	25.6	1	23.2	32 ⎫	1	35.5	1	34.7	36 ⎫	3	14.4	3	11.0
Head (below G3)	7	5.7	10	1.6	⎭	5	8.3	5	7.6	⎭	6	6.5	6	5.6	⎭	7	2.4	7	1.5
Deputy Head	2	19.3	3	15.7	16	2	17.3	4	15.7	14	2	11.5	4	13.9	18	4	3.7	6	3.0
Teacher Scale 2/3	1	26.1	1	34.1	23	3	12.5	2	17.8	20	3	10.2	3	14.5	19	5	3.5	4	3.7
Teacher Scale 1	5	7.8	2	16.7		4	8.7	3	16.0		4	7.7	2	15.2		8	1.9	5	3.1
OTHER EDUCATIONAL		68.9		73.8			72.4		80.3			71.4		83.9			25.9		22.3
Related Educational Work	4	9.3	8	3.3		9	5.0	10	1.9		9	3.6	10	0.8		6	2.8	11	0.0
Lecturer	8	5.7	9	2.3		8	5.1	7	3.7		10	3.3	9	1.1		9	1.7	9	0.2
Administration	11	1.9	11	0.6		6	7.1	8	3.2		5	7.1	8	2.0		10	1.1	8	0.4
OTHER EDUCATIONAL POSTS		16.9		6.2			17.2		8.8			14.0		3.9			5.6		0.6
Don't know	6	6.2	4	8.5		7	5.3	6	6.9		8	5.9	5	7.1		2	24.0	2	11.5
Retirement	10	3.5	7	5.0		10	3.0	11	1.6		7	6.4	7	4.3		1	43.6	1	65.4
Non-educational/emigrate	9	4.5	5	6.5		11	2.1	9	2.4		11	2.3	11	0.8		11	0.9	10	0.2

With age groups, an explanation of their expectations in terms of reality is more directly available to us. The teachers were asked to what they aspired and what they expected in 10 years time. We already know the distribution of in-school posts in ten-year groups. The aspirations and expectations of the current under-30 group may be seen against the current reality of our 30–39 group. This assumes, of course, comparable conditions in the promotion system and in supply and demand over the next decade. The youngest teachers appeared unduly pessimistic about getting a headship in 10 years time and over-optimistic about a post on Scale 2/3. The 30–39 year group had expectations that accorded well with the reality as experienced by our sample, and the 40–49 group were a little too hopeful about headships but underestimated the proportion of other posts to be awarded.

2. *Age groups—secondary*

The wish to be in the school ten years hence grew with each decade of age, 54 per cent, 64 per cent, 65 per cent, until the advent of retirement, when it fell to 27 per cent. This was the expected figure for the 49+ group too, though the expectation of the younger teachers indicated more expectation then, with 66 per cent, 77 per cent, 82 per cent. Thus some 13–17 per cent of teachers below 49 years see themselves in schools when they would like to be elsewhere. Nearly a third of the youngest group wished for some other job in education (a fifth liked lecturing), a quarter of the 30–39 group wanted a similar transfer, with lecturing being followed by a growing interest in administration. For the 40s one-fifth wanted 'out', with the same options favoured. In the oldest group, 45 per cent of teachers would have liked to retire in 10 years, and 62 per cent expected to.

Secondary teachers in their 20s had considerable ambition for the higher posts in their schools—and, it seems, they were not too unrealistic. Unless in the next decade the opportunities change there will be room for the one per cent of these young teachers who expect headships, and for the four per cent who expect deputy headships. The pinch comes at Scale 5 level, but they underestimate placements on Scale 3/4 somewhat and Scale 2 radically. For the next two decades the expectation increased but was only a little more generous than reality for deputies and heads; but it heavily overestimated opportunities at Scale 5 and seemed reluctant to recognize that the bulk of colleagues of the relevant age were now at Scales 2, 3 and 4. One might assume that these levels retain those who do not 'escape' into the other educational occupations wished for, expected by fewer and, in all probability,

TABLE 17.8: *Secondary teachers' aspirations and expectations—by age groups*

Status	<30 Years (N = 1100) Asp R	Per cent	Exp R	Per cent	Actual N=720 Per cent	30-39 Years (N = 736) Asp R	Per cent	Exp R	Per cent	Actual N=486 Per cent	40-49 Years (N = 502) Asp R	Per cent	Exp R	Per cent	Actual N=308 Per cent	Over 49 (N = 380) Asp R	Per cent	Exp R	Per cent
Head (G7 & over)	10	2.2	13	0.7	1 }	4	13.5	4	8.4	9 }	1	14.6	4	11.0	14 }	4	5.8	6	3.9
Head (below G7)	12	1.4	4	0.5		7	5.2	8	3.4		6	7.6	9	3.0		8	2.6	9	0.8
(G7 & over)	6	5.5	9	3.0	5 }	5	11.4	3	9.6	13 }	3	12.0	3	14.5	13 }	3	7.1	4	5.0
(below G7)	11	1.8	11	1.3		10	3.4	12	2.2		12	2.6	11	1.6		12	1.1	7	1.3
Teacher Scale 5	3	13.5	2	11.0	9	3	14.1	2	13.6	10	4	10.4	2	15.3	9	7	4.2	5	4.2
Teacher Scale 3/4	1	27.6	1	42.1	50	1	15.2	1	34.0	45	1	14.6	6	28.4	43	4	5.8	2	9.7
Teacher Scale 2	13	1.2	6	4.5	21	14	0.3	9	3.0	14	13	1.6	7	5.2	13	14	0.0	7	1.3
Teacher Scale 1	14	0.8	10	2.4		13	0.8	10	2.4		14	1.4	8	3.2		13	0.8	12	0.5
ALL TEACHERS	2	54.0	3	65.5		2	63.9	5	76.6		5	64.8	12	82.2		6	27.4	9	26.7
Lecturer		20.3		10.3			14.8		8.2			10.3		1.2			4.4		0.8
Related Educational Work	4	6.7	8	3.1		10	3.4	13	1.4		11	3.8	7	4.0		10	2.1	11	0.5
Administration	7	5.3	11	1.3		6	7.9	10	2.4		7	7.3	12	1.2		9	2.4	14	0.4
OTHER EDUCATIONAL POSTS		32.3		14.7			26.1		12.0			21.4		6.4			8.9		1.7
Don't know	8	4.4	5	6.9		9	3.9	6	6.5		8	5.2	5	7.6		2	17.3	3	8.7
Retirement	9	3.2	7	4.4		12	1.4	14	0.8		10	4.2	10	2.6		1	45.3	1	62.4
Non-educational/ emigrate	5	6.1	4	8.5		8	4.7	7	4.1		9	4.4	14	1.2		11	1.1	11	0.6

achieved by still less. Teachers who were unsuccessful applicants for head, deputy and Scale 5 posts will occupy these positions—a little regretfully perhaps.

Present Post

1. *Present post: primary teachers*

Certain issues stand out. Aspiration and expectation regarding staying at school were remarkably close (within five per cent) for all but those at the top of the promotion ladder. There the wish was to try some other educational occupation (21 per cent) with administration being the most preferred (15 per cent) specialism. The percentage of teachers who *wished* to remain at their current rank for the next decade varied from eight to 17 per cent—excepting the 46 per cent of Group 3+ heads who had no further level to aim for. *Expectations* followed somewhat the same pattern, with 12 per cent reluctantly expecting to remain at the assistant level, 14 per cent at deputy and head of larger school, and eight per cent at head of smaller school.

A very small number of promoted teachers, except heads of large schools, would apparently have liked to settle for a lower position, and some expected to do so. Naturally enough, with ascending responsibility, teachers had greater desires for headships (Scale 1, 12 per cent; Scale 2/3, 31 per cent; deputy, 55 per cent; and heads of small schools, 62 per cent). Though expectation is dampened by experience so that the percentages are lower, the trend remains (Scale 1, 6 per cent; Scale 2/3, 19 per cent; deputy, 45 per cent; heads of below Group 3 schools, 62 per cent). When aspiration and expectation are compared, we can see that they approximate with experience and the common situation where aspiration exceeds expectation for the highest promotion levels with a compensatory reverse at the current or immediate promoted level.

Wishes and expectations for education posts outside schools were fairly constant at 12–15 per cent and three–four per cent respectively for all but the most senior of head teachers, 20 per cent of whom had this wish to try something else in education. Uncertainly about the future ran between seven and 10 per cent with the single exception of the expectation of senior heads. The retirement percentage crept up, from eight to 21 per cent wishing for it and between 10 and 27 per cent expecting that they would leave.

Within the next 10 years one-fifth of Scale 1 teachers expected a Scale 2/3 post, one-tenth a deputy headship and six per cent a headship. Of the Scale 2/3 teachers, nearly a quarter expected a deputy position and nearly a fifth expected headships. Deputy headships, presumably of large schools, were preferred (and expected) to headships of small schools. Forty-five per cent of deputies expected headships within the decade, and nearly half of heads of the smaller schools expected to move to a larger school.

There are other relationships that the individual reader can trace from Table 17.9.

2. *Present post—secondary teachers*

You can trace through the hopes and expectations of any teacher below head from Table 17.10, but again a few general features are pointed out.

Whereas two-thirds of deputy heads both wished and expected to be in school in 10 years time, the unpromoted teacher was the least enthusiastic of the assistants (53 per cent wish and 64 per cent expect), with the discrepancy (expectation-wish) increasing with rank—nine per cent Scale 2; 13 per cent Scale 3/4; and 16 per cent Scale 5. More than a quarter of all teachers with scale posts wished to try an education post outside school, and 10–12 per cent expected this to happen. One-tenth of unpromoted teachers expected to have left teaching in England within the 1970s.

The target for unpromoted teachers is Scale 3/4/5, with the expectation that it will be Scale 3/4 (40 per cent). Certainly few wish (two per cent) or expect (six per cent) to remain on Scale 1. Scale 2 is not popular with Scale 2 teachers, seven per cent only expecting to be at that level by 1980. Scales 3/4/5 were again the targets, particularly Scales 3/4 (48 per cent). Once at this level, aspirations towards deputy head and head arise—ironically more for the larger than the smaller schools. One-third of Scale 3 teachers expect to remain there, one-third will do better, over a quarter look to education jobs outside teaching, and the rest envisage retirement. Scale 5 teachers would like (30 per cent) to assault the heights (head of Group 7 or higher school) but expectation was somewhat more sober, focussing attention on both head and deputy headships of larger schools, the same positions in smaller schools being virtually ignored. Over a third of Scale 5 teachers expected to remain at that grade.

Deputies of the smaller secondary schools had no wish to remain in that position, rather hoping for headships of smaller (38 per cent) or larger (23 per cent) schools. However, expectations again focused on deputy of a large school (26 per cent) and head of a smaller secondary

TABLE 17.9: *Primary teachers' aspirations and expectations—by status*

Status	SCALE 1 (N = 1582) Aspirations R	Per cent	Expectations R	Per cent	SCALE 2/3 (N = 526) Aspirations R	Per cent	Expectations R	Per cent	DEPUTY HEAD (N = 297) Aspirations R	Per cent	Expectations R	Per cent	HEAD (below G.3) (N = 144) Aspirations R	Per cent	Expectations R	Per cent	HEAD (G3+) (N = 317) Aspirations R	Per cent	Expectations R	Per cent
Head (G3 & above)	8	5.6	9	2.7	1	24.0	3	15.4	1	49.1	1	39.4	1	54.2	1	45.8	1	46.1	1	60.3*
Head (below G3)	7	6.8	7	3.2	5	7.2	6	3.4	5	5.4	4	5.8	4	7.6	3	16.0*		0.0		0.0
Deputy Head	2	18.2	3	11.5	2	17.9	2	23.0	3	9.4	2	23.9*	9	0.7	6	1.4		0.0	7	0.3
Teacher Scale 2/3	1	22.9	1	28.3	3	16.5	1	28.5*	9	0.7	8	0.3		0.0		0.0		0.0		0.0
Teacher Scale 1	3	11.8	2	24.0*	11	0.6	11	1.0		0.0	8	0.3							7	0.3
ALL TEACHERS		65.3		69.7		66.2		68.2		64.6		69.7		62.5		63.2		46.1		60.9
Lecturers	9	4.6	10	1.8	7	5.1	7	3.0	8	3.4	7	1.4	7	1.4	7	0.7	5	3.5	5	2.2
Administration	11	1.6	11	0.5	8	3.8	9	1.3	6	5.1	6	1.7	4	7.6	5	2.8	3	15.1	3	5.7
Related education work	5	8.1	8	2.8	8	3.8	10	1.1	7	4.0	8	0.3	6	2.8	7	0.7	6	2.2	7	0.3
OTHER EDUCATIONAL POSTS		14.3		5.1		12.7		5.4		12.5		3.4		11.8		4.2		20.8		8.2
Don't know	4	8.6	5	9.5	5	7.2	5	7.1	4	8.1	5	5.4	3	9.0	4	6.9	4	9.8	4	2.9
Retirement	6	7.9	4	10.6	4	11.8	4	14.5	2	14.1	3	21.2	2	15.3	2	25.0	2	21.1	2	27.1
Non-educational/emigrate	10	3.9	6	5.1	10	2.1	8	1.7	9	0.7	8	0.3	7	1.4	7	0.7	6	2.2	6	0.9

* Current level of group.

school (21 per cent). Only a tenth felt that headship of a large school could be expected. Deputies in general became more aware of retirement (20–28 per cent) and lost the interest and expectation of jobs outside teaching that graded assistants had shown. Deputies of the larger secondary schools were only really concerned with their own position (26 per cent wished and 40 per cent expected to stay at this level) and that of headship of a large school (wish 36 per cent, expect 24 per cent).

As a general observation, expectation is lower than aspiration for posts outside the school and the positions ahead of the improving teacher. On the other hand, in posts at or near the teacher's current post more teachers will find themselves there than would wish.

The picture for heads is that, of the 54 per cent who expected to be in teaching in the 1980s, 42 per cent would wish to. Twenty per cent would have liked to try an education post outside teaching, but only six per cent expected to. Of the 'outside' educational jobs, administration attracted 9.5 per cent, whilst lecturing (5.7 per cent) and other related educational jobs (4.8 per cent) were in a somewhat different category. Nine per cent of heads were uncertain about their future, and 29 per cent wished and 30 per cent expected to retire within the decade. A little over a third would have liked to be head of a large school, and 44 per cent expected to be just that in 1980 (perhaps some whom we surveyed already hold this position).

Subject Specialism—secondary (Table G17.11 in Supplement)

We made a brief analysis of what the different secondary school subject specialists hoped to do in the next ten years, confining this to those under 40 years old. Our main interest was whether they aimed at the school senior positions of head and deputy head or whether they hoped to remove themselves from working in schools, or indeed in education at all.

Some subjects had too few teachers in our sample to warrant analysis, but in Table 17.11 will be found those aspirations supported by at least 10 per cent of the teachers of any of the 19 subject specialisms sufficiently represented.

In 18 of the subjects, the aim of easily the largest proportion (31–46 per cent) of teachers was to hold a post on Scales 2–5 in the next 10 years. More art teachers hoped to become lecturers (38 per cent) than teachers in schools (31 per cent). The desire to cut all connections with educational work varied between 10 per cent of French teachers and 2 per cent of teachers of religious education, with most subjects fluctuating between 4 and 8 per cent.

TABLE 17.10: *Secondary teachers' aspirations and expectations—by status (below head)*

| | SCALE 1 (N = 802) | | | | SCALE 2 (N = 499) | | | | SCALE 3/4 (N = 972) | | | | SCALE 5 (N = 165) | | | | DEPUTY G7 (N = 53) | | | | DEPUTY G7 (N = 99) | | | |
| | As-pirations | | Ex-pectations | | As-pirations | | Ex-pectations | | As-pirations | | Ex-pectations | | As-pirations | | Ex-pectations | | As-pirations | | Ex-pectations | | As-pirations | | Ex-pectations | |
	R	Per cent	R	Per cent	R	Per cent	R	Per cent	R	Per cent	R	Per cent	R	Per cent	R	Per cent	R	Per cent	R	Per cent	R	Per cent	R	Per cent
Head (G7 & over)	14	0.6		0.0	12	1.0	14	0.2	7	8.1	7	3.3	1	29.1	2	18.2	2	22.7	4	11.3	1	36.4	2	24.3
Head (below G7)	13	1.8	12	0.6	7	4.4	9	1.8	10	3.2	12	1.1	8	1.8	8	1.2	1	37.7	3	20.7	5	4.0	5	4.0
Deputy (G7 & over)	8	2.6	10	1.5	4	7.6	9	1.8	3	13.0	4	10.3	4	10.9	3	14.5	4	7.6	2	25.4	2	26.3	1	40.4*
Deputy (below G7)	8	2.6	11	1.0	11	3.2	8	2.4	11	2.6	10	1.9	11	0.6		0.0		0.0	5	5.7*		0.0		0.0
Teacher Sc. 5	3	10.9	6	6.3	3	13.4	4	7.0	1	15.2	2	17.5	2	12.7	1	37.0*		0.0		0.0	8	1.0	5	1.0
Teacher Sc. 3/4	1	30.2	1	40.3	1	28.9	1	48.0	4	11.5	1	32.4*		0.0		0.0		0.0	7	1.9		0.0		0.0
Teacher Sc. 2	11	2.1	4	8.0	13	0.6	4	7.0	14	0.1	14	0.2		0.0		0.0		0.0		0.0		0.0		0.0
Teacher Sc. 1	11	2.1	8	5.9*	14	0.2	13	0.4	13	0.4	13	0.8	9	0.6	9	0.6		0.0		0.0		0.0	5	1.0
ALL TEACHERS		52.9		63.6		59.3		68.6		54.1		67.5		55.1		71.5		68.0		66.0		67.7		67.7
Lecturers	2	18.3	5	7.6	2	16.5	2	8.8	2	15.0	5	8.1	2	12.7	5	7.3		0.0		0.0	8	1.0	5	1.0
Administration	8	2.6	14	0.4	7	4.4	12	1.2	6	8.6	8	2.1	5	10.4	7	3.0	5	5.6	6	3.8	5	4.0	5	1.0
Related education work	4	7.7	9	3.2	7	4.4	9	1.8	10	3.2	11	1.3	8	1.8		0.0		0.0		0.0	8	1.0	5	1.0
OTHER EDUCATIONAL WORK		28.6		11.2		25.3		11.8		26.8		11.5		24.9		10.3		5.6		3.8		6.0		3.0
Don't know	6	5.8	3	8.4	6	5.6	6	6.6	8	5.1	6	6.3	7	8.5	6	6.1	5	5.6	7	1.9	4	9.1	4	8.1
Retirement	7	5.0	7	6.0	5	6.4	3	8.6	5	9.7	3	12.6	6	9.7	4	12.1	3	20.8	1	28.3	3	15.2	3	20.2
Non-educational/emigrate	5	7.7	2	10.8	10	3.4	7	4.4	9	4.3	8	2.1	8	1.8		0.0		0.0		0.0	7	2.0	5	1.0

* Current level of group.

There was considerable variation among the specialists in a desire to take up work in education outside schools (administration, lecturing and related educational work). Examples were—17 per cent of classics teachers, 22 per cent of maths teachers, 26 per cent of physics specialists,

TABLE 17.11: *Secondary teachers' aspirations by subject taught*

SUBJECT	N	Teacher S.2–5	Lecturer	Head	Deputy	Administration	Non-Educational	In* Teaching
Art	121	30.5	38.0	5.0	7.4	5.0	7.5	42.9
Domestic Science	103	47.6	19.4	1.0	5.8	5.8	7.8	55.4
Biology, Botany, Zoology	119	33.6	10.9	9.2	11.8	8.4	6.7	55.4
Chemistry	110	38.2	13.6	13.6	11.8	6.4	4.6	63.6
Craft, Needlework, Woodwork	108	44.4	28.7	1.9	5.6	8.3	7.4	51.9
English	299	36.7	17.1	8.7	7.4	6.0	6.7	54.1
French	137	36.4	19.0	7.3	7.3	5.1	10.3	52.5
General Science	96	37.5	18.8	9.4	9.4	6.2	6.2	59.4
Geography	171	39.2	16.4	15.2	11.1	4.7	3.5	65.5
German	39	38.5	18.0	5.4	15.4	0.0	7.7	59.0
Greek/Latin	36	30.5	(5.6)	11.0	24.9	5.6	5.6	63.4
History	171	35.7	18.1	12.3	10.5	5.9	4.7	58.5
Mathematics	258	40.3	14.7	8.1	17.4	3.1	4.3	66.6
Music	59	45.8	18.6	3.4	10.1	10.1	5.1	59.3
Needlework	69	42.0	23.2	2.9	7.2	2.9	7.3	53.5
Physical Education	258	39.1	19.4	3.1	7.4	9.7	6.2	51.1
Physics	103	44.7	17.5	9.7	9.7	6.8	5.8	64.1
Religious Education	99	41.4	(8.1)	6.1	14.1	5.1	2.0	61.6
General Subjects	134	30.6	(8.2)	20.2	12.7	6.0	5.9	64.3

* Includes teachers (Scales 1–5), heads and deputy heads.

29 per cent of domestic science teachers, 32 per cent of English and history teachers. Lecturing was the primary aim, only classics, religious education and general subjects not having 10 per cent of their teachers so inclined. It was common for between a fifth and a quarter of teachers to aspire to a lecturer's position.

At least 10 per cent of the teachers of general subjects, geography, chemistry, history and classics hoped for headships by the 1980s. Some of course might already have been in them and wish to remain. However, by confining the analysis to teachers under 40 years the percentages relate mainly to aspiration rather than retention. Teachers of more subjects felt that they were in the running for deputy positions, for in addition to the five mentioned there were biology, German, maths, music and religious education.

A glance back at Chapter 5 indicates that the hopes for deputy headships on the part of classicists and teachers of general subjects— and to some extent maths, history and geography teachers—were not misplaced; nor were the aspirations for a headship by history and physics teachers.

If the teachers' aspirations for posts outside the schools were realized, the percentage remaining in schools could be seen in the last column of Table 17.11. Over half of all art teachers would have left, and at least one third of the teachers of every other subject. Shortage subjects have always been a matter of concern, with attention usually focused at the training end. The other end of the pipeline appears to have been given little attention. Loss of a third of the teachers of shortage subjects, e.g. science, maths, appears to be the minimum loss that would follow fulfilment of teachers' aspirations outside the school, for the position is worse in other, 'non-shortage', subjects. However, what is a 'shortage subject'? Is the criterion determined entirely by national economic circumstances? Is it a balanced school curriculum? Would the fact that only 33 per cent of the current maths teachers want to stop teaching in school cause greater concern to planners than the fact that 48 per cent of metal/woodwork teachers, or 41 per cent of history teachers or 38 per cent of religious education teachers hope to leave?

Women—'Normal' and Re-entrant Career Type (Tables G17.12 to G17.17 in supplement)

Proportionately more of the re-entrant teachers wished and expected to retire in the next decade ('normal' 13 per cent and 18 per cent, re-entrant 22 per cent and 30 per cent). The highest overall level could well be due to the age of the re-entrants. Apart from this there were a few small differences.

Proportionately more re-entrants than 'normal' women wished to stay unpromoted (i.e. on Scale 1) during the next 10 years, especially in primary schools (16 per cent re-entrants, nine per cent 'normal'). An aspiration towards Scales 2 and 3 (in primary schools) and towards Scales 3, 4 and 5 (in secondary schools) was more pronounced for 'normal' than for re-entrant women. Among primary teachers, a deputy headship was desired by 16 per cent of 'normal' women compared with eight per cent of re-entrants. But in secondary teaching this was reversed—15 per cent of re-entrants hoped for a deputy headship compared with 10 per cent of 'normal' career women. Neither of the two secondary groups expressed much desire for a headship, but in both groups in primary schools about 15 per cent wished to obtain or to retain a headship status. Although only small proportions wanted to cease any connection with education, in both primary and secondary schools the 'normal' hoped for this more than the re-entrants.

In general, expectations for both 'normal' and re-entrant teachers were lower than aspirations for senior posts, and higher for the junior posts. The only difference appeared to be that among the primary teachers more re-entrants expected to get a deputy headship than wanted one (the reverse was true for 'normal' career women), and that the re-entrants believed their hopes of headships were doomed to disappointment much more than was the case with 'normal' career women.

CHAPTER EIGHTEEN

Summary and Conclusions

Summary

In 1971 the NFER undertook an inquiry which attempted to gather facts and opinions about teachers' careers, the promotion system, teachers' attitudes to teaching as a career, and aspirations. The work was sponsored by the Social Science Research Council, supplemented by a grant from the DES (Chapter One).

Evidence was collected by questionnaire from teachers and their employers. One was sent to every LEA in England and Wales, asking about various aspects of appointment procedure. A hundred and fifty-five (94.5 per cent) of the 164 questionnaires despatched were returned. A second questionnaire was sent to the heads of 963 maintained schools, seeking general information about school circumstances, and specific comments on each head's involvement in appointment procedures. These schools comprised a national random sample, structured to be representative of school size and type, and 881 (91.5 per cent) of the heads responded. A third questionnaire was sent to every teacher (including the head) in the 881 schools, and was concerned with each teacher's career and opinions—6,722 teachers responded (66.8 per cent). The non-response was proportionately similar among men and women and among different school types, so that, at least in these two main variables, no bias existed in sample response.

The bulk of the analysis of teacher data concerned those teachers who had followed a 'normal' career. Some analyses, however, related to teachers who had interrupted their careers for a period of five or more years (called 're-entrants') and to others who had begun their careers 15 or more years after leaving school (called 'late entrants').

To supplement the questionnaire data, personal interviews were conducted with a random sample of 135 teachers in different school types and geographical regions, and with 20 LEA officers. Additional evidence was gathered from a review of Burnham settlements since 1945, an analysis of application forms used by LEAs, an analysis of a sample of advertisements, and an analysis of responses to advertised vacancies (Chapter Two).

Teachers' salaries are negotiated at national level by means of settlements made by the Burnham Committee, but at the same time such settlements have determined the type and range of promotion posts that LEAs are permitted to establish in their schools. A review of these settlements since the last war revealed a steady expansion in the number of different status levels available. Two points were fundamental to all settlements. First, the criteria for deciding number and type of promotion posts available in a school were the number and age of pupils on roll. These were compounded into one basic operating principle called the 'unit total'—itself determining the Group to which a school was allocated. Secondly, all promotion posts were, subject to the LEA's discretion, associated with responsibilities additional to, or instead of, normal teaching tasks. The 1971 Burnham settlement dropped this second condition again, but in practice the association between promotion post and additional responsibility persists.

Any discussion of promotion structures or careers in teaching must be in the context of Burnham settlements (Chapter Three). Within this context LEAs may have differed in the exact form in which they have implemented settlements (e.g. in policy regarding allocation of head of department allowances). In operation, the unit total system has made more promotion posts available in secondary than in primary schools. Because of the larger number of primary schools, the posts of head and deputy head have been in far greater supply in the primary sector than in the secondary. But these primary posts have generally been much less rewarding in financial terms because of the unit total system and smaller size of the primary school.

Career patterns

The changing basic structure of available statuses made it impossible to construct a typical career pattern for an 'average teacher'. Patterns were constructed based on actual teacher careers, and different groups of teachers were compared in terms of the number of years of experience before corresponding statuses were reached. The number of years of experience at which teachers were first awarded a particular status varied greatly, but some typical figures follow.

In the primary sector, those who obtained lower promotion posts did so after about seven years (four for men, nine for women), deputy headship had been awarded after about 13 years (11 for men, 15 for women), and primary teachers who became heads achieved this after 17 or 18 years (16 for men, 19 for women). Little difference was found between graduates and non-graduates in primary schools.

In secondary schools, the first promotion of both men and women came after about three years. Teachers obtaining medium-sized departmental headships (present Scale 4) did so after about 10 or 11 years. And the few who were deputy heads and heads were awarded these posts after 16 and 18 years respectively. Men who became heads of medium-sized departments or deputy heads did so about four years before women. In general, the comprehensive and grammar teachers who held promotion posts had been awarded these four or five years before their counterparts in the secondary modern school. Non-graduates holding promotion posts had been first awarded these after serving longer than had graduates who held similar posts. A comparison of subject specialists was also made (Chapter Four).

A further comparison was made of the age when different 'genera-tions' of teachers, i.e. different quinquennial entry groups, were first awarded specific statuses. The general conclusion was that in both primary and secondary sectors, first and second promotions (present Scales 2 and 3) were being awarded about three and six years earlier respectively than during a decade previously. The trend to receive them earlier now than formerly was particularly marked among women secondary teachers.

How promotion posts were distributed

The survey showed how promotion posts were distributed among the sample (Chapter Five), and here the chief points are highlighted. 57 per cent of all full-time teachers held a promotion post of some kind—11 per cent were heads, eight per cent deputy heads, and 38 per cent held posts below deputy (present Scales 2 to 5).

Proportionately far more secondary teachers than primary held a promotion post of some kind (71 per cent compared to 44 per cent). The unit total system provided over three times as many posts below deputy head (present Scales 2 to 5) in secondary schools as in primary. How-ever, the actual number of schools existing determined that far more deputy headships and headships were held by primary than by secon-dary teachers (10 per cent of primary teachers were deputies and 16 per cent heads, compared with corresponding figures of 6 per cent and nearly 5 per cent for secondary teachers). The unit total system, however, dictated that in the main the primary deputy heads and heads were paid on much lower scales than were secondary deputies and heads.

In primary schools, about three-quarters of the men held promotion posts, compared with about 30 per cent of women. In the secondary sector the proportions were respectively about 80 per cent and 60 per cent. In both systems the difference was generally much more notice-able at the higher levels of responsibility than at the lower. The analysis of applications for posts showed that applications from men far exceeded those from women. When teachers were asked to indicate the level of appointment they would *like* to occupy in ten years' time, the aspirations of women were much lower than those of men (10 per cent of women wished to be heads compared with 36 per cent of men). These two pieces of evidence indicate that a major contributory factor to the difference between the sexes in distribution of promotion posts *may* be a far greater demand for promotion from men.

When comparing types of primary school, the size of school rather than the age of pupils determined the number of promotion posts available. Consequently the teachers in infant and smaller primary schools held proportionately fewer posts below headship than colleagues in larger primary schools. In the secondary sector, where age range of pupils became far more important, teachers in modern schools were found to have relatively fewer promotion posts below deputy head than comprehensive or grammar teachers, and far fewer large departmental head posts. The fact that more modern than other secondary schools existed accounted for the greater proportion of modern school teachers who were deputy heads and heads, while their smaller size ensured they were paid on lower scales. Little difference in the distribution of number or type of promotion posts could be discerned between comprehensive and grammar schools of equal size.

In primary schools there was no difference between graduates and non-graduates in the way promotion posts were distributed, but in secondary schools graduates held proportionately more of the senior posts than non-graduates.

The analysis of subject specialists in secondary schools showed that distribution of promotion posts within subjects varied according to level of promotion. All subjects, because of being taught in secondary schools, offered reasonable prospects of promotion of *some* kind, especially music, physics, chemistry, classics. Some, however, such as drama and physical education, offered little prospect beyond lower level promotion, while others, such as German and music, seemed to offer better prospects than others of obtaining a small-sized departmental headship. At higher levels physics, chemistry, English and maths were among the subjects where proportionately more teachers held promotion. Headships were concentrated disproportionately on a few subjects, history in particular.

In general, teachers who were late entrants were promoted more than re-entrants, and even more so in primary schools. Also, in primary schools promotion was awarded more to women who had pursued a 'normal' career than to those who had left and returned. There was no difference in the secondary sector.

Certain attributes of teachers who had been promoted were studied (Chapter Six), with findings as follows.

Internal promotion An important finding was that 57 per cent of all promotions had occurred internally within the school, over two-thirds of these without formal application (presumably by recommendation). In primary schools internal promotions accounted for 46 per cent of all promotions (26 per cent informally). In secondary schools 66 per cent of promotions were internal, including the 52 per cent by recommendation. These high proportions of internal appointments were found at all levels, e.g. over a half of primary and secondary deputy heads were internal applicants, as were a quarter of secondary heads. Where the internal appointment was not by recommendation but by formal application, the assumption is that the post was advertised. Excluding the 'recommended' promotions, it was found that nearly a third of the remaining 'advertised' vacancies were filled by candidates internal to the school—a situation that may have contributed to the widespread impression among teachers that some appointments were 'rigged' (but there was little concrete evidence).

Variety of schools Promoted teachers had taught in more schools than unpromoted teachers, which suggests that variety of schools played a bigger part in promotion than long service in one school. Yet nearly a fifth of the sample had served in four or more schools but remained unpromoted. Men had served in more schools than women, and teachers in modern and comprehensive schools had moved around more than grammar school teachers. Service in only one or in four or more schools appeared less helpful in promotion than service in two or three schools, and women's prospects were affected by number of schools more than men's.

Length of teaching experience was, as expected, associated with rise in status. The average length of experience was 11 years for lower level posts, 15 years for heads of departments, 20 for deputies and 24 for heads. These years refer to experience up to 1971, not when post was first awarded. Many variations were found, e.g. unpromoted teachers with 13 or 14 years' experience. Primary teachers had taught for longer than secondary teachers at the lower status levels, and for shorter periods at deputy and head levels. At corresponding status levels, women had had more teaching experience than men, secondary modern teachers more than comprehensive and grammar teachers, and re-entrants more than 'normal' or late entrants.

For teachers following a 'normal' career, *age* naturally parallels length of teaching experience. Among primary teachers the average age of holders of graded posts (on Scale 2) was 38 years, of deputies 43 years, of heads (Group 3 or more) 48 years. For secondary colleagues the average age of holders of graded posts was 33, of medium-sized departmental headships (Scale 4) it was 40, of deputy heads (Group 8 and over) 46, and of heads (Group 8 or over) 48.

Course attendance During 1961–71 men had attended courses more than women, modern school teachers more than other secondary teachers, and non-graduates more than graduates. Teachers of more experience had attended as often as less experienced colleagues. Increase in status seemed to be associated with course attendance for primary teachers but not for secondary teachers.

Change of subject Over a quarter of secondary teachers were teaching a subject different from the one they had studied for degree or initial training, and this had occurred much more with non-graduates than graduates. Non-graduates who held promotion posts had changed subjects much more than graduates of similar status. Apparently for non-graduates the subject, or flexibility, had become an important factor in promotion, while for graduates of comparable status their qualification was the overriding factor.

Mobility Three-quarters of the sample had not moved home in search of promotion, though secondary teachers had moved more than primary teachers. Half the promoted teachers had not moved home—a not unexpected finding in view of the high proportion of internal school promotions—but increasing status was associated with the number of home moves. In both primary and secondary sectors, men had moved home in search of promotion more than women, grammar and comprehensive teachers more than modern school teachers, and graduates more than non-graduates.

Half the sample had served in only one LEA, and about a third in two. The number of LEAs in which teachers had served was significantly associated with increase in promotion level, although the number of moves was greater for primary than secondary teachers at the lower levels of promotion, and the reverse at senior levels.

Factors operative in promotion

Chapters Seven and Eight were concerned respectively with what teachers believed to be the factors at present favouring promotion and what they thought ought to favour promotion. The chapters detailed the teachers' opinions according to the group to which they belonged— primary or secondary, men or women, older and younger and so on. Some comparisons were made between the factors believed by teachers to favour promotion, those they thought ought to favour promotion, and the factors that our survey showed in fact to favour promotion.

From among the 31 offered in the questionnaire, the ten factors most frequently selected by teachers as those which *ought* to favour promotion were—in order of size of 'vote'—flexibility in teaching methods, familiarity with new ideas, ability to control pupils, concern for pupil welfare, variety of schools, length of experience, good relations with staff, subject specialism, administrative ability and extra-curricular work. Of these ten, those that appeared among the ten most frequently selected by teachers as *actually* favouring promotion were—length of teaching experience (sixth), variety of schools (eighth), extra-curricular work (ninth) and familiarity with new ideas (10th). Thus, four out of the ten factors were believed to be both desirable and actual factors. A fifth should possibly be included, as subject specialism was eleventh on the list of 'actual' factors and eighth among the 'oughts'.

The *survey* findings were that length of teaching experience partially favoured promotion, though many long-serving teachers were unpromoted. Variety of schools was helpful in the limited sense that two or three schools favoured promotion, especially for women, but one school or more than three schools had little effect. Subject specialism was an extremely important factor. No comparison about extra-curricular work or familiarity with new ideas could be made as these were not, and could not be, measured by means of the questionnaire if it were to be kept to acceptable dimensions. One might conclude, therefore, that a correspondence between 'perceived', 'desirable' and 'actual' factors was moderately well achieved. There is, however, a large area of doubt concerning factors which teachers though desirable but about which no objective evidence was gathered, namely, flexibility in teaching methods, ability to control pupils, concern for pupil welfare, good relations with staff and administrative ability.

Among the ten most frequently 'thought' factors which were not placed on the 'ought' list were: being a graduate, specialism in a shortage subject, social contacts, conformity with advisers and good relations with the head. Of these, being a graduate was definitely a factor that the survey found to favour promotion in secondary schools. Quantitative measures of the other factors are not readily available, and subjective assessment in such delicate areas could be both unacceptable and misleading. One further factor, course attendance, was placed 12th in the 'ought' list and seventh in the 'thought' list. It was found in fact to favour promotion for primary teachers and teachers in comprehensive schools.

There were factors which from the survey appeared to influence promotion but which were *not* listed high on teachers' 'thought' or 'ought' lists. Being between 35 and 40 years old in secondary schools and between 35 and 50 in primary schools appeared to have helped promotion holders. An important factor proved to be local and particularly internal promotions. Factors like 'having taught in area where post advertised' and 'being native to area where post advertised' were clearly associated with 'local appointments' yet were not high on either of the teachers' lists. Perhaps the factor 'good relations with head', ranked high (fifth) as 'thought' and low as 'ought', was an oblique reference to this situation. Being a man was not placed frequently as a 'thought' or 'ought' factor, but was found to favour promotion. This tendency paralleled men's higher aspirations and application rates for promotion posts. School type, though found in the survey to be of the greatest importance, had not been included in the possible factors offered to the teachers, as it was related to a basic principle of the promotion structure, the unit total, rather than to individual teacher attributes. Where the comparison could be made, as with comprehensives and large grammar schools, the difference did not appear to affect promotion.

Significant by its absence in our preliminary discussion and subsequently in the questionnaires and interview data was any positive mention that how well children learned should be a criterion for promoting teachers. It might be thought too obvious to mention. It might of course be subsumed within the item 'concern for pupil welfare', but this is not evident. Success with examination pupils (a pragmatic if limited measure) was not regarded by teachers as a factor which ought to play a significant part in promotion. Presumably this reflected their view of the *negative* backwash effects of external examinations, limiting curricula, solely cognitive, affecting a minority of pupils. The outcome of good teaching should surely be improved learning, yet, consistent with most studies of teaching competence, pupil achievement did not emerge as a criterion.

Many of the factors considered desirable by teachers were factors which have not often been measured except by reference to subjective judgement, e.g. flexibility of teaching methods, familiarity with new ideas, concern for pupil welfare, ability to control pupils. If such factors are to be taken into account in promotion matters, ways would have to be found to assess them. Assessments of teacher competence would undoubtedly be controversial. Currently our criteria of teaching competence are imprecise and it is difficult to see how this could be overcome.

Despite the practical problems of making such assessments, the qualities teachers see as desirable factors in promotion are typically those of 'classroom teaching'. These attributes, albeit poorly defined and badly measured, at present have no formal recognition by Burnham as criteria for awarding promotion. Until 1971 promotion was associated with responsibilities additional to or substituting for classroom teaching. Oddly enough, the one quality which might have reasonably been considered a principal attribute associated with such additional or substitute responsibilities, namely administrative ability, was placed very low on factors thought by teachers to favour promotion and only ninth on the list of factors which ought to favour promotion. Teachers appear to think that classroom teaching qualities ought to be the chief criteria for promotion, and that they are not so at present.

Appointment procedures

General policy about appointment procedures was gleaned from analysis of the LEA questionnaire (Chapter Nine). In the five stages of advertisement, application, short-listing, interviewing and appointment one might discern a basic uniformity in procedure across most authorities. In practice considerable differences in executing this common procedure arose as a result of the different settings in which schools functioned, e.g. whether the school was voluntary or county, the articles and instruments of management or government laid down for the school, the relationship between the executive authority and the school, the relationship between the executive authority and the professional administrators, and the delegation of power to divisions within an LEA. The description of appointment procedures as given by LEAs was based on our asking about 'usual practice', and many made the proviso that local circumstances might dictate amendments to any general policy.

Advertising The general rule was open, i.e. national advertisement, but promotion posts in primary schools were more often advertised internally within an LEA than were posts in secondary schools. County boroughs rather than county councils restricted posts to internal applicants.

Applying Over 90 per cent of LEAs required applicants to complete an application form. Letters of application were required by between 30 and 40 per cent of LEAs. A very small proportion asked for a letter but no form, and both letter and form were requested by 40 per cent for headship posts and about 25 per cent for other posts. Between 40 and 45 per cent of LEAs asked for testimonials, but almost all asked for references.

Short-listing Applications were often processed at the education office, but secondary schools were allowed to sift their own more so than primary schools. Headship applications were of course always processed at the central office. There were many variations in the way short-listing was carried out, and the selecting panels might include advisers, heads, administrative officers, managers or governors, education committee representatives—all in varying combinations. The processing of applications, including short-listing, is the only stage where the qualities and qualifications of every single applicant can be judged, and is therefore crucial in the appointing process. Any subsequent panel appointed to interview and select have to be sure that the final group of applicants that they see and from whom they choose are indeed the 'best' applicants. For this vital stage of short-listing it is arguable that the best possible expert professional advice should be available, and that this is not always the case. The wide variations in short-listing procedure produced inconsistent treatment of applications across different authorities.

Confidential reports   Where a short-listed candidate was not in the LEA's employ, it was standard practice to send to the applicant's present LEA for a confidential report. Such reports were usually collated via the candidate's head or local adviser or both, but were usually despatched only after receiving the approval of the CEO or his deputy. Two purposes of the report were seen: they reassured the prospective authority of the applicant's bona-fide standing as a qualified teacher, and supplemented any evidence about the candidate's professional suitability for the post in question. Although these reports were compiled by professionals (administrators, advisers or heads), they nevertheless were documents recording subjective opinions. These 'confidentials', like references, played a large part at the final short-listing stage and/or at the interview. Yet they were not strictly comparable one with another, compiled as they were by different people using different criteria. This again seemed to introduce into the promotion procedure elements of inconsistency which might possibly introduce injustice or unfairness in the treatment of applicants. We would stress, however, that most officers and LEAs seemed intent on achieving fair treatment for all applicants.

The interview   Apart from a few exceptions, the usual method of interviewing was to invite the few selected short-listed applicants to appear before a panel of interviewers. The panel would see each candidate in turn, ask him questions and, when all had been seen, they would decide whom to appoint. The panels varied. For headship posts representatives of the education committee, of the professional administrators and sometimes of the managers/governors were present. For other posts any combination of these, plus the head and possibly other members of staff might attend. The parts played by members would vary, and usually the advice of the professionals was sought, but not always. The purpose of the interview was often seen to be a weighing-up of the personalities of applicants, their professional competence having been assumed to be established during the short-listing stage. Despite a surface uniformity, we were still left with the opinion that most interviews were not conducted very systematically. Panels with different members, representing varying factional interests, having varied roles and widely differing purposes in their questioning, all ensured enormous variation from one appointment to the next. Reliance was placed again on the subjective impressions received by interviewers, and often it appeared that the final decision on appointment depended as much on the relationship between the members of the panel as on the qualities of the applicant.

The description given us by heads of their part in the procedures for appointing to promotion posts (Chapter Ten) reflected the general impression given by the LEA account of policy. While secondary heads were allowed greater freedom than primary heads, in both school sectors heads appeared to be consulted more and given more responsibility in short-listing and interviewing than the LEA description had implied. The heads' accounts were probably based on experience rather than expressions of policy, and there could well be more consultancy practised in the local implementation of policy than the formal central statement of policy would suggest. On the other hand, these apparent discrepancies may have been due to the difference in sampling procedure for including LEAs and heads in the survey, reflecting differences between county borough and county councils, and between voluntary and county schools. During our discussions with heads we learned of heads having sole charge of short-listing and interviewing, and others having no say whatever. One general conclusion must be noted: most heads felt that managers or governors were happy to rely on the advice and opinions of the head (or of the other professionals involved) both at short-listing and interview. Many heads accepted that despite all precautions, the result of the total procedure rested firmly on subjective appraisals of candidates' ability and character. While heads were anxious to ensure that the views of the professionals should be paramount, there was considerable support for the involvement or at least presence of the lay personnel.

Sensitivity was evident over confidential reports, whether those formally requested on behalf of the LEA or informally between heads. About a third of the heads felt unable to comment in 'yes/no' terms on whether the practice existed or on what form it took. Another third thought it occurred fairly commonly, and another third rarely. Our talks with heads left little doubt, however, that the majority did seek confidential reports from the applicant's current head or, less usually, his LEA. These inquiries were often by letter, but quite frequently by telephone. While they did not necessarily accept all that was said (or written), they believed this was an indispensable precaution. They placed little trust in testimonials and were not always happy with references because they were frequently unrelated to professional matters. The heads were concerned not just with the candidate's general abilities but also with his capacity for fitting in with other staff. Essentially they wanted to be reassured that the applicant would be an asset to the school and pupils. 'Fitting in' was felt to be crucial, with the stress being on social compatibility not conformity of educational outlook. Indeed a fresh mind and approach to educational matters was one of the qualities sought by heads. Heads recognized that assessments made by present employers might be biased, but they generally relied on the integrity of colleagues and on their own capacity to appraise such assessments.

Most teachers took the same view about confidential reports. While making the reservation that they hoped the contents were confined to professional matters, the majority we spoke to had no objection to such assessments and indeed believed that the prospective head (or LEA) had every right to obtain them. The teachers' experiences of promotion procedures, as related to us in our talks with them (Chapter Eleven), illustrated clearly the wide variations in practice that had been implied in both LEA and heads' questionnaires, and some experiences went a long way towards explaining why there is a teachers' folklore about appointment procedures and factors favouring promotion. Opinions about the promotion procedures as such, as recorded in the teachers' questionnaire (Chapter Twelve), showed that the qualifications of the interviewing panel caused greatest dissatisfaction among teachers. There were other disturbing factors, chiefly the questions asked at interviews, testimonials, and the lack of opportunity to look round the prospective school and meet the staff. The personal discussions we held with teachers probed these opinions much further (Chapter Thirteen), and once again we found that these talks added enormously to our understanding and interpretation of questionnaire results. At the same time we asked for teachers' suggestions for improving the procedures, and found great uncertainty as to how the unsatisfactory aspects of the system might be remedied. Teachers' opinions and suggestions varied just as much as had their experiences.

(1) *Advertising* On one issue teachers were unanimous. The practice of advertising posts which for practical purposes had already been filled

was bitterly resented. This apart, where posts were advertised it was thought important to be sent further details of the post in question, and such details had been received by secondary applicants much more than by primary. Although there was a general demand for such 'job specifications', teachers were divided in their views of what should be the essential contents of these further details.

(2) *Applying* With a few exceptions, most teachers said their applications had been acknowledged. They were also notified of the results, though this was sometimes very late in coming. There was frequent criticism of the application forms issued by LEAs, and the advantages of a standard form were suggested. Teachers were divided about preferences for letters of application, as distinct from forms and indeed a third of the teachers preferred to use both in conjunction. While the teacher questionnaire indicated dissatisfaction with the use of testimonials in the procedure, over a third of the teachers interviewed wanted them retained. The majority, however, thought references were necessary, but expressed concern that the kind of reference required (e.g. professional or character) was not made clear to applicants. Nearly three-quarters of the teachers spoken to had no objection in principle to the use of the 'grapevine' method of finding out in confidence more information about applicants. They wanted assurance that only professionals (heads or LEA administrators) were involved. While conceding the feasibility of biased and unfair assessments, teachers generally had experienced little to warrant anxiety, and expressed trust in the impartiality and integrity of the heads they had known.

(3) *Short-listing* Almost unanimously the teachers believed the head should be involved in short-listing applicants. There was more division of opinion about other possible personnel involved, with over half the teachers seen wanting advisers, LEA officers and managers/governors to be consulted. Secondary teachers were particularly anxious for departmental heads to participate at the short-listing stage.

(4) *Interviews* The number of interviewers experienced by teachers varied from one to over 10, with an average of about seven. In general the teachers' view was that four to six was desirable. The teacher questionnaire had indicated that the qualifications of panel members were considered unsatisfactory by many teachers. The talks with teachers, however, showed that experiences included the usual wide variety of situations—head only, head and managers, advisers present, LEA officers present, and all permutations and combinations of these. While the head's presence was thought vital, teachers were divided on the attendance of others. Oddly enough, in view of the qualifications

issue, nearly half the teachers wanted the laymen managers/governors present. The division of opinion about the attendance of lay people on the selecting panel was linked to the teachers' concern about the questions asked at interviews, for, according to their experiences, the 'irrelevant' questions came from the laymen. The head's role at interviews was usually a major one, and this was preferred by most teachers. Despite isolated cases, teachers were generally satisfied with the arrangements made for interviewing, but their suggestions for possible improvements were noted and listed (Chapter Thirteen).

(5) *Unfair practice* We particularly attempted to discover, in our confidential talks, the teachers' experiences and views about suggestions of unfair practice, canvassing and so on. The overall impression left us in no doubt that while some 'rigging' had gone on, almost all evidence was from hearsay. If, however, 'unfair practice' was taken to refer not to canvassing or social contacts but to favouring the internal or local candidates, then teachers' experiences were often first-hand and could be supported by our other evidence. Teachers were divided about the merits of open and closed advertising, but they were insistent that whichever principle was adopted, it should be genuinely applied. More bitterness was expressed about the advertising of virtually 'locally rigged' appointments than about any other matter.

(6) *Reliability of the system* Despite criticism of individual aspects of the appointments system, there were many teachers who thought the system as a whole was reliable. Few could pinpoint or recall examples from their *own* experience of badly misplaced promotions. Even among those who were sceptical about the system's reliability, hardly any believed it could be radically improved or should be radically changed. Throughout all the evidence, among questionnaire analyses and interview material, we saw that teachers disagreed about specific grievances, varied in their concerns about prospects and procedures, and a large proportion were content with or not perturbed by the existing situation. The particular issue of school reorganization was a case in point—teachers who had experienced it were divided about its effects on prospects for promotion, and those who had not were also divided about what the effects might be.

It was unexpected that so few teachers, despite their experiences and criticisms, could offer so little in the way of improving the system. It was as if they saw that things were not all they should be, yet were afraid that change might make matters worse. The introduction of personality testing techniques, of seeing candidates in their teaching situations, of eliminating laymen from interviewing panels, and so on— all had counter arguments for retaining the system as it stands.

General aspects of teaching as a career

When teachers were asked about their views of teaching as a career generally, rather than in terms of promotion prospects, the same division of opinions found earlier was apparent (Chapter Sixteen). Few aspects were selected universally for approval or disapproval, but the aspects that appeared to be most satisfactory were holidays (selected by 58 per cent of teachers), the opportunity to practise one's own ideas, economic security, staff-pupil relationships and working hours. Two items, with 49 per cent of the teachers' vote, shared the most unsatisfactory spot— class size and the status of the profession in society. Other particularly unsatisfactory aspects were accommodation, promotion prospects and the non-professional tasks required of teachers.

To gain further insight into the teachers' appraisal of teaching as a career we asked whether they would encourage their own sons or daughters to pursue the career. Less than a quarter said they would recommend the career to a son, but more than two-thirds said they would to a daughter. Women felt even more strongly than men that they would not encourage a son towards a teaching career. It is hazardous to attempt to interpret this without knowing similar figures for other occupations, but it is a striking fact!

Despite the advice that might be given to sons to eschew a teaching career, despite the dissatisfaction expressed about this or that matter in the appointments procedure, despite the general grievances felt regarding class size, and so on, when we asked teachers whether, given another chance, they would themselves again choose teaching as a career, over half replied without hesitation 'I'd never do anything else', and only eight per cent said 'No'.

This 'feeling for teaching' was to some extent exemplified again when teachers were asked about their hopes and plans for the future (Chapter Seventeen). Only about four per cent of all the teachers wanted to leave the educational scene completely, while a fifth hoped to change from school teaching to a related educational field. The 'loss' to a related educational field, e.g. college lecturing, should in the long term be productive either of more teachers or more informed administration, etc. It would be valuable to know what *kind* of teacher leaves and who takes his place. We have commented on which teachers planned to leave, but we have no information on their replacements. To the heads, staffs, and especially the pupils of many schools, the most important issue is the rate of staff leaving regardless of destination or replacement, for on this rests the stability and continuity of school life. The analysis of the heads' questionnaires revealed that in 1970–71 the average leaving rate was about one in every five or six teachers, being slightly higher in primary than in secondary schools. With a fifth or sixth of a staff complement leaving each year, the concern about turnover and stability seems amply justified. General climate suggests that this figure may have become even higher since then, and it is known to be so in some areas.

That expectations were generally lower than aspirations is not peculiar to teaching as a career. In most occupations it will probably be found that employees do not expect to realize all their ambitions. It did indicate a willingness to make a realistic appraisal of the probabilities of achieving one's personal goals within the promotion structure and system in teaching. What we did find was that for the higher level positions even expectations were raised beyond what reality warranted.

Implications

The gap in communications: policy, practice and opinion

Chapter Fourteen revealed many discrepancies between the descriptions of the various aspects of the promotion system as seen through the eyes of LEAs, heads and other teachers. The opinions of various groups of teachers about the system also revealed disagreement between the groups and within each group. Some widely held views seemed to lack substance when probed in detail. On the other hand, some opinions often attributed to teachers were, at least in our sample, found to be only thinly supported. Some examples of conflicting facts or opinions, or conflict between fact and opinions, follow.

The analysis of the LEA questionnaire indicated that the general policy adopted by most LEAs was openly advertising promotion posts, yet the survey of teachers' present posts showed that a large proportion were appointments internal to the school. This was a conflict between policy and practice.

The teacher questionnaire revealed that most teachers regarded the qualifications of the interviewing panel as unsatisfactory in the appointments procedure. From preliminary discussions and a reading of the educational press it was apparent that the lay members (managers or governors) were the persons teachers objected to. Yet when we spoke to our subsample of teachers, the proportion who wanted managers or governors represented on the interviewing panel was larger than that which wanted LEA professional administrators or advisers. More important, despite the intensity of the teachers' views about these laymen, the issue was in reality purely academic, for in practice— according to heads and the LEA officers we visited—the managers or governors almost always leaned on the advice of the professional people and supported the head's recommendations. Here the conflict was between written and verbal evidence on a theoretical situation which in practice did not exist.

Very few teachers were aware of the fact that most LEAs requested a confidential report on any short-listed candidate from the latter's present employer. Here employer and employee knowledge of the same procedure was markedly different.

In our preliminary discussions we had heard a great deal about the 'scandal of the grapevine', whereby prospective heads wrote to or telephoned a candidate's present head whether or not the latter had been quoted as a referee. The heads' questionnaire left us in some doubt about the extent of the practice, but the talks with heads, LEA officers and teachers not only confirmed that the practice was common, but appeared to stress approval of the practice. This approval was particularly noticeable among non-heads, the majority of whom thought the heads were justified in finding out as much of a professional nature as possible about prospective staff. Here the 'scandal' became an approved, almost necessary step in practice.

Teachers supported very strongly the view that the head should always be concerned and usually take a major role in the short-listing and interviewing of candidates. This implies that teachers were happy to trust the judgement of the *prospective* head a great deal. However, teachers were not so happy about the role of the *present* head where the promotion prospects of his own staff, inside or outside the school, were concerned. Generally they trusted their present head to be fair, but hearsay had made them wary of possible abuse by the head of his powers. The paradox is there to be seen—the prospective head who is trusted to use his judgement impartially when appointing to his own staff does not receive quite the same confidence when he takes on the part of 'present head'. At the same time most teachers were content to trust in the head's integrity.

Hearsay provides one part of the answer to this problem of discrepancies between policy, practice and opinion. A major reason for the disparities in accounts is undoubtedly the actual differences in operation of the promotion procedures across different LEAs. A second is the different implementation of an overall policy within different sectors of an LEA. A third reason, however, is the lack of concrete information on the part of teachers of how the system operates. The circulation of second-hand and third-hand accounts of other teachers' experiences produces an atmosphere of distrust whereby dozens of satisfactory experiences may be swamped by exaggeration and distortion relating to one or two unsavoury tales.

In trying to piece together the descriptions and opinions conveyed to us, we became aware of a great need for increased communication about all aspects of the system between all the parties concerned. Much needless speculation is provoked by either deliberately or unintentionally drawing a veil of mystery over the methods used by LEAs or appointing boards. This does not mean that there should be no confidential procedures, but it does imply that candidates should be made aware of the practices. There is, for example, a strong case for preserving confidential reports, and this is accepted by many of those involved. Also it is doubtful if any official ruling forbidding a 'grapevine' will prevent a head from contacting another head if he believes this to be in his school's interest.

Lack of communication can create a situation where trust does not exist, and the latter in turn certainly breeds a lack of communication. To maximize trust there should perhaps be more recourse to career advisers for help in promotion matters. We were, to say the least, surprised to find an almost total absence of career development schemes and even more to hear that, where any existed, teachers found out about these only by a vague 'passing on' of information from other teachers. There is, however, a vast, unacknowledged, informal and often somewhat disorganized career development scheme existing in many areas, namely the policy of promoting internally in schools or internally within authorities. Formalization of the policy and its dissemination among the teachers could improve communication and local teacher morale.

While promotion procedures might have to vary according to local circumstances, teachers would appear to be justified in condemning a policy of openly advertising posts which have been assigned to local or internal applicants. In Chapter Fifteen there was support both for the idea of an LEA adopting a deliberate policy of internal promotion and also for the idea of open advertising. We can appreciate an LEA's dilemma, to guard against in-breeding and stagnation, and yet with a need to generate in local teachers a sense of loyalty to community or school, and to offer them a definite prospect of advancement within the LEA. But, as teachers pointed out, when different authorities adopt opposite policies, this results in an unfair distribution of opportunities for promotion. The teacher employed by the LEA which promotes internally can apply to his own LEA as well as to any other LEA which practises open advertising. A teacher in the 'open' type of authority cannot apply to the closed authority. It would perhaps be a step in the right direction if LEAs co-ordinated their systems, using local, open or mixed advertising in specified proportions or circumstances.

It is doubtful, however, whether all LEAs could adopt a uniform policy. Size alone might dictate that small authorities would wish to advertise most posts nationally. And high level posts, even in a big authority, reduce the pool of potential applicants. The point we would stress is that this issue should be aired thoroughly between LEAs and teacher associations, so that whatever policy was adopted, it was well publicized and teachers were made aware of it. As is so evident in much of what we have found, it is not so much that justice is not done as that it is not seen to be done, and improved communications between all parties would go some way to amend this.

Reliability of the appointments procedure

Considerable effort is expended by many LEAs to ensure fair play to teachers. Many teachers are satisfied with the system as it exists or at any rate cannot suggest a better. Yet at every stage, there is an amazing lack of uniformity in the systems adopted by LEAs and in some cases little evidence of any system at all.

The idea of a full job specification seems almost foreign to those who advertise teaching vacancies. Rarely do 'further details' explain clearly what the job entails, what additional duties are involved, and the kind of qualifications expected of an applicant. There appear to be exceptions, and the beginning of a change in this direction can be seen. The short-listing stage can be the most crucial of all, for this is the only occasion where the sifting process embraces all possible applicants. Those doing the short-listing obviously must have the job specification so that they can match specification against applicant.

At the interview the candidates are likely to be comparable as far as documentary evidence goes, and personality now counts. Lay persons might be able to judge character as responsibly as professional educators, and would therefore be more likely to exercise an influence at this stage than in the sifting of documentary evidence.

Confidential assessments, from LEAs or present heads, are considered necessary, yet there is the problem of lack of comparability. The prospective appointing body, and especially the prospective head, generally decides how much reliance is placed on such reports. It has sometimes been suggested that these assessments should be made 'open', but unless teachers had the opportunity to expand on or refute the comments made, it is difficult to see how this would help the procedure. It might placate the professional associations to have open rather than closed assessments, but such assessments would begin to look suspiciously like the testimonials so frequently held in contempt by most teachers and prospective heads alike. There might well be doubts about their authority. Advisers and LEA administrators are by no means universally trusted by teachers as having expert knowledge of the teachers' competence or capabilities. Heads might still be accused, as with testimonials, of falsifying assessments, either to retain a good teacher or to get rid of a bad one. If such assessments could be objectively arrived at, this would be a different matter. This would be less a question of closed or open assessment as of validity. And this, from the teachers' recorded comments, is really what is being questioned, not the confidentiality.

Validity of procedure is the real stumbling block. Even if all professional decisions were delegated to professionals, the decisions would still be based on subjective judgements at short-listing and especially at interview stage. A different approach to appointments, whereby testing techniques replaced interviews, was rarely supported by the teachers. There is certainly a case for experimenting with new approaches, e.g. using testing techniques to provide *supplementary* information. Such experiments should involve close consultation between LEAs, heads, applicants and teachers' associations.

In the present situation it is undoubtedly the head who has most influence over actual appointments. Our survey shows that teachers approve of this. The degree of their approval, however, may depend on the fact that it is difficult to imagine how else the promotion system might be organized, and staff trust heads in preference to any other individual figure who might be an alternative. This does not mean that teachers would not welcome innovations which could be seen to be fair. The most immediately needed innovations, however, are perhaps to do with the appointment of heads themselves, for at present this is the key to all other school appointments. It is essential that staff have faith in the head's impartiality and good judgement. LEAs, governors and applicants will have to rely on the soundness of his appraisals and also on his receptivity to colleagues' advice and other sources of judgement.

Apart from his influence on the ethos and policies of the school, the head is the point around which revolves teachers' acceptance of and satisfaction with appointment procedures. If career development schemes were pursued by LEAs, training for the kind of work and responsibilities expected at succeeding levels of promotion could be ensured, up to and including headships. Such schemes, drawing on wide experience in the schools, would provide more suitable candidates and therefore more efficient selection at each stage including headship.

The basic principles underlying career prospects

The history of Burnham is the key to an understanding of the present promotion structure and of the way the system functions (Chapter 3). It reveals the basic approach adopted by the combined forces of the employing authorities and the teacher associations to the promotion system. In so far as Burnham settlements have always had to receive approval from the Secretary of State in charge of the nation's education, Burnham reveals the policy of successive governments, that is to say national policy.

(1) *The concept of the unit total*

The number and type of promotion posts permitted in schools are determined largely by the school's unit total. A school's unit total is not based solely on the number of pupils but also on their age. From thirteen years of age onwards, the units allocated to each pupil increase with age. Each pupil under thirteen adds one-and-a-half points to the unit total, those aged thirteen to fifteen, two points, fifteen to sixteen, four points, sixteen to seventeen, six points and over seventeen, 10 points. The result is that two schools of equal size will have different unit totals and hence offer different promotion prospects to teachers if one school has more older pupils than the other. Thus it is evident that in general every primary (or middle) school will offer its teachers fewer promotion posts than a secondary school of the same size. Any eleven to sixteen years comprehensive or secondary modern school will have fewer intermediate promotion posts than an eleven to eighteen school of the same size. There has been a systematic policy to weight the teaching of older pupils more than the teaching of younger pupils. The net result is that primary schools have never been able to offer the number or range of promotion opportunities that have been available in the secondary sector.

It may be that the present reward system is based on the notion that the work done with older pupils is of greater importance. No such reasoning, however, has been explicitly stated, and it is unlikely that the management side of the Burnham Committee would endorse it if it were. The points and unit total system was originally introduced to determine the responsibilities and therefore the salaries of head-teachers of schools of varying sizes. Subsequently the same system was extended to become a guide to the number of above-scale posts in schools covering different age ranges. The reasoning behind this was that the staffing structures of secondary schools were likely to be more complex than in primary schools—there would be a need for more specialists, the organization of the timetable would be more difficult, and the work of the headteacher would therefore be more complex. For similar reasons there would be more promotion posts in secondary schools. None of this necessarily implies that teaching an eleven-year-old is any less difficult or socially important than teaching a sixteen-year-old, and there is nothing in the present system which requires that a teacher of eleven-year-olds should automatically have a lower above-cale post than a teacher of sixteen-year-olds.

It remains true, however, that in general, teachers of the lower age groups *are* paid less, and the feeling cannot therefore be avoided among some teachers that their work is therefore valued less. Growing evidence of the fundamental importance of early learning (such as that found in the Plowden and Plowden Follow-Up reports) may add weight to any movement to reconsider the relationship between salary distribution and age-group taught. A first valuable step would be for the reasons for unit differentiation to be clearly stated so that they could be evaluated. In terms of contribution to the unit total, 20 twelve-year-olds (or six-year olds) add the same as 15 fourteen-year-olds and 3 eighteen-year-old pupils. Can we assume that employers, teachers, teacher associations, government, parents and pupils themselves support the view either that the eighteen-year-old is more important than the eight-year-old or that teaching a sixth former is more valuable or harder work than teaching a six-year-old? It may be that debate is not often focused on this issue because there is not a widespread knowledge of just how it works.

Apart from the inferences that might be drawn about differences between the primary and secondary sector from Burnham, we also noted that LEA policy differentiated between them on a number of points, usually giving more freedom to the secondary sector. Some obvious reasons related to school size spring to mind, and the availability of full-time secretarial help to the head is related to school size, thus militating against the smaller primary schools. In a small school the head often has a considerable teaching load, leaving less time for administration. Because of their size the number of primary schools is greater, and it becomes administratively convenient to centralize procedures such as appointments. Out data, gathered in interview, and from free comment on many questionnaires, conveyed the impression that the policy of delegating more responsibility to secondary rather than primary heads was a matter of attitudes as well as administrative efficiency.

(2) *The purpose of promotion*

Until 1971 the essential qualification for the award of a promotion post was the assumption of responsibility that was additional to, or a substitute for, normal teaching duties. Since 1971 this stipulation has only applied to the posts designated as head and deputy head (or equivalent). The remaining promotion Scales 2–5, plus senior teacher, are no longer associated with any additional responsibilities advocated by Burnham. Part of the reasoning behind this was that it ought to be possible to reward teachers for a high standard of accomplishment *as* teachers, not merely for having extra duties. The 1971 structure introduced, therefore, the intention that a teacher's progress in the profession could depend on his qualities as a teacher. However, this reasoning does not yet play a major part in promotion patterns. There were cases in our study where no noticeable additional duties could be observed in a promoted teacher's work, but there was little doubt that the general rule was still understood to be that promotion ought to entail other duties. This notion has persisted even since 1971, and the majority of advertised posts specify a responsibility for supervision or other activity over and above (or instead of) teaching duties.

In short, then, the purpose of promotion is still generally seen as being not so much to reward competent teaching as to invite applicants to do work other than teaching, usually administration. It is considered that teachers with a talent for exercising administrative responsibility should be given incentive to undertake this kind of work. But this is but one of many talents needed in school. Those who are skilled at teaching and who seek higher salary or status are still virtually compelled to seek positions that involve giving less and less time to exercising their talent in the classroom. Heads who wish to retain the teaching services of a member of staff sometimes 'invent' a post at the school in order to give that teacher the incentive to stay. Many teachers we interviewed pointed out that the general result of the Burnham approach to promotion has been—albeit unintentionally—to denude the classroom of those who are good teachers but want promotion.

It would seem to be contrary to educational sense to deny teachers promotion because their talents and aspirations lie in the classroom. The problems are, how would teaching competence be assessed, and would a promotion system based on the suggestion that some teachers are more competent than others stimulate greater teacher divisiveness and discordent? Assessments of teaching competence are already *taken into account* when arriving at decisions on promoting to posts of responsibility, so this sort of assessment is evidently possible. Would assessments of teaching competence be less ethical or more difficult to justify than assessments of character and personality? Most teachers accept the commonsense view that some teachers are better at their jobs than others. Would they find it any less acceptable because the idea was incorporated into the promotion structure? At any rate, the award of promotion to teachers on the basis of teaching competence as well as (rather than instead of) the potential for administrative responsibility, deserves far more serious consideration than it has so far received.

(3) *The future*

The promotion structure and the appointment procedures in teaching have developed over many decades into the form they now take and there is no reason to suppose they have reached their final form. As the history of Burnham settlements shows, the changes in teacher supply and demand in national and local contexts, organizational and educational evolution in the schools, and local government developments, have all influenced changes in the promotion system over the past 30 years. Yet if anything has been revealed from this survey, it is that no system and no changes will please all teachers or LEA officers. They are too diverse in their professional interests and in their personal circumstances to permit that any system would receive unanimous support.

There is much that can be done to improve the current system. Both teachers and employers obviously shared the common goal of improving the educational service to the nation. Such was the goodwill and co-operation among the large numbers of teachers, head-teachers and LEA officers we met personally or through the questionnaire in this study, it is evident that progress will be made—there are too many dedicated and determined people who will not accept second best.